5 - 04

Rights of Inclusion

PUBLIC LIBRARY OF
SELMA & DALLAS CTY
1103 SELMA AVENUE
SELMA, AL 36701

D1044395

Chicago Series in Law and Society

Rights of Inclusion

*Law and Identity in the Life Stories
of Americans with Disabilities*

David M. Engel and
Frank W. Munger

The University of Chicago Press
Chicago and London

David M. Engel is professor of law at the State University of New York at Buffalo. He is coauthor of *Law and Community in Three American Towns* and has published numerous articles about legal consciousness in America and Asia. **Frank W. Munger** is professor of law at the State University of New York at Buffalo and at the New York Law School. He is the editor of *Laboring below the Line: The New Ethnography of Poverty, Low-Wage Work, and Survival in the Global Economy.* Both authors have served as president of the Law and Society Association, and together they were awarded the 1997 Law and Society Association Article Prize.

The University of Chicago Press, Chicago 60637
The University of Chicago Press, Ltd., London
© 2003 by The University of Chicago
All rights reserved. Published 2003
Printed in the United States of America

12 11 10 09 08 07 06 05 04 03   1 2 3 4 5

ISBN: 0–226–20831–1 (cloth)
ISBN: 0–226–20833–8 (paper)

Library of Congress Cataloging-in-Publication Data

Engel, David M.
    Rights of inclusion : law and identity in the life stories of
    Americans with disabilities / David M. Engel and Frank W. Munger.
        p.   cm. — (Chicago series in law and society)
    Includes bibliographical references and index.
        ISBN 0-226-20831-1 (cloth : alk. paper) — ISBN 0-226-20833-8
    (paper : alk. paper)
        1. People with disabilities—Civil rights—United States.
    2. People with disabilities—Legal status, laws, etc.—United States.
    3. Discrimination against people with disabilities—Law and
    legislation—United States.   4. People with disabilities—United
    States—Biography.   I. Munger, Frank W.   II. Title.   III. Series.
    KF480 .E494   2003
    342.73'087—dc21

                                                    2002151373

⊚The paper used in this publication meets the minimum requirements of the American National Standard for Information Sciences—Permanence of Paper for Printed Library Materials, ANSI Z39.48–1992.

To our children: Anya, Jacob, Mark, and Sam

And the possibilities for the future they may discover
in their recollections of the past

———————— ❦ ————————

In memory of Dina Goldstein,
daughter of our friends Bruce and Betsy Goldstein

Contents

Preface

This book began with a discussion in Frank Munger's kitchen shortly after passage of the Americans with Disabilities Act (ADA) in 1990. One of us, Engel, was then engaged in a study of the parents of children with disabilities and their often difficult dealings with school district special education committees. The other, Munger, had a long-standing interest in civil rights and the debates that had engaged scholars and activists for two decades. Passage of the ADA, we agreed, presented an extraordinary opportunity to explore from the very outset what rights actually did and how they mattered, or did not matter, to their intended beneficiaries. We shared an interest in the role of law in everyday life and in the consciousness of ordinary men and women. We could think of no studies in which these interests were brought to bear on a major civil rights law from the time it was enacted. The ADA was certain to be the last major civil rights statute of the twentieth century and perhaps the last we would see for many years. We agreed to collaborate on a study of its effects.

As we look back on the path our research took, we are more conscious than ever of the contribution our interviewees made to the framing of key issues and the methodology we eventually adopted. With a grant from the Fund for Research on Dispute Resolution, we began to interview individuals with disabilities and local employers. We also held a series of focus group interviews with participants who had learning disabilities or used wheelchairs. Originally we had planned to study the effects of the ADA in specific work settings, but that research design proved infeasible. Gradually, as we listened to the conversations in the focus groups, we realized that the interviewees were pointing us in a rather different direction. Again and again, these conversations referred back to childhood and to the influences of parents, siblings, teachers, and other mentors. Our interviewees were telling us, and one another, their life stories, although it took us some time to appreciate the significance of what they were saying. The remembered past was central to their conception of who they were, how they perceived their disability, and what future they could envision for themselves. These self-concepts, in turn, made law seem more or less relevant. Life stories, we concluded, held a key to the role of rights and the significance of the ADA.

We decided to undertake a broader study based on the life story narratives of a number of men and women with physical or learning disabilities. Our research was supported by a grant from the Law and Social Sciences Program of the National Science Foundation (No. SBR-9411919), and by generous supplemental funding from the Baldy Center for Law and Social Policy of the State University of New York at Buffalo. We must offer the usual embarrassed acknowledgment of the number of years separating our original conception of the study from the publication of this book. Delay did, however, yield two unplanned rewards. First, by stretching out the span of time between passage of the ADA and our final interviews, we were able to discern greater complexity in the effects of the new law (and in its subsequent interpretation by the courts). Second, since our collaboration had become an integral part of our friendship, each suggestion for further revision seemed more attractive than bringing the project to an end.

We have been fortunate to conduct this research within an academic setting where sociolegal study is valued and rewarded. The community of scholars at the UB Law School and those affiliated with the Baldy Center have provided encouragement, advice, and insight from beginning to end. Everyone familiar with the Baldy Center knows the invaluable role played by our friend and colleague Laura Mangan, who is the center's associate director. To Laura we extend our deepest thanks and appreciation. Colleagues in the Baldy Center's Program on Community and Difference have listened to our presentations and guided our research. We thank them all. For their suggestions and encouragement, we thank James B. Atleson, Dianne Avery, Guyora Binder, Rebecca French, David Gerber, Bruce Goldstein, Fred Konefsky, Melinda Saran, and John Henry Schlegel. For their tireless contributions to the fieldwork as well as to our writing of this book, we thank a group of exceptional secretaries: Joyce Farrell, Dawn Fenneman, Anne Gaulin, and Sue Martin. We thank UB's director of audio visual services, Terry McCormack, for technical assistance in recording our interviews, and other members of the Law Library staff, particularly John Longo, Marcia Zubrow, and Mary Ann Wachowiak, for their help along the way. We thank Tom Ruffino for facilitating communication between us when we were both on the move and for helping to keep things short.

Dorothy Engel, whose life and commitment to others provided inspiration, deserves special thanks for her comments on our work.

This study evolved within a broader community of friends and scholars, nearly all of whom are members of the Law and Society Association (LSA). We have presented our research in numerous panels and conferences and have benefited from the comments of many colleagues in these settings. We want to acknowledge our deep affection for and appreciation of the LSA, and should mention in particular a few individuals who have been especially influential in the evolution of this book: Ruth Colker, Patricia Ewick, John Gilliom, Dirk Hartog, Michael McCann, Neal Milner, Margaret Montoya, Stuart Scheingold, Susan Silbey, Mark Steinberg, and Barbara Yngvesson. For their generous and helpful comments on this manuscript, we are indebted to William O'Barr and Austin Sarat. Colleagues who offered comments at two recent conferences were especially helpful—the workshop "What Do Rights Do?" held in Buffalo in April 1999, and the Ohio State Law Journal symposium "Facing the Challenges of the ADA: The First Ten Years and Beyond," held in Columbus, Ohio, in April 2000.

We also acknowledge the helpful comments of Beatrice Wright, whose scholarship on persons with disabilities influenced us from the earliest stages of our work.

Over the inordinately long lifespan of this study, we have been the beneficiaries of an outstanding group of research assistants. Most have now graduated and some of the earliest participants are well along in their own successful careers. We thank all of the following individuals for their help and their important contributions to our work: Dana Campbell, Shelley Chao, Li Chen, Mary Collins, Sara Davis, Mariely Downey, Sara Faherty, Christine Farley, Ruth Hogan, Rashondra Jackson, Rochelle Jones, Jeffrey Lindenbaum, Amy Martoche, Johanna Oreskevic, Leslie Platt, Kathleen Rose, James Ross, Dana Schulman, Denise Yates, and Kareen Zeitounzian.

Personal thanks are given by David Engel to Jaruwan Engel, for her love, patience, generosity, and insights throughout this project, and by Frank Munger to Judy Munger, for her love, support, and mentoring over the long course of our research.

Finally, we must acknowledge a debt that can never be adequately expressed or repaid. The sixty individuals who participated in the in-depth interviews, and their predecessors in the initial focus groups and employer interviews, contributed far more than their time. They entrusted us with recollections, perceptions, experiences, and aspirations that had immense value to them. We are deeply conscious of our responsibility to understand and convey the significance of that which they have given us. If at times our powers of interpretation may have fallen short, we have nevertheless made every effort to treat their stories with respect and dignity and to glean whatever insight we are capable of. We thank them for their participation and for teaching us how to write this book, and we hope it will offer them in return some small measure of the contribution they have made to our lives.

Introduction

The nursing supervisor approached Jill Golding in the hospital ward and thrust a newspaper at her, exclaiming, "Look at this. They're advertising for readers for the Board of RN exams. . . . My opinion is that if they can't read, they shouldn't be sitting there and asking people to read for them." Jill felt a surge of fear. Although she was a successful young nurse who had an excellent relationship with her supervisor, Jill, too, had difficulty reading because of dyslexia. She always arrived at work early to allow herself extra time to sort out the medications and the paperwork. She, too, would be taking her licensing exam with the testing accommodations to which she was legally entitled. Wasn't her boss aware of Jill's disability? Hadn't Jill already told her? Had her boss forgotten or misunderstood what Jill had said?

Jill finally responded, "Do you think you're being fair?" and her boss answered, "Yes, I do." If her supervisor thought that nurses who required testing accommodations were unqualified for their work, would she recommend against certification for Jill? Would she find a way to fire Jill or prevent her professional advancement? Jill made a quick decision and reminded her boss bluntly: "You know, I have dyslexia, and there are some things that I have to stop and I have to ask myself, what does this say? I have to slow down so that I don't misread it or misspeak it. But you cannot generalize everyone and say, if you can't read you can't take the test, because that's not fair. . . . You knew I had dyslexia. . . . I guess I work very well with it, don't I?" Jill's boss looked at her for a moment and then said, "I guess you do."

Jill has never invoked the Americans with Disabilities Act of 1990 (ADA). Although she had the ADA in mind during the encounter with her supervisor, she never referred to it explicitly. Nevertheless, Jill overcame her sense of fear by reminding herself that rights can become active even in casual encounters around the coffee pot at work. Rights can affect the way people talk and think, usually in social contexts far removed from courts, lawyers, and regulatory agencies: "So I decided, what do I have to lose. You've got to start somewhere. And if you approach it then, you deal with the consequences at that time. *You can't live in fear."*

Life Stories and the Paradox of Rights

Individual life stories like Jill Golding's weave in and out of the fabric of public events and social history. Autobiographical narratives by ordinary people reflect the influence of political change, of cultural transformations—and, at times, of legal innovations like the ADA. Yet the threads of individual lives also make up this fabric: through the choices and struggles people experience in their everyday lives, such as Jill's distressing conversation with her supervisor during their coffee break, events are channeled in particular directions and history is carried forward. The telling of life stories is part of this process. By drawing selectively on elements of the remembered past, the autobiographical narrators create an identity and a destiny for their protagonist.

Our study, based on interviews with sixty individuals during the years following the enactment of the ADA, grows out of a puzzle, an inconsistency in two views of law and society in America at the turn of the new century. One view emphasizes the centrality of rights. It sees rights as a defining characteristic of American citizenship and an indispensable guarantee of "life, liberty, and the pursuit of happiness." Americans not only believe they have—or should have—rights; they also believe that rights are the appropriate solution to a broad range of social problems (see Scheingold 1974). Rights are thus expressive of citizenship, but they are also assumed to have instrumental value in fixing what is wrong in American society. As new problems come to the attention of social activists, lawmakers, and judges, it is not unusual for new rights to be framed in the expectation that they can provide solutions.[1] Thus, it is not surprising that the growing strength of the disability rights movement in the later part of the twentieth century

1. Many social critics argue that America has gone too far in its devotion to rights. Elshtain (1995:41–42), for example, writes: "[E]verything I 'want' gets defined politically as a 'right.' Thus, for example, my desire, now a right, to have easy access to a pornography channel on cable television is conflated with my right to be safe from arrest or torture for my political views. Civil rights are trivialized in this process. Political ideals and private desires are blurred or collapsed. By extension, of course, there is no such thing as an authentically private sphere." Other critics (see, e.g., Glendon 1991) contend that Americans too often look to the legal system to protect their ever-expanding concept of rights, that their expectation level is unrealistically—and dangerously—high.

ultimately found expression in a statute, the ADA, guaranteeing rights to men and women with disabilities.

Another group of writers, however, presents a different view of rights in American society at the turn of the new century. These writers (e.g., Galanter 1983b; Trubek et al. 1983) say that Americans seldom turn to the law and do so with strong misgivings. They assert that Americans usually deal with legal problems by absorbing perceived wrongs without overt response. Americans seldom consult lawyers when they believe themselves to be the victims of rights violations, and lawyers seldom bring lawsuits on behalf of those who consult them (see generally Curran 1977). From this perspective, America is a nation of "law-avoiders." Potential claims of rights tend to be repressed, wrongdoers are often free to repeat their transgressions without fear of legal reprisal, and relatively powerless individuals suffer the consequences of an inability or unwillingness to invoke the law to protect their interests.

These two perspectives raise fundamental questions about the role of rights in American society. Are the two views, taken together, inconsistent? Perhaps the first refers to a way of thinking and talking about law and society,[2] while the second refers to actual behavior. But this, too, would be puzzling: Why should Americans think and speak in terms of an exuberant commitment to rights but refuse to seek legal enforcement when those rights are actually violated?

The paradox of rights talk and rights assertion has special significance for civil rights law in the new millennium. Civil rights differ from other forms of legal entitlement. They concern themselves not only with the legal interests of those who belong to civil society but also with the issue of membership itself. Civil rights are rights of inclusion for the individual whom society otherwise excludes. They go against the grain; they often violate social norms rather than institutionalizing them in legal form; they annoy, they outrage at the very moment when they most effectively insist on an identity and a legal status for the person who invokes them. When civil rights are *not* asserted, the consequences can be profound: invisibility, the erasure of the individual from membership in the community. Yet it appears that civil rights are among the least invoked of all laws (see Mayhew and Reiss 1969; Curran 1977; Miller and Sarat 1980–81). Even as the rights paradigm is extended from racial minorities and women to new groups defined by such factors as disability,

---

2. Glendon (1991), for example, focuses on the *discourse* of rights rather than the actual assertion of rights, but she does not place great emphasis on the distinction between talk and behavior. Examples of literature discussing rights talk include Tushnet 1984; Haskell 1987; Williams 1987; Milner 1989; and McCann 1994.

sexual orientation, stigmatizing disease, or age, the actual use of civil rights laws by their intended beneficiaries remains highly problematic.

We are interested in the paradox of civil rights in American society. We want to know how these issues and debates play out in the lives of individuals caught in the crossfire between contending views. We ask how the declaration of new civil rights for historically marginalized groups actually affects their lives, and how individuals navigate between expanded opportunities for rights claims and the widely documented tendency of most individuals to shun the law when rights are violated. We listen to the words of individuals who are the potential beneficiaries of new civil rights legislation; we talk with them about their views, their experiences, their use or avoidance of the law, and their thoughts about the relevance of rights claims to their own lives and their hopes for the future. Through the narratives of Jill Golding and others, we explore the surprising variety of ways in which rights become active in the lives of potential rights holders, including conversations around the coffee pot in the workplace. Although relatively few have actually asserted their rights by using the legal mechanisms made available under the ADA, many have found their lives and careers changed by the indirect, symbolic, constitutive effects of rights. In the chapters that follow, we document these effects.

Tracing the Effects of the ADA

Few studies have attempted to trace the interconnections between a new law and the everyday lives of ordinary people who are its potential beneficiaries. In our research, we try to understand the life stories and "legal consciousness" of a group of individuals during the time when a major civil rights law is being implemented, a law that might potentially transform their lives and their very identity within American society. We focus on the ADA and, in particular, the provisions of Title I (ADA §§12101–12117) addressing the employment rights of persons with disabilities. We ask how this law interacts with the social and cultural processes that construct an identity for persons with disabilities and shape basic assumptions about their ability—and their right—to participate in mainstream social settings such as the American workplace. We present a number of life stories, drawn from interviews with sixty individuals in western New York who have learning disabilities or use wheelchairs, individuals who could potentially invoke the ADA as they seek employment or on-the-job accommodations that would enable them to work.

Persons with disabilities are among our society's most numerous (43 million by congressional estimate in 1990)[3] and least understood minorities. Their social history has been one of stigmatization, isolation, marginalization, dependency, and, in many instances, abuse, mistreatment, and unnecessary institutionalization. A disability rights movement first emerged in the 1960s, calling attention to the history of injustice and advocating autonomy, independent living, and an "equal opportunity to participate in all aspects of society" (West 1993:9; see generally Shapiro 1993). Legal protections for persons with disabilities evolved gradually in the wake of this movement, reflected in federal statutes such as Section 504 of the Rehabilitation Act of 1973 and the Education for All Handicapped Children Act of 1975 (renamed the Individuals with Disabilities Education Act [IDEA] in 1990).[4] But it was not until 1988 that Congress began to consider comprehensive legislation that would provide broad rights for Americans with disabilities (Mayerson 1993; O'Brien 2001). In 1990, overwhelming majorities in the House and Senate approved passage of the ADA; and on July 26, 1990, President George H. W. Bush signed the bill into law.

The ADA represents Congress's most ambitious effort to protect the interests of persons with disabilities and to grant them full membership in American society. The statute aspires to eliminate the "major areas of discrimination faced day-to-day by people with disabilities" (§12101(b)(4)). This transformation of "day-to-day" life extends in Title I to the employment arena, where the statute prohibits discrimination in hiring and failure to provide "reasonable accommodations" to an otherwise qualified individual with a disability (§12112(b)(5)(A), (B)). Reasonable accommodations include "making existing facilities . . . readily accessible" and restructuring work and work schedules, acquiring or

---

3. "The Congress finds that . . . some 43,000,000 Americans have one or more physical or mental disabilities, and this number is increasing as the population as a whole is growing older" (ADA §12101(a)(1)). Other estimates vary. For example, Colker and Tucker (2000:1), citing U.S. Department of Commerce statistics for 1989 reported in McNeil 1993:5, conclude that in 1989 "there were 48.9 million Americans with disabilities, which encompassed 19.4 percent of the total U.S. population of 251.8 million." Uncertain definitions of disability and problems of self-identification make it difficult to draw a legitimate conclusion about the number of people with disabilities in American society. Zola (1993:xix) observes that estimates vary from 25 to 60 million. He questions all such estimates, because they perpetuate misconceptions of disabilities as "finite and static" and of people with disabilities as a separate and distinct minority group. Instead, Zola argues that *everyone* belongs, or will at some time belong, to the group in question: "The empirical reality is that everyone, unless they experience sudden death, will in fact acquire one or more disabilities with all their consequences."

4. For a discussion of disability laws predating the ADA, particularly Section 504 of the Rehabilitation Act of 1973 and the Education for All Handicapped Children Act of 1975 (renamed the Individuals with Disabilities Education Act [IDEA]), see O'Brien 2001; Colker and Tucker 2000.

modifying equipment or devices, exam modifications, and providing readers or interpreters for employees with disabilities (§121111(9)). The ADA mandates such accommodations as long as they do not impose "undue hardship" on an employer—that is, "significant difficulty or expense" in light of their nature and cost and the capacity of the employer to provide them (§12111(10)). The enforcement provisions of the ADA are the same as those Congress provided under earlier civil rights laws prohibiting discrimination on the basis of race or gender.[5] Individuals who believe their rights have been violated may file a claim with a state or federal agency and, after exhausting their administrative remedies, may bring a lawsuit.

Although passage of the ADA was a landmark in the disability rights movement, activists who supported it soon began to express concern and even dismay. In large part, critical attention has focused on judicial interpretations of the ADA, particularly a series of decisions that narrowly define the "person with a disability" who holds rights under the statute (Feldblum 2000). Some commentators, according to Tucker (2001:339), perceive a backlash against the ADA resulting from "judicial and societal hostility," a failure by courts to understand the law, and a general antagonism toward those who seek to invoke it. Preliminary evidence suggests that relatively few claims of employment discrimination have actually been filed under the ADA (see pages 90–92).

Most analysis of the ADA since its enactment has focused on formal claims, litigation, and appellate court decisions. Few researchers have inquired into the ADA's role in the lives of ordinary men and women with disabilities. The ADA articulates a bold aspiration to transform the social status of its intended beneficiaries, and it provides sweeping antidiscrimination measures and extensive accommodation requirements to achieve this aspiration. As much as any recent federal legislation, the ADA represents an extension of the "rights paradigm" to new persons and social arenas. Yet there is a real question whether—and how—legislative enactments of this kind actually intersect with the "day-to-day" experiences of persons with disabilities (to quote ADA

5. The enforcement provision of the ADA incorporates the power, remedies, and procedures set forth under prior civil rights laws (ADA §12117). These statutory provisions authorize persons alleging discrimination, the Equal Employment Opportunity Commission (EEOC), and the attorney general of the United States to invoke the administrative and judicial powers of the state and federal governments. While the EEOC and the attorney general have the power to enforce the ADA, achieving compliance is left largely to the employer and employee. When employers fail to conform to the ADA, employees are expected to raise issues of discrimination or accommodation. Further, the employee bears the burden of seeking intervention by the appropriate governmental agency or court if the employee believes that an employer has not complied with the ADA's provisions.

§12101(b)(4)). Research in the field of law and social science has consistently demonstrated that the announcement of new rights and standards by legislators and judges is seldom translated directly into the transformation of day-to-day life in the sense that the ADA seems to contemplate. This is not to say that such laws have no effect but rather that the relationship between law and actual life experiences is extraordinarily complex and merits close and careful study. In this book, we attempt one such investigation of the role of the ADA in American society by studying the life stories of a diverse group of individuals with disabilities.

The approach in this book differs from conventional studies of legal impact or legal mobilization in that we do not confine our inquiry to a survey questionnaire nor to questions that pertain to a narrow slice of time or isolated incidents in the life experiences of our interviewees. Instead, we ask how newly enacted civil rights, such as those in the ADA, become interwoven with the life histories and the legal consciousness of individuals who might assert them. We began our research in 1991, shortly after passage of the ADA, by conducting a series of focus group interviews of persons with disabilities as well as individual interviews with employers in the western New York area. Our focus group interviewees, in particular, taught us how crucial it was to learn about childhood and early education experiences in our quest to understand differences in individuals' orientation toward inclusion and rights.

In order to trace the effects of the ADA in the life stories of differently situated individuals, we needed to find interviewees with diverse backgrounds and experiences. Most studies of rights tend to focus on the viewpoints of persons who bring claims, file lawsuits, or participate in social action movements. By contrast, we wanted to interview not only those whose rights consciousness was high but those who tended to be indifferent to rights, those who endured as well as resisted, those who were loners as well as joiners, and even those who were unaware that the ADA existed. The quest for a diverse group of interviewees led us to create an initial pool of 180 individuals through a variety of unrelated contacts. Using numerous sources to solicit participants not only guaranteed a diversity of viewpoints but also assured us that we were not tapping into a single network of individuals who tended to know one another and share similar perspectives.

We then conducted 180 preliminary telephone interviews, from which we selected sixty interviewees for lengthy, in-depth interviews about their lives, which we undertook between 1994 and 1997, with follow-up interviews from 1998 to 2000. We chose the sixty interviewees according to specific criteria, but they were not intended to be statistically representative of American society as a whole nor did we design the sample to predict frequencies in some larger universe. Instead, this diverse group of sixty interviewees illuminates the social and cultural effects of the ADA on the lives and careers of individuals whose circumstances varied in particular ways. Thus, the interviewees were divided equally along gender lines and came from three different age groups: (1) high school seniors, who were in the early stages of career planning; (2) persons in their early twenties, who had already acquired some experiences with employment and job-seeking; and (3) persons in midlife, who had substantial employment histories (or, in some cases, unemployment histories) and whose careers began before the enactment of the ADA.

Within each age group, we interviewed individuals with two quite different types of disabilities: learning disabilities and physical disabilities requiring the use of a wheelchair. We selected these two disability types in order to contrast the experiences of persons with visible and invisible disabilities. Wheelchair users are universally recognized as belonging to the social category "persons with disabilities," while individuals with learning disabilities are members of a group whose circumstances are poorly understood and whose very status as people with legitimate disabilities is often questioned. We anticipated—and actually encountered—significant differences in the experiences and orientations toward rights of these two groups of interviewees.[6]

The interviews themselves were designed to reveal the presence or absence of rights consciousness and the influence of law at various moments in the interviewees' employment experience and career planning. We did not ask directly about the law, or even mention its existence, until the conclusion of the interview. Rather, we invited the interviewees to use their own language to describe their life histories, beginning with early childhood experiences, and including recollections of family and early education, the onset or diagnosis of disability, the formation of ideas about careers and adult life, influential mentors, job training, early work experience, problems, conflicts, and achievements. As we listened to the life stories, and as we later studied the interview transcripts, we tried to discern whether and how the interviewees themselves incorporated legal concepts in their narratives and whether the law in some obvious or subtle way had shaped their experiences. We

6. Four of our interviewees at the high school level were members of a control group. As far as we knew, they had no disabilities. Because of the special difficulties associated with discussing careers and employment with high school seniors, we found it especially useful to compare the views and experiences of students without disabilities to those who had disabilities.

encouraged the interviewees to explain their perceptions of situations they themselves identified as problematic or unfair and to describe the framework they used to analyze such situations and respond to them. We asked them to talk in some detail about their actions or inactions in the past and to describe their plans for the future. We asked them to describe the behavior and attitudes of family, friends, employers, and coworkers. Near the end of each interview, we asked more explicitly about the interviewee's awareness of legal rights and his or her readiness to invoke them.

After completing the sixty interviews, we then selected eight for a somewhat unusual form of repeat interview, six of which we completed. Knowing that their life stories would have particular importance in this book, we shared with these interviewees what we had written about them and asked for their comments and criticisms. We are not aware of other sociolegal researchers who have engaged their interview subjects in quite this way, but we thought it important for several reasons. First, we wanted to emphasize that all narratives, including the life stories we present in this book, are inevitably interpretations that are shaped by the narrator's purposes, perspectives, and assumptions and those of the researcher. To this end, we thought it appropriate to provide the interviewees with an opportunity to comment on our interpretations of their stories, just as we comment on theirs, and to reflect further on the ideas they expressed during our first interview.

Further, some scholars have argued that every life story is produced in dialogue with a listener and that the dialogic quality of ethnographic fieldwork should be highlighted and not hidden (Mannheim and Tedlock 1995; Emerson 2001:306–15). While not disguising the fact that this study is ultimately our own interpretation, we wanted to acknowledge and expand the role of our interviewees in our project. Consequently, in the full-length life stories we present throughout this book, the interviewees' later comments, criticisms, corroborations, and scoldings are interpolated within our text, where they appear in italics. We hope this approach underscores our argument that life stories (and legal consciousness) are not fixed and forever unchanging but are constantly questioned, revised, and reinterpreted by the narrators themselves as well as the researchers who record them.

A Perspective on Rights and Identity in Everyday Life

Our life story interviews provide us with an understanding of the remembered past. Although these narratives contain important factual material, it is their constructed and recollected quality that we particularly value. That is, we recognize that people tell and retell their personal histories in different ways under different circumstances. These narrative variations enable individuals to go out and meet the world, to engage with different kinds of people and experiences, to present themselves to others and to return with a sense of who they themselves are. We have a great deal more to say about "identity" and our use of the term in this study. For now, we observe simply that our interviewees have convinced us that rights and rights consciousness hinge on the sense of identity that is reflected in the ever-changing life story narratives of individuals with disabilities. Life stories open a window onto identity, and the sense of who one is and where one belongs is a fundamental consideration in tracing the role of rights in everyday life.

Our thesis, then, is twofold. First, we argue that research on rights can be enriched by the study of life stories. Prior studies of legal impact, mobilization, and legal consciousness have tended to focus on a narrow time period in which to discern the effects of new law. By contrast, we ask whether and how new and old laws become active over the course of a lifetime and to what extent legal innovations such as the ADA play a role as individuals progress through different experiences and life stages. Our broader autobiographical inquiry illuminates several aspects of individual life stories that help us understand both the relevance and irrelevance of law. Among these, we consider the shaping of individual identity from childhood to early adulthood; the significance and patterning of relationships with others; the evolution of career plans and work experiences; and the capacity of an individual to negotiate conflicts and seize opportunities in the life situations she or he confronts.

The second part of our thesis grows out of the first. We argue that viewing individual autobiographies over a broad sweep of time reveals the variety of ways in which rights can become active or remain inactive. Traditional studies of legal mobilization and legal implementation have typically been conceptualized in terms of a simple alternative: individuals either invoke the law or they do not. Our study suggests that such a view is too limited, and that rights become active in many other ways beyond the relatively rare situations in which they are explicitly invoked. Further, traditional studies have tended to assume that the decision to invoke or not invoke the law can be analyzed in terms of its "rationality" and that, given sufficient knowledge and resources, individuals will choose to use the law whenever it would objectively appear to remedy a wrong or improve an unfair situation. Our interviewees, however, do not think about law this way. For many of them, even in situations of extreme unfairness and disadvantage, the provisions of the ADA are largely irrelevant to their lives. In some instances, the interviewees simply accept as natural the very conduct by employers that the ADA prohibits. In other instances, they think the law creates an inappropriate relationship to employers and coworkers regardless of the benefits it appears to offer. Thus, in our research we do not assume as a starting point that the normal or proper response to unfair treatment is the assertion of rights, or that the lives of our interviewees would invariably improve if they were to invoke the ADA. Instead, we try to understand the experiences, preferences, and aspirations of our interviewees from their own perspective, while keeping in mind that the ADA represents one resource among many that could play a part in their lives.

As we have said, we think it essential to consider the many ways in which rights can become active in day-to-day life even when individuals do not choose to assert them. Rights can transform the sense of self simply by increasing individuals' perceptions of their own worth, or by reminding them of opportunities they could pursue if they could assume reasonable accommodations and nondiscriminatory behavior by employers. Further, rights can emerge in day-to-day talk among friends and coworkers, such as Jill Golding's conversation with her supervisor. The very enactment of civil rights can subtly shape the terms of discussion or the images and conceptual categories that are used in everyday interactions. Rights may enter social settings indirectly, by changing institutional practices although no one has explicitly voiced a complaint. Such subtle yet profound effects may be overlooked in traditional studies of legal impact, yet they can be detected through the analysis of life stories.

Like other scholars who have emphasized the "mutually constitutive" relationship between law and its social context (e.g., Yngvesson 1988, 1993), we argue that legal rights and social and cultural settings "mutually shape" one another (to borrow Yngvesson's useful phrase). Law is one of the elements that constitute the categories and routines of everyday life; and, in turn, these very categories and routines—and the individuals who participate in them—give form and meaning to the law (see also Harrington and Yngvesson 1990). The term "legal consciousness" is now widely used to characterize this two-way process and the behavior and cognition of the social actors who participate in it. Thus, McCann (1994:7) emphasizes the processual and constructed quality of "legal (or rights) consciousness," which he defines in terms of "the ongoing, dynamic process of constructing one's understanding of, and relationship to, the social world through use of legal conventions and discourses." Ewick and Silbey (1998:39) also emphasize the reciprocal and interactive aspects of the process through which legal consciousness emerges from the actions of individuals within the practices and meaning systems they find available in society: "[C]onsciousness is understood to be part of a reciprocal process in which the meanings given by individuals to their world become patterned, stabilized, and objectified. These meanings, once institutionalized, become part of the material and discursive systems that limit and constrain future meaning making."

In this study, we view legal consciousness through the life stories narrated by our interviewees, tracing the emergence of identity and orientation toward law from experiences in early childhood, through adolescence, and continuing into the years of employment and adult life. Bruner (1990), whose research also uses autobiographical narratives to track the emergence of the self through a lifetime of interactions with others, speaks of identity as "distributed" among those with whom the individual shares significant experiences. Social and cultural factors, including the law, affect these interactions and shape the distributed self that emerges from them. The life stories we present in this study confirm Bruner's insight that identity and the relationship of the self to fundamental categories and routines of everyday experience, such as disability, capability, work, and rights, are the products of many factors, some under the individual's control and others not. For our interviewees, these factors include experience and disposition, family and social context, individual choice and happenstance, social class, race, religion, and gender. As some of these elements or their experiential significance change over time, the self described in each life story also changes and develops. Thus, our concept of identity and legal consciousness assumes that the "distributed self" continually evolves with experience, incorporating along the way multiple and sometimes contradictory elements and perspectives. We also assume that the telling of life stories is an important act in the evolution of the self, since these ever-changing stories give meaning to past experiences, prepare the individual for future experiences, and help to integrate the individual's understanding of social interactions, disability, employment, and rights.

Others have tended to treat legal consciousness in more categorical terms—as potentially composed of a set of fixed orientations that appear in particular incidents or interactions.[7] We do not approach legal consciousness that way. Our study attempts to discern the *process*

---

7. For example, Ewick and Silbey (1998) describe three such orientations, which they call "before the law," "with the law," and "against the law."

through which the self continually evolves and redefines the relevance or irrelevance of law. In short, we seek to discern the significance of ADA rights in everyday life by listening to potential rights holders describe how identity emerges from interactions with others over a period of many years. We suggest that identity, constituted in this way, holds a key to understanding the effects of rights. The individual's sense of self in relation to others and to society as a whole determines how and whether rights should play a role. In life story narratives we can discern what we think are the traces of rights, although they are not always apparent to the narrator. We can also discern the narrator's sense of fairness and unfairness, an essential precursor to a perception that rights might be relevant. Although law is often only implicit or even absent in these narratives, at times we hear the narrator discuss law explicitly, resolving to invoke the law to protect rights or rejecting it as having no useful role to play or as being unfair or even destructive. In these stories, replete with change and contradiction, we find the most direct and dramatic evidence of the role rights actually play in everyday life.

Employment and Disability Rights

Because we view identity as central to the role of rights in everyday life, we are particularly concerned with the aspiration of the ADA to *change* the identity of persons with disabilities. By extending new rights to those who have been excluded because their identities have been distorted by stereotype, fear, and stigma, the ADA aims to integrate persons with disabilities into the social mainstream. The employment provisions of the ADA are particularly relevant to its goal of identity transformation. In American society, where independence and self-sufficiency are prized, employment is a fundamental element of identity. Status and social position are determined most importantly by the type of employment one holds (Blau and Duncan 1967; Lauman 1970; Newman 1988). Supporting oneself by earning and spending money legitimates one's status as a full-fledged, adult member of the community. Conversely, people who do not work are doubly disadvantaged, not only by the absence of self-generated income but also by the moral stigma of dependency attached to any form of public support for those unable to work (Handler 1987–88; Oliver 1990; Munger 2002). In an earlier study of rights consciousness, McCann (1994) chose for this very reason to focus on the efforts of women to mobilize their rights *in the workplace* in order to achieve fair wages, social equality, and inclusion.

We think it critically important, therefore, that the drafters of the ADA chose to apply the rights paradigm to the issue of employment for a group that has historically been excluded from ordinary jobs and career options. Yet the very concept of rights for persons with disabilities who suffer employment discrimination is itself a problematic idea. For centuries, law, culture, and social practices have contributed to the misimpression that disability and employment are necessarily mutually exclusive categories. An extensive research literature examines the cultural images associated with disability and their effects on individual identity (e.g., Goffman 1963; Gliedman and Roth 1980; Livneh 1983; Wright 1983; Scheer 1984; Groce 1985; Murphy 1987; Fine and Asch 1988; West 1993). Thus far, however, scholars have not explored how employment rights under the ADA affect these well-documented identity distortions, nor have they asked how the intended effects of rights on identity are influenced by differences in family background, social class, race, religion, gender, and other factors. Our life story interviewees provide us with some insights into these questions, which in turn suggest how and when rights under Title I of the ADA become active.

In order to explore the relationship between identity and employment rights, we examine the images and social practices associated with two different types of disability: physical disabilities involving the use of a wheelchair and learning disabilities. From a sociological point of view, it is important not to treat "disability" as a homogeneous category. The term serves as a broad umbrella for circumstances and life experiences that may have little in common except the stigma society imposes on them. As Asch and Fine (1988:6) observe, writing in particular about women with disabilities:

> [T]he very category . . . "disabled girls and women," exists wholly as a social construct. Why should a limb-deficient girl, a teenager with mental retardation, or a blind girl have anything in common with each other, or with a woman with breast cancer or another woman who is recovering from a stroke? What they share is similar treatment by a sexist and disability-phobic society. This is what makes it likely that they will be thrown together in school, in the unemployment line, in segregated recreation programs, in rehabilitation centers, and in legislation.

We found that physical and learning disabilities are associated with very different life experiences, including employment. Our study draws frequent contrasts between individuals who are identified with these two different categories, and compares these individuals in terms of their efforts to obtain employment and their interactions with employers and coworkers. Since the identities of persons associated with these two disability types are strikingly different, we find that belonging to one group rather than the other has very significant consequences for the role of employment rights under Title I of the ADA.

Thus, we suggest that rights connect with identity in rather different ways, depending on a variety of factors related to the individual, the disability type, and the career he or she has chosen. The drafters of the ADA assumed that, in order to enable employment, the identities of persons with disabilities had to be changed by providing them with rights. But this assumption raises broader questions about the capacity of rights generally to change identities. In chapter 2, we suggest that discussions of rights have often had, at their center, implicit understandings of how rights affect identities, but these implicit understandings are typically unsupported by evidence of what it is that rights actually do. By examining the consequences of the ADA's employment rights in the lives of ordinary men and women, we are able to put forward an explicit theory of how rights become active to change the identity of the law's intended beneficiaries.

Plan of the Book

A study drawing extensively on the sweep of individual life stories must confront decisions on how to accommodate not only the authors' words and thoughts but those of the interviewees as well. The format of this book reflects the choice we have made in this regard. In 1996, we published our first article based on this research (Engel and Munger 1996), an article we began by presenting the life stories of Sara Lane and Jill Golding.[8] Their stories, which we rendered in some detail, preceded our own analytic text, which in turn concluded with an epilogue containing further comments by Sara and Jill. The decision to alternate our text with life stories was itself inspired by the dialogic pattern used by other researchers, particularly anthropologists such as Shostak, whose study, *Nisa: The Life and Words of a !Kung Woman* (1981) we found inspiring.[9]

The format of this book follows the one we adopted in our 1996 article. We include seven life story sections, each a rendering of the narrative of one of our interviewees. These sections alternate with the six substantive chapters of our book. By presenting the summaries of life story narratives in alternation with our six chapters, we intend to

8. Because of our assurances of confidentiality to all of our interviewees, the names we use in this book are our own inventions.

9. Shostak (1981) alternates between the transcribed narrative of her subject, Nisa, and the author's own interpretive text.

make clear that our interviewees taught us new ways to think about disability rights and careers; and when we attempted to express our new understandings, they criticized and corrected us and they contributed additional insights and theories. In a sense, our interviewees are the true researchers. It is they who lay out the issues and themes we explore throughout the book. We think the reader will be struck by the subtlety of their observations about the many ways in which rights influence— or fail to influence—their lives. The substantive chapters of the book represent our own efforts to elaborate the insights we have gleaned from such narratives.

As we have already explained, the life story sections of the book consist not only of our summaries of the initial interviews, but also of the interviewees' interpolations and critiques of our own interpretive efforts, which appear in italics. These critiques should not be regarded as corrections of our mistakes (although the reader may conclude that is in part what they are) but as an additional interpretive layer that enriches the insights they and we have already provided. At different times, each of us may tell a different life story, shifting the emphasis, highlighting one factor rather than another, darkening or lightening the story, or drawing different conclusions. These inevitable interpretive variations are often very important. People continually shape the past, even as the remembered past continually shapes them, and by fashioning different accounts of the self, they make possible new pathways for the future.

Our life story presentations begin with Sara Lane and Jill Golding. These two stories played a particularly important role in shaping the ideas we present in this book, and we think it appropriate to begin by presenting them together. Sara and Jill are both successful professional women. Sara, who uses a wheelchair, is a journalist; Jill, who has a learning disability, is a nurse. After we reinterviewed Sara and Jill and incorporated their comments into our renderings of their life stories, the two women expressed a wish to meet one another. Thus, the pair of life stories concludes with an extraordinary dialogue between Sara Lane and Jill Golding, in which they compare their life experiences and their thoughts about the role of rights. We present an excerpt from this dialogue as a short third section following the two life stories.

Chapter 1, which draws heavily on Sara and Jill's life stories, presents our approach to the issue of identity in relation to rights. Here we argue that the sense of self determines the perceptions of fairness and unfairness that precede any consideration of rights. We also suggest that the challenges of identity formation differ for persons with physical and learning disabilities. This chapter, which compares Sara and Jill's experiences to those of three other interviewees, emphasizes two aspects of identity that we find particularly important: its interactive, intersubjective quality and its narrative component. We relate both of these aspects to the emergence of an orientation toward rights among our interviewees.

Raymond Militello's life story introduces chapter 2. Raymond, a college student and young businessman, conveys a cautious and at times cynical view of rights that contrasts markedly with those of Sara and Jill. His life story demonstrates how rights can affect identity in ways that the rights holder views as both positive and negative.

Chapter 2 continues our exploration of identity and rights by asking what our life story interviews tell us about the capacity of rights to transform identities and achieve their intended purpose of social inclusion. In this chapter, we examine the implications for identity transformation that are implicit in three prevailing theories of rights: classical rights theory, the rights versus relationships model, and critical rights theory. We consider each of these theories in relation to the experiences of our interviewees and, based on our own findings, present an alternative approach suggesting that rights tend to affect identities primarily through their indirect, symbolic, and constitutive effects. We describe and document these effects in the life experiences of several of our interviewees, including Sara, Jill, and Raymond.

Sid Tegler's life story presents the perspective of a middle-aged small-town accountant who has used a wheelchair since adolescence. Sid's strong commitment to the values of self-sufficiency, independence, and political conservatism leaves him unsympathetic to the ADA's employment rights in particular and to disability rights in general.

Chapter 3 examines more closely the connections between work and identity for persons with disabilities. The historic opposition between disability and work creates a challenge for the ADA in its attempt to ensure that those who have a disability *can* work with the support of reasonable on-the-job accommodations. In a sense, the ADA contemplates a reversal of the historically sanctioned process of defining jobs in terms of prepackaged sets of tasks and in terms of the ideal worker who can perform those tasks according to routines specified by the employer. The traditional concept of jobs has shaped the system of education and job training in which our interviewees spent their early formative years. The transformations contemplated by the ADA's drafters must somehow overcome the identities of rights holders as they emerge from this system, which has often defined them as poorly suited to many mainstream jobs. The ADA must also persuade employers to abandon their assumption that jobs and job routines can be entirely predefined, and instead make them willing to negotiate different routines and on-the-job accommodations for workers with disabilities. Our interviews suggest that neither of these challenges will be easily met.

Georgia Steeb's life story illustrates the difficulties some individuals with physical disabilities experience when they attempt to attend college and enter the workplace. Georgia, who suffered a spinal cord injury in junior high school, has found greater fulfillment in her family relationships than in her career as a teacher. Her religious faith has also sustained her and, in some respects, exists in tension with her inclination to invoke her rights.

Chapter 4, building on insights obtained from Georgia Steeb's life story, examines three discursive frameworks that affect the way individuals think and talk about rights: the discourse of racial justice, the discourse of the market, and the discourse of religious faith. We argue that these three discourses, and others like them, offer our interviewees the opportunity to incorporate rights into their day-to-day perceptions and experiences; but they also affect the ways in which rights are conceptualized. The discourses we discuss may facilitate the operations of ADA rights in the lives of our interviewees, but at times they also tend to make rights appear undesirable or irrelevant.

Rosemary Sauter's life story portrays a middle-aged woman with a learning disability who is undertaking a new career as a nurse after many years working at home to raise her son. Rosemary, like several other interviewees, grew up without having her disability diagnosed. Identity formation during her earlier years was profoundly affected by a disability no one recognized or understood, yet Rosemary and her parents found creative and unusual ways to accommodate her talents despite her academic struggles. Now that she understands her disability and has successfully trained for a professional career, Rosemary views employment rights under the ADA as legitimate but not particularly relevant to her life.

In chapter 5, we explore some of the social factors—family, social class, race, and religion—that shape the role of disability rights in the lives of our interviewees. We argue that factors such as these affect the resources individuals can tap as they attempt to construct an identity that is consistent with employment and a career. We also emphasize the timing of a disability's onset or diagnosis as a critical factor for the role of rights. At different times in their lives individuals have access to different kinds of resources, and the social factors we consider tend to vary in their salience over time. In this chapter, we consider the ways in which individuals mobilize resources—including rights—to create an identity and a career from the moment when disability first intersects their life.

Beth Devon's life story illustrates the resilience and adaptability of a woman who suffered from polio as a child and used a wheelchair almost all her life. We interviewed Beth when she was in her early sixties, nearing the end of a successful professional career. Sadly, she died before we were able to arrange a second interview. Like Sid Tegler, Beth valued independence over rights, yet she was a committed activist who counseled other men and women with disabilities as they embarked on their careers.

Chapter 6 explores the complex connections among gender, disability, employment, and rights. Gender resembles the social factors we discuss in chapter 5—such as family, social class, race, and religion—in that it can help to determine what resources are available to individuals at different stages in their lives and how they go about utilizing those resources. But gender proves to be significant in these life stories in another way as well. We have seen that work is itself a definer of identity and that conventional concepts of jobs affect the early process of identity formation by suggesting that persons with disabilities may or may not have a place in the social mainstream. But the culture of the workplace is affected by the male/female dichotomy as well as the able/disabled dichotomy. The gender coding associated with many jobs has historically directed men and women into different kinds of work or different roles or statuses in the workplace. In this chapter, we ask how the existence of a disability affects and is affected by the male/female divide in employment and, more broadly, what significance gender has for the role of the ADA in the lives of the men and women we interviewed.

These, then, are the seven life stories and the six substantive chapters of our book. We begin by introducing two of the individuals whose stories we found most surprising and provocative: Sara Lane and Jill Golding.

one

Life Story: Sara Lane

[We remind the reader that, after preparing our summaries of the life story narratives, we returned to our interviewees and showed them what we had written. We invited them to comment on our efforts and, if they wished, to revise or add to what they had previously told us. These later comments, revisions, and additions appear in italics.]

We interviewed Sara Lane at her desk in the bustling newsroom of the *Midwest Tribune*, where she works as a reporter and editor. In this setting, everyone is visible to everyone else, and low partitions separated us from Sara's colleagues. During the interview, her fellow reporters at adjacent desks spoke in such loud voices that our transcriber would later have difficulty making out what we said. The newsroom is the hub of Sara Lane's professional life. It is not a place for those who crave privacy and quiet. Reporters and editors are crowded together, and there is constant noise and movement. The work and talk of one employee impinges on others; all can see and hear the activities of their coworkers; there is continual interaction and cooperation among employees. It was immediately apparent that Sara Lane had chosen a professional environment and a career different from those of the other participants in our study. We sought to understand why she had made this choice.

Sara Lane contracted polio before her first birthday. Her memories of childhood include many summers of operations and convalescence. Nevertheless, her parents—particularly her mother, who later became a special education teacher—attempted to place Sara in mainstream settings throughout her childhood. Sara recalls meeting other children with comparable disabilities who led far more sheltered lives. These children, she now realizes, were destined for segregated and dependent adult careers. By contrast, Sara's family always expected her to pursue an education and a career in fully integrated settings. They made few concessions to her disability: she remembers rough and tumble physical play with her siblings ("They'd try to trip my crutch."). She also remembers being urged by her doctor as well as her parents to use crutches rather than a wheelchair, to resist "giving up" the struggle to walk. Her home was never modified for accessibility. Sara crawled up the stairs to her room on the second floor and thought nothing of it.

Yes, I think because my disability was so integrated into our family as a community, it just made it obvious to me that that's how it would be in the rest of my life. I mean, my parents accepted it, and they worked around it, and they did what they needed to do; but they never made it into this monstrous deal, in terms of, oh, we can't do that because of Sara, or we'll leave Sara home. That was never an option. . . . I just know that, because I was treated as an equal, as a peer, when I went to get a career, I went to college, those barriers didn't exist in my mind—that they're going to leave you out because you're disabled.

Sara played with other children in the neighborhood. She participated in sleepovers. Although she attended segregated classes in first through fifth grades, in order to receive physical therapy available only to children in the special education program, Sara's mother had her transferred to a regular education program for her junior and senior high school years. She saw greater opportunities for Sara in the mainstream environments, and Sara remembers that she was indeed a successful and popular student. In Sara's recollections of her childhood, her mother plays a critical role by creating expectations and selecting social and educational settings where self-sufficiency and a "normal" identity were most likely to emerge. She prepared the schools for Sara's arrival by talking with teachers ahead of time. "They were ready for me," Sara recalls of her mother's behind-the-scenes activities, and her teachers did in fact prove to be very supportive.

During this time, however, Sara Lane does not recall talking openly with her parents—or with anyone else—about disability issues. She did not learn how to make her surroundings physically accessible or how to communicate with others about accommodations. It was not until she entered college that she saw how beneficial a truly accessible physical environment could be for a young adult who used a wheelchair. Her college was more enlightened than most at that time and had removed many physical barriers on its campus and in its buildings. For the first time in her life, she was able to enter and use a library. While in college, Sara met other active and independent students with disabilities. She became more conscious of disability as a social issue and learned strategies necessary to involve herself in mainstream social activities.

It was very paternalistic, though. . . . They really kept you under their thumb. . . . We weren't really integrated into the university as such. We were more responsible for going to this place called the rehab center, where we would report in for activities and if we needed counseling or we needed this or we needed that. And then, outside of that, you would take classes. . . . But we were really watched and overseen. Most of us tried to really back away from it toward the end of our college career. It was way too paternalistic. We weren't allowed to have that same kind of freeing experience most college kids go through. At first it was quite comforting, because for many of us it was the first time we had ever been away from home. I mean it was terrifying. Into the first year or so it felt very comforting, and then it was like, get out of here. Let me have my college experience. Let me make my mistakes and figure this out myself.

College was enlightening and liberating in many ways for Sara, yet it was there that she first encountered the perception that her disability could actually limit her career. In pursuing her journalism major, she met professors who told her that no newspaper would hire her as a reporter because of her mobility restrictions. Instead, she should accept what she considered a less desirable desk job as a copyeditor. A well-known television journalist visited the college and told her to give up journalism entirely because of her disability. She rejected this advice and kept her expectations high.

Sara Lane's disability did affect her first job application, but in a positive rather than a negative way. The *Ardmore Gazette* is a midwestern newspaper owned by the Gannett Company, which in 1973 was a leader on the issue of affirmative action. Sara says that both her gender and her disability were considered pluses for the newspaper. She recalls that the editor thought it was "cool" to have Sara there.

I heard that later down the line: they thought it was quite cool. But the day that I went in for that interview, what he liked was that I graduated with a prestigious program and I was homegrown. And it was later that I saw the wheelchair play into it. But then there's prejudice. I mean they'll hire you, but then they'll stick you at a desk and they won't let you really show what skills you have. They put you at a copy desk, and they say, write headlines for the rest of your life, and don't move, and don't even ask us to be a reporter. And it was women editors all the way through who would give me my breaks. It was never a male editor; it was always the women. Because you would befriend them and they would get to know you, then they would say, well, go write something.

The same pattern was to hold true when Sarah was hired by the *Bayside Tribune,* a California newspaper where she worked in the early 1980s. The *Tribune* was also owned by Gannett, and its editor advocated hiring qualified persons of color and women. Sara was his second employee with a physical disability, and, once again, she says that this was a positive factor. In both Ardmore and Bayside, rights appeared to have played a part in the decision to hire Sara Lane. The law did not compel these employment decisions, but a growing disability rights movement had already affected the consciousness of some employers and employees, who placed a positive value on the inclusion of persons with disabilities.

Although Sara's early career benefited from the women's and disability rights movements, she advanced professionally because her employers perceived her achievements as genuine. At the *Ardmore Gazette,* she says, she had a good relationship with her employers, who took a cooperative and low key approach to physical accommodations: "They just kind of made sure I had what I needed without making a point of that." Sara drew on the skills she learned in college, and she guided her employer through the steps required to make her environment accessible:

> I think when they interviewed me for the job, they pretty much said, "What do you need?" . . . And I said, "Well, I have to have good entry and parking, and I need to get into a bathroom stall." "Well, what's the easiest and cheapest way we can do that?" they always say. And you have to know, you have to teach them. And in those days, what you would do would be to take the bathroom door, the stall door off, and drop a curtain. And that's what they did.

She notes that accommodation was relatively simple when the costs were small. The door on a bathroom stall, for example, was replaced with a curtain; and, she recalls ironically, when the newspaper's offices were renovated a few years later, the management actually saved money because they had to buy sixty desks but only fifty-nine chairs. When costs were high, however, accommodations became more problematic. For example, when the newspaper moved her section to the second floor, they refused to provide an alternative to a dangerous freight elevator, which she could not operate without assistance.

Although Sara Lane initially worked as a copyeditor, she eventually achieved her goal of becoming a reporter. Her disability sometimes affected her reporting style, but it never became the insuperable obstacle her college professors had predicted:

I know that when I do an interview I have to maybe approach it a little differently from another reporter. And . . . I have to judge them on an individual basis, whether or not I'll mention something about the disability to the person I'm interviewing—try to make them feel more comfortable. Sometimes I just try to weave it into the conversation later, because I feel some people send me language, where they want to know. . . . I mean, I'm interviewing them, but they want to know about me. . . . I've done a lot of face to face, and . . . at some point you just kind of bring it back to yourself and try to address it . . . in order for the interview to go on, so they'll stop obsessing about it.

Sara's experience at the *Ardmore Gazette* established a pattern for her employment elsewhere. She left the Ardmore area for a number of years and obtained jobs at two other newspapers in part because the editors who hired her thought her disability helped to establish a desirable identity for their papers. Her disability was one factor in her being hired, but not the only factor, since she had accumulated considerable experience in positions of responsibility. Editors also valued her other qualities. Sara says that the *Bayside* editor particularly liked her offbeat sense of humor. Her growing network of friends and professional associates also provided her with another resource not related to her disability. Her career has been shaped uniquely, but by no means exclusively, by her disability.

Sara mentions the law just once during this portion of her life story, when she describes a destructive encounter with the judicial system following a horrifying event. Shortly after beginning work on the night shift as an editor for the *Bayside Tribune* in California, Sara was attacked and raped as she returned to her home in Berkeley. Her attacker was caught, tried, convicted, and sent to jail, but not until Sara had been subjected to a humiliating cross-examination by a defense attorney who repeatedly challenged her for not running or fighting off her attacker. During the cross-examination, he forced Sara to describe her disability before the jury again and again. The judge, on the other hand, fearing reversal on appeal, struggled to prevent the jury from seeing her in her wheelchair so that her disability could not be cited by the defense as having unfairly prejudiced the jury against the defendant. She remembers feeling more discrimination in the courtroom than she ever faced at a job or in any other setting. She was shamed and humiliated both as a rape victim and as a person with a disability. Her family also had problems dealing with her attack and failed to provide the support she expected.

The negative responses of the court and Sara Lane's family contrast with the practical and supportive responses of her employer and colleagues. They were concerned and protective and made immediate arrangements to restructure her schedule to avoid the risks associated with leaving work at night. Nevertheless, Sara decided to leave the Bay Area and return to Ardmore several years later, just before her attacker's release from prison. The attack and its legal consequences caused severe dislocations in her life.

A second reason for this move was the birth of Sara's child. About two years after the assault, while still working for the *Bayside Tribune,* Sara developed a romantic relationship. When Sara became pregnant, the man was unwilling to marry and they separated. Single parenthood as well as the imminent release of the convicted rapist convinced her to return to the Midwest, where she hoped that family and friends might provide a more supportive network and enable her to pursue her career while raising her child. That network also provided a job contact at the *Midwest Tribune,* her current employer.

Sara's experience at the *Midwest Tribune* was initially quite different from her other jobs. When they hired her, the *Tribune* seemed less attentive to her needs than had her prior employers, who had made diversity in the workplace an explicit goal. Although the newspaper is—and was—subject to state and federal laws that prohibit discrimination, it has only one other employee with physical disabilities and little experience with accessibility issues. The editor who hired Sara asked about accommodations she would need and provided a protected parking space. But the only accessible bathroom was not on her floor, and the newspaper refused to provide one until Sara's coworkers protested on her behalf. When the paper agreed, she notes, they said " 'Okay, we'll do it, what do we have to do?' And then I went through the whole thing about the curtain." One of the problems she faced in dealing with accommodations at the *Midwest Tribune* was that she had expensive medical needs and, for a short time, difficulties with her supervisor as well. Although she acknowledges that she could have brought the accessibility issues to the paper's attention and fought for them, she was reluctant to do so "because of all the other complicated factors." Having no other source of income and a great many medical needs, she felt that her ability to negotiate with her employer was undercut by her dependence on her job and her problematic relationship with her immediate superior.

The passage of the Americans with Disabilities Act (ADA) in 1990 brought some significant changes to Sara Lane's status at the *Tribune,* but these changes occurred through the unilateral actions of her employers and not because Sara herself chose to invoke her rights under the act. At first, she recalls, the newspaper assumed that the ADA applied only to customers, not to employees. But when the paper realized, much later, that it also applied to employees, "somebody actually said to me, 'We treated you terribly. And we'll now try to make up and try to do something.' Yeah, it really took that law to get them to realize it." Sara believes that the paper's attitude has improved since then, and some accommodations have been made for her. She attributes the change in part to the increased value they place on her work but also to the ADA, which, unlike earlier civil rights laws for persons with disabilities, "has more teeth in it." She is negotiating with the publisher for paid leave while she has carpal tunnel surgery, "and I'm sure after some give and take we'll work something out. But he's very, he's now become extremely accommodating."

Yet even in this period of post-ADA improvements, Sara Lane feels reluctant to ask for accommodations specified by the new law. Instead of invoking the ADA to obtain flexible hours and permission to work at home, she would prefer to wait until the newspaper guild, the union that represents all employees, makes such a demand on behalf of all of its members:

> I would work more . . . with the guild, with our union, than I would ever work with a lawyer or whatever on ADA issues. I think that's less threatening to them. . . . As much as [the publisher] respects me and does for me what he says he can, you have to play the game, you have to be careful. And there is a point in my career where I don't want my disability to be out there that much. You know, so that by going through the guild it's the more proper way to do it.

Although Sara sometimes feels frustration and even anger because of inadequate accommodations, she sees risks in invoking legal rights that might remove barriers and improve her work. She fears that invoking the ADA would have a negative effect on the professional identity she has created over a period of many years and might prevent her from advancing to a higher position at the newspaper. The invocation of rights might suggest dependence, not the independence they were intended to promote. Sara realizes that the law has, at several key points in her life, played a critically important role in helping her to forge a career that conformed to the active self-image she has held since childhood. Yet she believes that the assertion of rights could also undermine that career by suggesting to others that her disability really does make her different, less capable, less independent. When it comes to issues of identity and rights, she observes, "You have to be careful."

At the end of the interview, we paused to reflect on a life story that simultaneously spoke of independence and of helpful interventions by others, of barriers impeding access and of accommodations that facilitated a successful career, of egalitarianism and paternalism, of laws and a legal culture that opened doors at important moments and of laws and a legal system that posed great professional risks and inflicted pain and humiliation. We asked Sara Lane to reflect on the complexity of the story she had told and the subtle and sometimes contradictory roles law had played in her life:

Q: Is this a success story?

SL: Is this a success story? It's too early to tell. I have a lot of physical problems right now in my body. Now that I'm forty, it's breaking down. From the use of the wheelchair, from carpal tunnel. And, to be perfectly, honest, I don't know if I'll make it to retirement. If my body will allow me to work, what I'm hoping is that technology will allow me to start working from home. And maybe part-time editor, part-time writer.

Her dilemma puts her ambitions at risk. She would like to ask for a promotion, but her need for carpal tunnel surgery interferes with this plan. She does not think she can ask for a raise and then leave work to have surgery. If she decides to stay at home, work part-time and take a pay cut, she may not have enough income to raise her daughter. But a pay cut is only part of the dilemma that working at home would pose. As she observed, "part of being a newspaper person is being here, and having face-to-face contact with the writers and news sources. And while someone from IBM can maybe work their program at home, the newspaper's an inherently different business."

The noisy, bustling newsroom is indeed a microcosm of Sara Lane's career. It has been a source of sustaining relationships. To banish herself from it would cut her off from the roots of her professional work. The newsroom has also defined the meaning of her disability. Early in her career, it defined that disability—in some respects, at least—as an asset. Now, her disability may force her to work at home and rely on technology to maintain contact with her work. She understands that such a move poses a fundamental threat to her professional identity.

Q: Where have you fallen short?
SL: Where have I fallen . . . I'm not running this newspaper, yet.

It's interesting to talk to you . . . and then to read it all together, because actually I don't think when you live this you pull all these things together. I didn't really think a lot about how my disability played out in terms of my career or how it maybe led me to the next level of the career. But seeing it in black and white made so much sense. I mean it put it in perspective for me, which I thought was kind of unusual, because when you're living it you don't really think about it.

I guess that I'm a pretty optimistic kind of person; and I guess when you're living a lot of this, it doesn't seem quite as easy or quite as happy as it sounds when you put it down and you look back on it years later. But I did feel prejudice in the newsroom, and I did feel often to be an outsider, and I did feel that I had to work a lot harder to prove myself on a daily basis. . . .

And you did get very, very, very tired of it after awhile. When you're out in the real world and you take your kid to the mall and you find that everybody who walks past you stares at you, that really starts to get at you after awhile. And there were times in the newsroom where that kind of staring was going on, that you just didn't feel they took you seriously or that they really wanted your opinion. And there were times when I would really lose my temper. . . . I said to the editors, how long do I have to be here before we get beyond this point, before this is not an issue anymore? . . .

Personally, it's been very degrading. . . . And the fact that they wouldn't give me a bathroom stall on my own floor for three or four years was just degrading beyond belief. It was infuriating; and you would just kind of go along for awhile and be a nice happy-go-lucky kid, but deep down it was really eating away at you. . . . I didn't feel that I could go to them one more time and say, I've got to have a bathroom stall on this floor, because you are perceived as a whiner. And you are perceived as someone, oh, well, we didn't realize you'd be so much trouble when we hired you. You're always thinking, what if somebody comes after me? You don't want to spoil it for them. You don't want them not hired because you're perceived as a whiner, because you want a bathroom on your floor. So there's always weighing heavy that the next generation of disabled employees are going to be screwed because they didn't like you.

The women at the Tribune have had a terrible time, and we do not have a lot of senior women officials there. We have a few more now but not enough. We all have our little crosses to bear, but being a woman and being disabled and being a single mother with special needs has been very difficult. The Tribune is definitely nineteenth century in its thinking. So that's how I would change it [i.e., the telling of her life story]. I would darken it quite a bit.

Life Story: Jill Golding

Jill Golding, unlike most of our interviewees with learning disabilities, speaks openly about her dyslexia; and when she speaks, she often invokes the language of rights and antidiscrimination law. For many others, concealment is a daily practice, and exposure—to employers, coworkers, and friends—is a constant threat. Their disability becomes the center of a secret life, vast and significant to them but hidden from those with whom they work or interact. Jill Golding is more forthright. Her learning disability was not diagnosed until 1991, when she was in her mid-twenties. The diagnosis came at a time when, through psychotherapy and self-reflection, she gained other insights into her identity and her upbringing. It coincided as well with an upsurge in social awareness of disability issues and new rights guarantees for persons with disabilities, particularly through implementation of the Americans with Disabilities Act (ADA) of 1990.

In the intersection of Jill's life history and evolving disability law, we find the origins of a distinctive legal consciousness in which the commitment to caring is closely linked to the language of rights. Jill observed that social and legal norms concerning disabilities have changed significantly in recent years. In the past, "nobody cared"; today, accessibility rights, particularly for persons with mobility impairments, are commonplace: "And where did that all start? Well, it started with one person." Throughout the narration of her life story, she links the themes of caring and of individual rights assertion. By asserting employment rights, she can become a nurse, who will care professionally for others; by asserting rights, she can ensure that employers and others will care for her, although she was not always cared for as a child; by asserting rights, she can be sure that other children, including her own, will be treated in the future with the care that she was denied during her own painful childhood.

Now in her late twenties, Jill Golding maintains a positive and hopeful outlook despite difficult experiences throughout her life. Her grade school years were, as she recounts in her narration, marred by illness, abuse, and humiliation. As early as kindergarten, she was sexually abused by a teenage boy, and she now realizes that this experience led to extreme discomfort in the presence of all her male teachers. At the same time, an undiagnosed learning disability impeded her classroom work and left her constantly in fear of exposure and ridicule. After her fourth-grade teacher spanked her with a ruler for misspelling an easy word on the board, Jill became terrified of being asked to read or spell in front of the class. Recollections of sexual abuse and anxiety over her learning disability merge and overlap as she tells her story. She became depressed and bulimic; she feigned illness in order to escape from the classroom and from contact with male teachers. The school nurse's office became her refuge.

The school nurse offered care and comfort. At an early age, Jill experienced direct connections between childhood disability, illness, and the compassion of a professional nurse. The humiliation and fear she experienced in school—when translated into stomach aches, vomiting, or even "fevers" produced by running hot water on thermometers—gave her access to a substitute mother who comforted and praised her. It is not surprising that Jill would later choose nursing as a career for herself.

Jill's own mother was, in her telling, a more distant and less understanding figure, whose attitude toward most difficulties was the same: "You prayed about it and God would take care of it." Her parents were public-spirited people, strongly committed to helping neighbors with their problems; but Jill recalls that they were not attentive to their own children. Jill's mother was also a nurse. In this complex mother-daughter relationship, Jill followed the service ethic and the career that shaped her mother's public life, while simultaneously identifying her mother's indifference as an important source of the pain that led her as a child to the office of another nurse and another mother figure.

When Jill was twelve, she assumed primary responsibility for her younger siblings. After school and through the night, it was up to her to feed them, change their diapers, and care for them in place of her parents. At the age of twelve, she acted out a commitment to caring—becoming a mother to her siblings even as she searched for someone who would be a mother to her.

Reading became increasingly problematic for Jill as she advanced into middle school. Told that she was a bad student, she became "mouthy" at times or else shy and withdrawn. Since no one ever recognized her disability, she received no special educational services or support. Even when help was offered—she recalls that a friend's father, a teacher in another school, was particularly generous in helping her with her schoolwork—her feelings of gratitude were mixed with fear and anxiety: "I was still really scared. He was a guy, you know, and until I was diagnosed as dyslexic I still always, in the back of my mind, thought I was stupid. And I didn't want people to pick up on that, so I didn't always, I tried to avoid situations." The signs of a learning disability were evident if anyone had taken the trouble to read them. Jill learned easily in courses that used a workbook but failed in courses where the teacher lectured. She could not write or think fast enough to keep up in the less structured classes and would find herself staring at a blank sheet of paper at the end of the hour.

In high school, I thought that I was just stupid. There was a blank, broad "NO" in my head that said, you're never going to be an A student. Now I realize that there's different degrees of everything. Dyslexia does not mean everything is upside down, backwards, or whatever. And there's different avenues of how to deal with it.

An incident while Jill was in middle school helped shape her career interest in children with disabilities. A small class of developmentally disabled students was bused to Jill's school, where they became the objects of curiosity and hostility. A friend told Jill to write a note to one boy in this class, saying "Fuck you." Without knowing the meaning of what she was writing, Jill did as she was told. The school suspended her for three days, and her mother made her apologize to the boy. Jill recalls her mother saying, "You had no right to write that note to that child. You gave that note to that child because you didn't think he'd understand it. Well, he's a human being, and he has feelings. And he is just as smart as the rest of us. He might have a different way of showing it or using it, but you do not abuse him because he's in a different program."

Jill's mother also made her write a report on children with disabilities. In researching this report, Jill contacted the United Cerebral Palsy Association and became fascinated with pictures in brochures showing therapists working with young children. The incident, and the report Jill had to write as a consequence, made her decide that when she grew up she wanted to work with children with disabilities. Through such a career she could make up for mistreating her classmate and could also channel her own generous and caring impulses into work that comported with her mother's value system. In her teenage years, Jill not only cared for her own siblings but did volunteer work at a local hospital for children who were sick or had disabilities. The school nurse sponsored Jill's work at the hospital, which was also where her mother was employed. Early in her life, following the incident in which she had betrayed the commitment to caring, Jill began to forge a career path that affirmed her mother's public values yet simultaneously allowed her to nurture children with whom she closely identified because of her own painful childhood.

Working in the hospital, Jill received praise and encouragement, unlike the humiliation and criticism she experienced in school. She recalls that doctors told her, "You're going to be a good nurse, or you're going to be a good doctor, but you're going to stay in this field because you've got the heart, and you've got what it takes to be a good one." Upon graduation from high school, she resolved to study either nursing or physical therapy. She was accepted into a physical therapy program in college, but withdrew almost immediately when she learned that she would have to dissect cadavers. She married and worked as a hospital aide for a time, but the marriage proved to be a mistake: her husband abused her and refused to allow her to reenter college. Jill became depressed and her eating disorder worsened. Receiving little comfort from her husband or her family, she entered therapy.

Therapy, in Jill's narration, marked a turning point: "A lot of the truths that had been secrets for many years came out." She gained a perspective on her life that allowed her to understand the connections between her experiences growing up and her illness and depression. She also gained enough confidence to confront her parents, to insist that they, too, undergo therapy. She countered what she characterizes as a repressed and religious ethos in her family ("If you pray about it, God will take care of it") with a more assertive, even legalistic approach: if her parents refused therapy, she threatened to have Social Services take away her younger siblings, who were also experiencing considerable distress growing up.

I was never brought up thinking that you could set goals and attain them. I don't know what really triggered that. Probably the biggest thing is my therapist. And then of course getting involved with [children with disabilities]. That certainly sets you up for seeing what they've accomplished. I mean you see these people doing amazing things. . . . [Therapy] gave me the self-esteem and the confidence. At the same time, I met my [second] husband, and he's so supportive. I think that was the strongest turning point.

My husband says I'm over-assertive, too demanding in some sense, but I think we all have some degree of overdoing certain things. And I'd rather be over-assertive and considered too demanding than be taken advantage of. But I feel bad that not everybody has had that opportunity. I think God gives us little paths. I'm not a horribly religious person like my family, but I do believe that He has a reason for everything, but you have to use those things to your advantage. You have to seek out why is He doing this? What is this going to lead me to?

For several years after returning to college, Jill floated from one program to another, dissatisfied with her course of study and frustrated with her difficulty in reading. Eventually she realized that she had a learning problem and insisted on an evaluation. As she describes this period in her life, she explicitly connects the discovery of her learning disability with the discovery of a capacity to advocate her own interests: "It was only because I'm very demanding at this point in my life that I went on and demanded that someone find what was wrong." Although Jill was then in her mid-twenties, she told her parents it was their responsibility to pay for the costly evaluation because, had they cared for her properly as a child and recognized her educational *rights,* she would have been diagnosed at a much earlier age and her childhood would have been far less painful: "There's someone at XYZ Clinic that will test me. Would you be interested in paying for it? I feel it's your responsibility, because this is something that should have been picked up on eleven years ago, when I was in your care. So I think it's your responsibility."

I was determined. I wanted to find out what was wrong. And if I had to drive two hours, that was acceptable to me, because I wanted an answer. Some people don't want answers. Some people are not willing to go to that length simply because they don't either have the self-esteem or the income.

Armed with a professional evaluation of her learning disability for the first time in her career as a student, Jill received the accommodations recommended by the learning specialist, and her academic work improved significantly. She completed her nursing program and continued her work with children as a professional nurse. She loves her job, her health is improved, and she is happily married to an understanding and supportive husband. Jill's discussion of employment rights for persons with learning disabilities reflects her own recent transformation. She is aware that her reading difficulties might affect some aspects of her work, such as preparing medications for the children. She arrives at work half an hour early to give herself time to go through the orders slowly and carefully. She is happy and comfortable in her present job but worries that she might encounter misunderstanding if she had to apply for work with a new employer. If an employer refused to hire her because of her learning disability, she describes her likely reaction in unusually legalistic terms:

> Oh, I would go to court and I would fight back, because that is not right. . . . They have to let me prove myself. If I proved incompetent, if I proved that I was giving meds in error or that my order was incorrect, if they have reason to not hire me, that's fine. But don't create a reason unless it's there. . . . They're saying that I can't do my job, and I can. And unless they show me just reason why I can't, or how this interferes with my job, then they can't discriminate.

Few of our interviewees with learning disabilities viewed their situation through such a rights-tinged lens. Jill's perspective is distinctive because it equates learning disabilities with physical disabilities ("If I had one arm, that is no different") and with the issue of racial discrimination ("It's as equal as black and white or minority versus majority"). To enforce such fundamental equality rights, Jill feels she must be "hardheaded" and "demanding," by which she means, "I would fight as much as I could." Jill distinguishes, however, between discrimination in the hiring process and discrimination on the job. If her job application were rejected because of her disability, she would fight hard "to prove to them that they better not do it again"; but in the end she would probably not take the job. She would not want to work in a setting where her employer had doubts about her and hired her simply because the law required it. She would fight them so that their attitudes would begin to change, but she would seek work elsewhere.

Fighting for accommodations on the job is a different matter. Here, too, Jill would be tenacious, but there is no question of moving on to another job after winning a legal victory. Jill's reasoning is important and reflects the close connections she makes between caring and rights claims. An employer should not, she insists, refuse to accommodate her disability on the grounds that she must follow the same routines as all the other nurses or be disqualified: "Oh, then I would fight back. . . . I need you to work with me. You deal with the situation. I'm a nurse and, especially in this field, no situation is identical. Do I treat my patient like the patient in the next bed? No, every person is different. So don't tell me that there's anything concrete."

The analogy is revealing. Jill compares the relation between herself and her employer to that of patient and nurse, inverting the professional relationship in which she works every day by equating herself with the patient rather than the caregiver. By asserting her rights, she can guarantee that her employer will treat her with the same individualized care that she, as a nurse, provides her patients. In some sense, Jill views her own altruism and compassion toward others as originating in the caring that others have—or *should* have—extended to her: her employer, the school nurse, and her own mother. Although she struggled to receive such care in her childhood, she now views caring as an entitlement—for employees as well as for children and hospital patients. The entitlement is now connected in her mind to legal rights under the ADA: if she is not treated with respect for her individual differences and needs, then she will invoke antidiscrimination law to assert her interests.

Jill's perceptions of employment rights are thus connected to her identity, past and present: as a child, as a "patient" who was cared for by the school nurse, and as a health care professional who now cares for others. For Jill, rights claims can enforce the commitment to caring that is the core of her adult value system. Although she is personally entitled to the benefits of disability law, she also sees its value for others. Because she now has a child, she must protect her employment rights for her child's sake. More broadly, however, Jill asks, "What about all the kids who don't have parents that either care or don't have avenues that are accessible or whatever? I have to really do my part." Again, her perspective is simultaneously self-referential and concerned with children growing up as she did—that is, without understanding and support. By asserting her own employment rights, Jill can pave the way for children who might otherwise have to suffer all the difficulties she experienced. A rights claim is not just a matter of entitlement for Jill, or of financial security for her own child, but an act of caring for children who, like Jill as a child, are vulnerable, frightened, and in pain.

I wouldn't disagree with any of the interpretations. I do have to apologize. There was one part in there where you said that "she" was able to incorporate a theme throughout her thing; and I'm thinking, there have been so many times when people—well, my husband in particular—will say, you jump from topic to topic. And I know I was with that interview. Of course it is more evident when I am nervous or in a new situation. But that was the one thing, I interpreted that as being, well she rambled on and on and on. But I don't think it was meant that way, and I certainly don't think that someone reading it would interpret it that way. It's just my own insecurity. . . . So that was the only part that I laughed and thought, oh that's so cute. I wonder if anybody else sees it that way.

The interview was very good in that you were able to get me on track. You kept it in order, basically. You were able to say, okay, now, let's start here and let's work our way up; and I think that that's important in something like this. And you were able to get up to the employment part of it. And fortunately I was employed at the time. I don't think I would change anything. I think that my views are still the same, and I don't foresee them changing.

I think anybody reading this will get a sense of, first of all let's say that it was somebody with a learning disability, or anyone really, they can read this and say there's certainly people out there that have accomplished things, based on whatever their history is. You can accomplish things. And that no person is the same. . . . Or they're reading it so that they can get some hope for something, and I think that they're going to gain that, too.

Life Stories: Sara Lane and Jill Golding Together

[After completing our work on the life stories of Sara Lane and Jill Golding, inserting their later comments into the texts, we sent the final versions to both women and invited them to participate in a joint interview. Sara and Jill were eager to meet and wanted to speak with us and with each other about the issues addressed in an article we had just written that drew extensively on their stories (Engel and Munger 1996). Since we had last seen them, changes had occurred in their lives. Jill Golding had passed her licensing exam and was now a registered nurse. Sara Lane had undergone orthopedic surgery and anticipated a second operation in the near future. She observed that she had become more willing than in the past to request special leaves and accommodations and was increasingly inclined to present such requests in terms of her legal rights. She now viewed the individual rights framework as preferable to a strategy that relied on union intervention, for it had become clear to her that the union had no interest in advocating home work arrangements for any of its members. As discussion continued, Sara and Jill compared their current attitudes toward social change, rights, relationships, and the employment setting.]

Sara: I don't think we're ready though to even sit down and say to ourselves, "We did good. We got far." Because it always seems like there's another challenge that's on the horizon.

Jill: Exactly, exactly.

Sara: There's always something.

Jill: We're always critical of ourselves.

Sara: And it's always the same frigging issues. They never change. . . . I sometimes feel like I'm talking to a wall except that I have this great woman supervisor who gets it and who puts her job on the line for me all the time. And I know she meets these incredible "Are you kidding?" kind of responses. So I think, bottom line, they feel sorry for me, and that's why they're doing what they're doing. It has nothing to do with my rights; they feel sorry for me. . . .

Jill: I would tend to agree that a lot of people do feel sorry, but I think we have to say, "I don't care if you feel sorry for me or not. Is the end result what I want?" I might be the sorryass that got everything I wanted and everybody [pitied] me, but I don't have to accept the pity. I have to accept the just reward in the end. . . . So sometimes I think that it is hard to get what you want. But if the end result is to get what you want, it doesn't matter why you got it. Just be thankful that you got it. And make sure the reasons you wanted it were appropriate also. . . . Unfortunately you and I are the fighters. We're the front line in this battle; and as much as we're uncomfortable with it, it is still our duty as a human being to take care of that. To do it for ourselves, to do it for our family, to do it for the future generations. It doesn't mean it's going to be easy, and it certainly doesn't mean that we're going to get our rights met, but at least we can rest assured that we tried. . . .

Sara: I think that our kids will have it better only because there's a better education process going on. And if passing the ADA boosted this education process, which I think it has—the mainstream media has done some good work since the ADA came out—that's more important to me than actually what the law will do. It's more how people's minds are changed, and that's education and that's what we're doing, unfortunately. . . . I think the only way that this will ever really come to fruition is in the workplace. I mean, where else in our lives are we peers as we are in the workplace? So it's critical for the education and for the whole implementation of the rights to be done on the job where people are equal. I mean, you're not going to do it in your church; you're not going to do it in the supermarket; it's got to be [on the job]. And that's so unfortunate, because of the dinosaur that the American corporate world is, that that's the critical place. It wasn't that long ago when I was in college and I was told I couldn't be a teacher because a disabled woman could not handle a class of children. I mean, that's so bad to think about. Think about it: that's the only way to educate children, is to have a disabled teacher. You get them young, and you convince them right away.

Jill: Certainly family education has to fall into place, too. I mean, old-fashioned thinkers that are parents, they have to, they can't sit there and stereotype. I don't know how to get that other than if they get it from their workplace. I think the workplace is the key—and then schools, because those are the two places that everybody falls into. But there's going to be a gap before everyone meets, and how long that gap is I don't know. But I think it's going to be shorter than we might have thought it would be years ago. . . . It's just unfortunate that they hold the key. They really do hold the key, you know.

Jill: Rights or not, when it comes right down to it, if they fire you, yeah, you can sue, but what do you do in the year's time to support your family while you're fighting this lawsuit? It's great to have rights, but sometimes they aren't as helpful as we want them to be.

Sara: It's not practical. It's just not practical for real life.

Jill: It isn't . . .

Sara: [But] the symbolism of them I think is effective.

Identity and Rights

How do rights become active in the lives of their intended beneficiaries? Studies of the effects of civil rights usually address this question by examining the frequency with which individuals make claims, hire lawyers, and file lawsuits. Consciousness of rights, in such studies, is defined as the extent to which rights holders understand the law, gain access to lawyers and legal institutions, and weigh the costs and benefits of legal action. We think such approaches are inadequate. The life stories of Sara Lane and Jill Golding, like those of the other interviewees in this book, suggest that identity, rather than legal competence or rational choice, is the appropriate starting point for exploring how rights become active. In this chapter, we examine the relationship between disability and identity, and we argue that this relationship is key to understanding the effects of the Americans with Disabilities Act (ADA) and of civil rights in general.

The issue of who one is and where one belongs precedes the issue of the rights one might choose to assert. Viewed from this perspective, law is often of secondary importance to those it is supposed to help and is at times an irrelevancy. The more fundamental question is how and when individuals view themselves as inappropriately situated in the social framework, as excluded from activities in which they should take part, as unfairly separated from mainstream settings by barriers that have been improperly constructed or placed. The perception of boundaries wrongly marked is inseparable from the sense of self. The perception that exclusion is appropriate or inappropriate, indeed the *awareness* that exclusion has occurred, hinges on the way in which individuals and those around them define their identity. Jill Golding's childhood identity as an unintelligent and uncooperative student was consistent with the perception that it was fair to exclude her from mainstream educational opportunities; but her adult identity was, at least in her own mind, inconsistent with exclusion from the nursing profession. What appeared to be "normal" treatment of Jill Golding as a child now appears to be unfair and perhaps a violation of her rights as an adult. Perception of a potential role for legal rights turns on such assumptions about inclusion and exclusion and is thus inseparable from identity.

When we speak of "identity" in this book, we refer to concepts of the self that emerge from interactions among individuals and groups over time. As Bruner (1990:110) observes, the creation of the self is not an isolated process but involves the society and culture in which the individual lives: "The Self, then, like any other aspect of human nature, stands both as a guardian of permanence and as a barometer responding to the local cultural weather. The culture, as well, provides us with guides and stratagems for finding a niche between stability and change: it exhorts, forbids, lures, denies, rewards the commitments that the Self undertakes. And the Self, using its capacities for reflection and for envisaging alternatives, escapes or embraces or reevaluates and reformulates what the culture has on offer." Identities may be consensual or contested, imposed or voluntarily assumed. They are the products of already familiar images and stereotypes, and they also emerge spontaneously from surprising acts of creativity and struggle. Identities are not like product labels or street addresses. They continually evolve and may be read differently depending on one's position, relationships, and circumstances. As the narratives of Sara Lane and Jill Golding illustrate, even the individual in question may define her identity differently from one moment to the next or from one context to another. Society as a whole may project an identity onto an individual who rejects the social consensus and views herself in entirely different terms.

The protean quality of identity is a key to our study. The capacity to view oneself as unique and distinct from social stereotypes explains the success some of our interviewees have enjoyed. The ability to reimagine oneself, to create ever more expansive identities, is part of the process through which successful careers are constructed. As individual identity changes, the individual's position in society may be perceived in new and different ways—by herself and by others. These perceptions may lead to the conclusion that the individual is positioned on the wrong side of a social boundary, that she is being treated unfairly, and even that her rights have been violated. Until the perception of exclusion arises, the law's protections do not appear relevant. Sara Lane was prevented by architectural barriers from entering a library until she became a college freshman. She and others assumed that the absence of a ramp was a normal part of the world in which they lived, and Sara as a child accepted that her place was outside and not inside those libraries. As an adult, however, Sara assumes that she is entitled to enter public buildings, that her exclusion is unfair, and that the absence of a ramp—or an accessible bathroom and elevator at her workplace—is a violation of her rights.

In this chapter, we consider some of the distinctive features of identity formation of individuals with disabilities. Using the life story narratives of our interviewees, we present different patterns of identity formation that vary in the extent to which the disability overwhelms or remains separate from other aspects of the self. To put it another way, some of our interviewees viewed themselves as persons with disabilities, while others viewed themselves (and were viewed by employers) as disabled persons. We consider some of the differences between physical and learning disabilities in this regard, since these two disability categories raise different issues of identity and accommodation. Having suggested some of the basic features of identity formation over time, we then explore how identity leads some individuals but not others to perceive their experiences in terms of rights.

Disability and Identity

Identity and the positioning of the self in relation to the social mainstream determines whether individuals experience a sense of unfairness that might lead them to invoke their rights under the ADA. The identities of persons with disabilities take shape over time in a symbolically charged environment. As Goffman (1963) observed, disability can impose a stigma that "spoils" identity, impairs normal social interactions, and excludes the individual from participating freely in everyday activities, including employment. The stigmatizing effects of disability are sometimes powerful enough to create an identity whose natural place appears to be outside the mainstream and whose position on the margins of society may seem fair and appropriate, even to the individual herself. We do not always see ourselves as others see us, but their views have lasting effects.

It is remarkable that Sara Lane, whose disability was highly visible from early childhood, resisted a marginalized identity so effectively throughout her life. As a child, according to the story Sara now tells, she learned in elementary school that she was bright, energetic, active, and popular, and that she should participate in the same activities as her peers. For children with physical disabilities, this sense of self does not often emerge so clearly at such a young age. Sara accounts for her positive self-image in terms of the experience of a generation of children with polio—the "type A" children whose parents and doctors pushed them to be self-reliant, independent, and socially integrated with classmates who had no disabilities. Sara's life story narrative is notably consistent: the resilient, independent, and confident self of childhood is clearly the predecessor of the journalist Sara was later to become.

For Jill Golding, because her disability was invisible and for a long time went undiagnosed, it was more difficult to resist a marginalized identity. Her dyslexia tended to relegate her to the margins of society because it affected her behavior rather than her appearance and limited her efforts to participate fully in the academic and social life of her peers. Her disability tended to spoil her identity because its effects made Jill appear—even to herself—less intelligent, hard-working, and well-intentioned than other children. Despite the negative social consequences of Jill's disability, however, her identity took shape during childhood in ways that would ultimately influence her pursuit of a professional career. Her devotion to service and caring when she was very young—acting as a primary caregiver for her younger siblings, for example—eventually translated into a commitment to nursing. The choice of career was strongly influenced by the two women who most affected her childhood: the motherly school nurse and her own public-spirited but emotionally distant mother. Jill's identity, her sense of who she was, thus developed in step with her sense of a vocation. She was a child who needed nurturing, but she was also a child who provided nurturing to others; the approval and sense of fulfillment that she sought throughout her childhood were most available to her when she played this role.

Sara's and Jill's life story narratives highlight two aspects of identity formation that are central to our discussion throughout this book: (1) identity's interactive and intersubjective development, and (2) the importance of the narrative process itself in the formation of identity. Many theorists have emphasized the interactive and intersubjective development of identity. Most would agree that identity is not simply assigned by others or unilaterally adopted by the individual, nor is identity fixed and unchanging. Rather, identity reflects a *process of interaction* over an extended period of time. Habermas (1979:107), for example, asserts that individual identity is a product of "communicative action" involving persons and social groups who participate interactively in the creation of the self: "No one can construct an identity independently of the identifications that others make of him. . . . [The ego] presents itself to itself as a practical ego in the performance of communicative actions; and in communicative action the participants must reciprocally suppose that the distinguishing-oneself-from-others is recognized by those others. Thus the basis for the assertion of one's own identity is not really self-identification, but intersubjectively recognized self-identification."

Similarly, Bruner (1990:114) argues that identity must be understood in terms of the network of family, friends, and acquaintances among whom we "distribute" various facets of the self, almost like using different filing cabinets for important documents. Jill's identity was distributed among her parents, her siblings, her school nurse, and her friends. Among them, her sense of herself as a competent and caring future nurse took root. Yet her distributed identity also reinforced negative images of incompetence, shame, and failure. Her teachers and some of her classmates viewed her as stupid, lazy, "mouthy," and unfocused, and Jill also accepted and internalized these unfavorable perceptions throughout her childhood. They became—and to some extent still remain—a part of the self that persists into her adult years. Jill's evolving sense of self thus contained a volatile mix of elements, some of which were potentially highly destructive. It is significant that Jill could eventually transcend the more limited and negative elements of her identity, which were continually reinforced in her dealings with others.

Sara's account of her childhood and adolescence also illustrates the concept of distributed identity, but in a more positive and less destructive way. The elements of her identity that her parents shared and reinforced were those of a child who belonged in the mainstream despite her disability. She apparently saw herself as they saw her, belonging within the context of typical school social life, although there were surely times when such perceptions were stretched to the limit by medical treatment and rehabilitation and by the restrictions created by a physically inaccessible environment. Nonetheless, her dealings with teachers and peers were much more fulfilling and positively reinforcing than Jill's. Sara's distributed identity, the self she shared with others around her, was consistent with an adult life in mainstream settings performing challenging professional tasks.

The interactive process of identity formation shapes a sense of self that is consistent with inclusion or exclusion in mainstream society. One's distributed identity continually changes because one tends to interact with different individuals and groups as time passes. Different groups may reinforce significantly different self-understandings. To some extent, these changes are the product of choices individuals themselves make as they gravitate toward some relationships and away from others. Jill, for example, chose to spend time with the school nurse and with the doctors, nurses, and patients at the hospital where she volunteered; and they, in turn, reinforced her self-image as a competent care provider. Yet sometimes it was luck, happenstance, or someone else's choice that placed Jill and Sara in one social context rather than another. Sara might have remained forever in segregated special education programs had her mother not intervened to force Sara's inclusion in regular elementary school classrooms; and Sara's identity would have formed very differently apart from the social mainstream. Similarly, after high school, Sara chose to attend a college well known for its supportive and accessible programs. Yet it was a somewhat fortuitous combination of friendships and public events—particularly the emergence of a national disability rights movement—that caused Sara and some of her classmates to chafe under what they considered an overly paternalistic college administration and to view themselves as persons entitled to a more complete form of social integration.

The second key element of identity formation is the role of narrative in shaping the self over time (see generally Bruner 1990:111–16). It has been clear, at least since the advent of Freudian psychology, that identity and life history narratives are inseparable. Goffman (1963:57) asserts that life stories become identities, in the sense that people's life histories are told in order to characterize the unique self who lived that history, and *also* in the sense that new experiences and facts, as they occur and are narrated, "stick" to the identity and are regarded as further illustrations of the self who is narratively constituted: "Personal identity, then, has to do with the assumption that the individual can be differentiated from all others and that around this means of differentiation a single continuous record of social facts can be attached, entangled, like candy floss, becoming then the sticky substance to which still other biographical facts can be attached."

The important role of narrative in constituting identity is further elucidated by Rosenwald (1992:272–73), who views the evolution of identity in terms of a "dialectic of telling and living life." The ever-changing stories people tell themselves and others about who they are alternate with "new living action." That is, narratives of the self follow and explain past experiences, but they also *precede* new experiences in which individuals attempt to act out the selves they have narrated and the desires and aspirations associated with those selves: "New living action follows a new story partly as a way of catching the life up to the account of the life and partly to express what is missing from the story. Each story falls short of expressing the full potential of the subject, and each action is somewhat false to the story it bodies forth" (274–75).

Rosenwald posits a dynamic, forward-moving process in which retrospection and experience alternately propel the individual through new activities and life stages. This process may stall or "stultify" if opportunities for new living action are obstructed or if the imagination falters and individuals cannot create new stories of the self with new possibilities for social experience (283). Both risks are very real for people with disabilities: society often creates barriers that sharply limit new living action; and individuals themselves sometimes lack the imaginative resources to envision life options beyond those they have already experienced. As Rosenwald observes, "there are many ways to run aground" (ibid.); and the dangers are especially acute for individuals who have disabilities.

A key question for all of our interviewees as they narrate their life stories is the extent to which disability overshadows other elements of their identity. Goffman's classic study demonstrated how identities can be "spoiled" by the stigma associated with disability. We discovered that the extent of spoiling varies greatly among our interviewees. For some of them, the effects of disability—social, physical, and cognitive—pervade every aspect of their identities as they and others perceive them. For other interviewees, however, disability is one of many elements constituting the self, and its effects on identity are balanced by numerous other attributes and experiences that emerge in the life stories.

We think a fundamental issue for individuals with disabilities is their capacity to narrate a forward-looking life story, to use the past in order to establish a pathway for "new living action" (Rosenwald 1992); and those who were best able to create such narratives without "running aground" were the individuals who could most often differentiate their disability from their sense of self. For these individuals, disability was not the all-pervasive fact of their identity but merely an objective feature of their life experience that had its place among many other features. For them, *the disability was not the self,* although it was a part of their life experience that sometimes had great importance.

Furthermore, we see the capacity to distinguish disability from self as a key to opening a space in which rights might become active. For the individual who perceives and describes herself as a "disabled person," it is less likely that exclusion from mainstream social activities will appear to be notable or unfair treatment. Such an individual is unlikely to consider using rights to change a situation that strikes her as normal and appropriate. On the other hand, to the individual who perceives and describes herself as a person with many attributes and capabilities, of which the disability is but one, there is a greater chance that exclusion will appear unfair, because it precludes her participation on the basis of one aspect of her identity while ignoring the many others that make her similar to people who participate freely in mainstream activities and settings.

The life stories of Sara Lane and Jill Golding illustrate both of the key features of identity that we seek to highlight in this book: the interactivity of identity formation and the importance of narrative in constructing a self that can either run aground or move forward in productive ways. Furthermore, both Sara and Jill eventually achieved a relatively clear sense of self that was not dominated (or "spoiled") by their disability, and thus both of them discovered a space in their lives in which rights could operate.

Sara's social interactions during childhood, guided by her parents, shaped an identity compatible with an education and professional career in the mainstream. Her earliest experiences as a child with family, professionals, and friends made her aware that several very different social identities were available to her. Each could have led to profoundly different adult personas and career paths. The story she tells about her own childhood highlights the choices she made and the unproductive paths she avoided. Polio imposed on her the necessity of hospitalization, treatment, surgery, and rehabilitation. It created a risk that her primary identity would be that of a patient. Institutional practices at that time accentuated the physical separation and social distinction between children who were patients and those who were not. Furthermore, the images of childhood polio patients were familiar throughout American society from newspapers, magazines, and March of Dimes posters and pamphlets. Certain well-defined cultural connotations were associated with these young patients, who were viewed as plucky but extremely unfortunate, as "crippled" by their illness, as struggling against crushing circumstances beyond their control, and as unlikely despite their "courage" to attain meaningful independence. A second form of potential social identity connected with the first was the noninstitutionalized but nevertheless "handicapped" child. In Sara's description of the summer camps she attended, children with disabilities were segregated from all other children and were defined as a distinct group for whom social activities and relationships had to be programmed apart from the mainstream. Such programs could be supportive and nurturing, but Sara now believes that the children who participated in them were generally destined for segregated lives as "handicapped" adults.

Sara and her family steered away from these two kinds of identity toward a third, the one Sara still embraces and offers spontaneously in her interactions with others: that of the independent self who desires—and deserves—a place in mainstream social settings. Sara's mother cultivated this identity and made sure that Sara participated in sleepovers with friends, attended neighborhood schools in regular education classrooms, and took part in extracurricular activities. Her mother apparently shared the doctors' view that children who used crutches were less handicapped than those who used wheelchairs and that most forms of physical accommodation in the house would signify weakness in the face of Sara's disability. Sara learned a great deal about independence and social integration during her childhood, but she learned somewhat less about bringing appropriate physical accommodations with her into the social mainstream.

Sara's identity developed in the context of these conflicting social images of children with polio, filtered through the family members who helped her negotiate the social interactions that make up one's childhood. With her mother's guidance, Sara self-consciously chose to emphasize the social identity that created the greatest opportunity for her to pursue a nondisabled career despite her disability. Consequently, although Sara's disability affected most aspects of her life, the story she tells is one in which *her disability is not her self.* Her identity includes the fact of polio and its physical effects, but she was more able than most children in her circumstances to objectify her disability, to separate her disability to a large extent from her sense of who she was. She was a child who had had polio; she was not a polio victim. We do not suggest that this process of objectification and distancing was or ever could be complete; it always remains an issue. One's disability is always a part of one's identity; and, at times, one's identity may seem to collapse back into the powerful effects of the disability. The disability may succeed for a time in recolonizing the self. Many people who have disabilities struggle with this dilemma; yet Sara's story is distinctive because she addressed the dilemma so forcefully at such an early age in order to achieve some measure of separation between disability and self.

Jill Golding's life story also illustrates the two key elements of identity formation: its interactive and its narrative qualities. By the time Jill told us her life story, she, like Sara Lane, had achieved a sense of self that was separate from her disability, but during her childhood this was far from true. Jill's early sense of self, affected by her invisible and undiagnosed learning disability, emerged from painful and humiliating interactions with her family, her teachers, and her schoolmates. Jill came to see herself as they saw her: a lazy and unintelligent child without prospects. Unlike Sara, Jill lacked a mother who understood her problems and could guide her effectively through the childhood interactions that shape identity. Growing up in the 1970s and 1980s, Jill attended school with other children whose learning disabilities were diagnosed and who received special education services, yet no one seems to have considered that Jill might have belonged with them. Jill today is obviously bright. It is doubtful that anyone would consider her an unintelligent adult, but as a child she apparently warded off potentially helpful

grownups through shyness and "mouthiness." She was intensely fearful of adult males because she had been sexually abused at an early
age. Adult females, such as the teacher who spanked her in front of the
class for a spelling error, were also potential sources of humiliation and
degradation. As a consequence of these destructive social interactions,
Jill thought of herself as an essentially incapable and stupid person.
Her strategy in dealing with adults was not to display her considerable
intellectual strengths—of which she was not necessarily aware—but to
minimize her interactions with them, to make herself as small and in-
conspicuous as possible. She describes only one fulfilling connection
with an adult—the school nurse—and that connection was established
by presenting herself as a sick person in need of treatment. The contrast
with Sara, who assiduously avoided the category of "sick child," could
not be more vivid.

For Jill during childhood, unlike Sara, *her disability was her self.* Although at some level Jill may have suspected that she had a learning
disability, she did not succeed as a child in objectifying the condition
that affected the way she thought, learned, and processed information.
Unlike Sara, Jill could not look in the mirror and see that she had a
disability; and no adult told her that one existed. It is hard to objectify
a disability without knowing that you have it. Jill's process of identity
formation, based on a series of negative interactions with the people
around her, was a downward spiral until she underwent successful psychotherapy as a young adult. At that time, in Rosenwald's terms, she
learned how to tell a different version of her life story that enabled her
to pursue a more affirmative and productive life. A significant part of
Jill's new life story narrative was a diagnosis of her learning disability
that made it possible for Jill to perceive herself as a highly intelligent
person who had difficulty reading. Gradually, she was able to differentiate her disability from her sense of self. It became only one aspect of
an identity that included many other qualities and capabilities. As Jill
discovered the capacity to narrate an entirely different story of her life,
one in which she was a child with special needs that adults had failed
to recognize and accommodate, she changed the direction of her life
and embarked on "new living action" leading to a career as a nurse.

The role of rights emerges in Sara's and Jill's narratives as the result of a process of identity formation in which the sense of self separates itself from the disability that threatens to "spoil" identity. Sara
had found it possible since early childhood to "objectify" her disability
and maintain some degree of separation between it and her sense of
self. Although Sara's story evolved over time and in different circumstances changed from "lighter" to "darker," her sense of entitlement

to mainstream educational and professional settings is a thread that runs throughout her narrative. With the enactment of the ADA, it was natural for Sara to adopt the language of rights to describe what she perceived as unfair acts of exclusion from the mainstream.

By contrast, the incorporation of the language of rights in Jill Golding's narrative marked a dramatic autobiographical transformation. When Jill as an adult eventually realized that she was a capable person with good career prospects, she also recognized that *in the past* she had been unfairly excluded from access to educational opportunities that should have been available to her. The recognition of unfairness and exclusion created a consciousness that rights—or rather the disregard of her rights—had played a role in her experiences. Jill began to retell her life story in terms of the violation of her rights to educational services and accommodations rather than her own shortcomings. In this new narrative, Jill's parents were accountable for the violation of her rights, as were many of the adults with whom she had interacted during her childhood. Moreover, as Jill reinterpreted her past in terms of rights violations rather than personal failures, she created a new self for whom "new living action" might include a role for rights as she pursues her career. Her new narrative of the past is also a story of Jill's future, in which she is a bright and capable professional entitled *as a matter of right* to participate fully in the workplace.

By the time of our interviews with Sara and Jill, they drew in similar ways on the language of rights to tell their life stories and express their sense of identity. Yet they had arrived at this similar perspective through dramatically different life experiences. Some of these differences arise from the fact that Sara's disability was open, obvious, and associated with a set of widely recognized cultural images and assumptions, while Jill's was invisible and culturally uncertain. These differences between physical and learning disabilities are important to our discussion throughout the book. In the next section, therefore, we explore in greater detail how the two disability types affect the process of identity formation among our interviewees.

Physical and Learning Disabilities: Identity Formation and Rights

We have suggested that the process of identity formation is central to an individual's orientation toward rights, and that identities develop in relation to the social environment in which the individual experiences the world. Interactions over time shape the self who is a potential rights bearer under the ADA. These interactions, however, are not the same for all types of disabilities. The use of the single term "disability" may suggest, misleadingly, that individuals in very different circumstances have more or less the same experiences and social interactions and form very similar identities. Yet our discussion thus far has pointed to some of the differences in the life stories of Sara Lane, who contracted polio as a child, and Jill Golding, who has dyslexia. In this section, we address these differences more fully and draw explicit comparisons between the identities and rights orientations of individuals with physical and learning disabilities.

The contrast between physical disabilities and learning disabilities is central to our study. We sharpened this contrast by selecting for interviews only those persons with physical disabilities who use wheelchairs, since the wheelchair has become a universal symbol of disability. For those who use wheelchairs, moreover, a classic and widely understood argument against discrimination is available: people should not be judged by superficial physical differences. The chair in which they sit does not limit how they can think or, in many instances, how they can act. Here the contrast with learning disabilities is very significant. There are often no physical differences to identify an individual with a learning disability. The only important difference may be in the way she thinks or acts. Moreover, these cognitive differences can be subtle, highly variable, and usually not well understood by the general population. Unlike the universally recognized symbol of the wheelchair, there is no familiar symbol or cultural category for a learning disability. People with learning disabilities, consequently, find themselves misunderstood and miscategorized. The fact that their disability affects cognition leads to the erroneous assumption that they are intellectually incapable. The invisibility of their disability, therefore, creates an almost irresistible temptation for them to conceal it and to attempt to "pass" as a person who has no disability, for the risk of an occasional public slipup—in reading, writing, processing information, directionality, or computation—is less than the risk of being perceived as intellectually deficient. These and other differences in the process of identity formation, as they relate to perspectives on rights under the ADA, are the subject of the discussion that follows.

Physical Disabilities

The existence of a physical disability, particularly one requiring the use of a wheelchair, appears to be a manifest, objectively verifiable aspect of one's identity. Yet even this type of disability raises fundamental definitional issues. Wright (1983:11), for example, defines physical disability as a "limitation of function that results directly from an impairment at the level of a specific organ or body system." But the "handicapping" effects of a disability—the "limitations of function" in their broadest sense—very often flow from social or cultural responses to a physical impairment rather than from its tangible physiological aspects.[1] Thus, the World Health Organization in 1980 (27–29) issued a widely cited tripartite definition that distinguishes among *impairment* ("any loss or abnormality of psychological, physiological, or anatomical structure or function"), *disability* ("any restriction or lack [resulting from impairment] of ability to perform an activity in the manner or within the range considered normal for a human being"), and *handicap* ("a disadvantage for a given individual, resulting from an impairment or a disability that limits or prevents the fulfillment of a role that is normal [depending on age, sex, and social and cultural factors] for that individual").[2]

Even these distinctions are not entirely persuasive, because they are based on the dubious assumption that physical impairments and disabilities are not themselves cultural constructs. It would seem obvious that concepts concerning "limitation of function" vary according to the kinds of function a society considers significant. Wright (1983:11) herself cites the example of foot binding among Chinese women, which was considered at one time to be a mark of nobility, but which contemporary American society would regard as an important limitation of function—and a disability. Finkelstein (1980:34) illustrates the culturally constructed aspects of physical disabilities by imagining a world designed and inhabited primarily by wheelchair users: "Door and ceiling heights . . . could be lowered substantially. If, now, able-bodied people were to live in this community they would soon find that they were prevented from 'normal' social intercourse—they would be constantly knocking their heads against the door lintels! Apart from bruises the able-bodied would inevitably find themselves prevented from using the wheelchair-user-designed environment and aids. They would lack jobs and become impoverished—they would become disabled!"

Physical disabilities and the obstacles and impairments that flow from them are, in many important respects, social constructs (see generally Gliedman and Roth 1980). The identities of individuals who bear

---

1. In enacting the ADA, Congress found that discrimination against individuals with disabilities resulted from "stereotypic assumptions not truly indicative of the individual ability of such individuals to participate in, and contribute to, society" (§12101(a)(7)). Similarly, the legislative history of the ADA contains findings that "[s]uch discrimination often results from false presumptions, generalizations, misperceptions, patronizing attitudes, ignorance, irrational fears, and pernicious mythologies" (H.R. Rep. No. 485, 101st Cong., 2nd Sess., pt. 2, 1990 at 30).

2. The term "handicap" has fallen out of favor because of its historically pejorative and demeaning connotations. We, like the majority of writers, prefer the "people-first" terminology, "people with disabilities," although we recognize the problematic character of the term "disability" itself.

this label, particularly those like Sara Lane who use wheelchairs, are perceived in terms of prevailing cultural conceptions of normal physique and physical function and of the significance of any deviation from that norm. Undoubtedly, some positive connotations are associated with physical disability, and Sara's own life story suggests that people who use wheelchairs may be viewed as sympathetic, admirable, intelligent, and hard working. Yet the testimony of our interviewees and of numerous writers with disabilities also suggests that social interactions—the experiences that shape their identities—are often "spoiled" (to use Goffman's term) by the negative cultural images associated with physical disability. Murphy (1987:116–17), an anthropologist who became quadriplegic, observes: "We are subverters of an American ideal, just as the poor are betrayers of the American Dream. And to the extent that we depart from the ideal, we become ugly and repulsive to the able-bodied. People recoil from us, especially when there is facial damage or bodily distortion."

Murphy suggests that individuals with physical disabilities evoke negative reactions because they represent to the observer a "fearsome possibility" (117), a reminder that injury or illness could happen to anyone. In addition, physical disabilities are often perceived in the same terms as communicable diseases ("They act like it's contagious" [Scheer 1984]) or as phenomena likely to "spread" to other aspects of the personality, such as cognitive or social processes ("I expected his thoughts to be jerky also" [Wright 1983:61]). Murphy (1987:131) and others have argued that the social identities of people with physical disabilities are compromised because they exist in a *liminal* state, suspended between illness and health, for which no "normal" social status seems appropriate: "They are not ill, for illness is transitional to either death or recovery. . . . The sick person lives in a state of social suspension until he or she gets better. The disabled spend a lifetime in a similar suspended state. They are neither fish nor fowl; they exist in partial isolation from society as undefined, ambiguous people."

Liminality, the perception that individuals with physical disabilities cannot fit readily into any familiar social role or activity, produces anxiety and avoidance among those with whom they interact: "The lasting indeterminacy of their state of being produces a similar lack of definition of their social roles, which are in any event superseded and obscured by submersion of their identities" (135). For wheelchair users, Murphy observes, the consequences are apparent in everyday social interactions: "Their persons are regarded as contaminated; eyes are averted and people take care not to approach wheelchairs too closely" (135).

There is some risk in describing only the negative and oppressive imagery associated with physical disability, for one-sided descriptions can reinforce the stereotypical assumption that disability is associated only with misery and pain. Our purpose is not to deny that our interviewees enjoy many of the same pleasures and achievements as non-wheelchair-users, but rather to emphasize hazards that are present in the cultural environment in which their identities take shape over time. This environment shapes many of the interactions, relationships, and professional experiences that become part of their life stories; and it also creates obstacles of many kinds that they must overcome as they pursue their careers.

Sara Lane's life story narrative does not dwell on the identity-compromising quality of social interactions with people who regard her as "contaminated" or avert their eyes and maintain their distance from her because she uses a wheelchair. Much of her career success derives from her capacity to tell a different story, to emphasize successes, achievements, and "normal" social experiences in her private and professional life. Particularly in our second and third interviews, however, Sara makes it clear that she has always had to contend with misperceptions and negative stereotypes, from the time in college that she was told she could never be a newspaper reporter to the "staring" that she still encounters from strangers in the mall and even from colleagues in the newsroom. She has attained success as a journalist by continually overcoming doubts about her ability to do her job "despite" her disability, doubts that originate in her anomalous identity as a woman in a wheelchair who claims a "normal" professional status within a mainstream work setting.

Sara's success in forming a professional identity despite many years of identity-compromising encounters and experiences can be appreciated by comparing her story to that of Rick Evans, a man with cerebral palsy who is about Sara's age and also uses a wheelchair but has found it more difficult to overcome social and cultural barriers. Early influences were critical in the formation of both Sara's and Rick's identities. While Sara's parents treated her and her siblings as equals and guided her to the social and academic mainstream, demonstrating to her the possibilities for inclusion, Rick's parents made choices that unintentionally led to isolation and exclusion.[3] Rick has no siblings, and his

3. Our findings about the causes and negative effects of social isolation are complemented, to some extent, by the arguments of some critics of contemporary disability-related social welfare policies in the United States. These critics maintain that the United States, unlike many European welfare states, places too much emphasis on income support through Social Security Disability (SSD) and Supplemental Security Income (SSI) benefits and too little emphasis on work. Such policies in fact create negative incentives for work.

parents' second-floor apartment made it difficult for him to meet other children. Unlike Sara, Rick does not describe efforts by his parents to facilitate such friendships. Rick's parents urged him to use a wheelchair, even when he was still capable of walking, unlike Sara's parents who insisted that she use crutches in order to avoid what they considered the appearance of helplessness. Rick, unlike Sara, attended primary and middle schools operated exclusively for children with disabilities. No separate high school existed for such students, and most of his classmates with disabilities were not expected to continue their schooling, but Rick had showed exceptional academic promise and he was finally placed in a mainstream school setting when he reached the ninth grade. By that age, Sara had extensive experience in the public schools. Rick, by contrast, had almost no experience in the social mainstream before he was abruptly transferred to the local public high school, where he was the only student with a physical disability.

Rick's childhood identity was affected by his social isolation, but it was also influenced by negative and degrading experiences after he began high school. His relations with other students were difficult. A few of his classmates chose to express their discomfort with his presence by writing obscenities on his wheelchair. He believes that the students feared him because they had never before been exposed to people with disabilities. As he progressed beyond high school, he experienced fewer and fewer such indignities, but the memories have never left him. Describing his long and unsuccessful search for employment as an adult, he says that he has been the victim of subtle discrimination by employers and fellow employees for the same reasons that he experienced isolation and discrimination earlier in his life, namely, their feelings of discomfort and their fear of persons with disabilities.

Although early experiences indelibly linked his disability with dependency and exclusion, Rick also knew he was intellectually talented. His teachers and family encouraged him to attend college and graduate school, and he eventually chose to enter a master's degree program in rehabilitation counseling because "it turned what I had considered a liability into an asset." His progress through college and graduate school

---

The result, say the critics, is a life of dependency that starts at an early age, even after the ADA and contrary to its spirit. See Yelin and Katz 1994; Burkhauser 1997. Our research suggests that isolation can also result from circumstances having little to do with the income-support policies of the government. In a broader sense, however, the income-support policies that discourage work and the specific institutional pressures experienced by Rick Evans and Sara Lane—the unwillingness of educators or employers to create accessible schools or workplaces voluntarily—arise from a common source, namely, the underlying belief that persons with disabilities are not capable of participating in everyday life activities and, therefore, may be excluded from many social settings, thereby isolating them and making them dependent on public subsidies.

was slowed by a change in majors, failure to gain immediate admission to a graduate program, and, finally, surgery and an unexpectedly long period of rehabilitation. When Rick finally entered the job market for the first time, fifteen years after graduating from high school, he was thirty-three years old.

Rick's professional career has been far less successful than Sara's. It took him three years to obtain his first job offer as a counselor in a center for persons with disabilities that was located thirty miles from his home. Within a month, Rick resigned because wheelchair accessible housing, which had been promised to him, proved to be unavailable, and Rick was unable to find substitute housing or to manage the commute from his parents' home. Ironically, solving such problems for others was among the responsibilities of the job Rick was forced to abandon. During the decade that followed, Rick has had thirty or forty job interviews but he has held only one short-term job and never made another attempt to live on his own. He rejects the possibility of pursuing a job in another city or state, because he thinks his disability ties him to his current home and support system. His only hope for the future is that his efforts to learn to walk again will enable him to find work, or, that he will be able to develop a small business of his own, perhaps as a computer consultant. He believes he may never become an employee as long as he uses a wheelchair.

Although they are about the same age and share many personal attributes, Rick and Sara's identities evolved in very different ways. Both of them had to contend with the social consequences of disability—stigma, stereotyping, exclusion, and discrimination—which marred social interactions and experiences throughout their lives. Yet Sara, unlike Rick, is able to offer an account of her life that demonstrates not only her ability to overcome obstacles in the past but also her assumption that she will continue to pursue a successful career in the future. For Rick, the story of his past is primarily a story of the limitations associated with his disability; and his thoughts about the future are constrained by the things he and others cannot or will not do as long as he continues to use a wheelchair. Rick believes that he has limited capacity to persuade an employer to hire him, rendering his long search for employment futile. His isolation from the social mainstream from childhood to the present has led him to conflate his disability and his identity.

The differences between the identities offered in Sara and Rick's narratives have implications for their orientations toward rights. Rick believes that the most formidable barrier to his employment is discrimination by employers against people with disabilities, but, unlike

Sara, he has little faith in his ability to overcome this barrier. Both Rick and Sara are well aware that the ADA prohibits discriminatory employment practices, but Rick does not believe that invoking rights under the ADA can help people with physical disabilities. Indeed, Rick tends to attribute his unemployment to the ADA's ineffectiveness. He believes the ADA has failed because it lacks the teeth of civil rights laws that protect racial minorities. Further, even if the ADA provided stronger remedies on paper, he believes that in practice it could never overcome the overwhelming prejudice of employers against persons with disabilities. "[T]here are forty-six ways to, you know, if you don't want to hire somebody, and you really don't, there are a whole bunch of ways. . . . It just means you have to work harder to not hire them. . . . You just have to be more creative at avoiding hiring these people."

The similarity Rick perceives in the barriers to employment experienced by persons with disabilities and racial minorities is consistent with his perception that he has failed to obtain employment primarily because of discrimination. Many other interviewees who had difficulty finding employment believed that the main obstacle is employers' exaggerated concerns about the costs of accommodations. In contrast, Rick believes that persons with physical disabilities are excluded from the workplace for the same reason he has experienced social isolation for most of his life, namely, discrimination that results from stigma, fear, and stereotyping. Attitudes will change, he believes, only when there is more contact with people who have visible disabilities. Social interactions may increase when more people with disabilities enter the workplace and work alongside nondisabled employees, but laws alone will not change perceptions. Characteristically, Rick does not mention a part for himself in this process. He assumes a passive role or, more accurately perhaps, justifies his passivity by making such changes a precondition for employment. Thus, in a direct but surprising way, Rick's identity renders the law relevant but impotent to change his life. His interpretation of the role of law suggests to him that he has only two unsatisfactory alternatives: invoke the ADA's ineffective remedies or passively accept society's discrimination.

Rick's orientation toward the ADA, his "rights consciousness," is an integral part of the identity that formed during a lifetime at the margins of society. Comparison to Sara Lane's rights consciousness is revealing. Although Sara faced similar obstacles and had similar intellectual and material resources at her disposal, her identity evolved through experiences with people who did not have disabilities and institutions that were not isolated or segregated. Sara, like Rick, is familiar with the ADA, but she views it as a potentially useful tool to maintain her position at the newspaper and to advance her career. Although she has not invoked her rights in a formal sense, she believes that the ADA has already caused her employer to make her workplace more accessible. When she thinks of the future, she envisions a career made possible by the rights that protect individuals with physical disabilities, despite the cultural and physical barriers they face in American society.

Learning Disabilities

The ADA prohibits discrimination and mandates reasonable accommodations for individuals with learning disabilities, just as it does for individuals with physical disabilities. The identity-shaping effects of both types of disability, moreover, have some elements in common, since individuals in both groups experience stigma, prejudice, and social exclusion. Yet the life story narratives of our interviewees in these two groups diverge in a number of significant ways. The dilemma for many adults with learning disabilities arises from the invisibility of their condition, whereas the dilemma for individuals who use wheelchairs is that their condition is too visible, making the participants in social interactions constantly aware of its existence. Many adults with learning disabilities prefer to conceal their condition, an option that is not available to those who use wheelchairs. Furthermore, the nature of the disability of an individual in a wheelchair is sharply focused and readily understood by most observers. Its significance is so obvious that it can be conveyed by a simple logo—the universal symbol for disability. By contrast, the nature and significance of learning disabilities are poorly understood, uncertain, and ambiguous in the eyes of the general public. The very existence of learning disabilities is doubted by some observers, while others may have only a vague comprehension of what a learning disability is and how it might affect an individual's life.

Identity formation for individuals with learning disabilities therefore differs in certain ways from the process we have considered for individuals who use wheelchairs. Jill Golding's life story is exceptional in some respects, for she chooses to acknowledge her learning disability much more openly than many of the adults we interviewed. Yet her childhood account of humiliation, self-doubt, failure, fear, and loneliness is echoed by most of our interviewees. Such stories are familiar in the rapidly expanding literature on learning disabilities. Simpson's eloquent autobiography, *Reversals: A Personal Account of Victory over Dyslexia* (1979), is now complemented by other narratives describing the paradoxical stigma associated with a disability that "doesn't exist" (see, e.g., Gallet 1988–89; Gerber and Reiff 1991; Weis 1998). Middle-aged adults with learning disabilities typically recount a childhood in which their difficulties were completely misunderstood by their families and teachers, for the history of learning disabilities as a recognized category in American schools is relatively recent.

The term "learning disability" was first used by Samuel Kirk in the early 1960s to distinguish a group of children whose academic difficulties arose from neither mental retardation nor other impairments. A federal mandate requiring special education programs for children with learning disabilities was first issued in 1975.[4] Some of our interviewees came of age before any of these developments occurred. Their identities evolved without reference to the concept of "learning disability" or the educational programs and legal protections now available to children classified in this way. The interviews with younger adults who have learning disabilities tell a different story. Most of them describe childhood experiences in special classes. These stories typically reflect their narrators' ambivalence toward the identity-shaping aspects of their disability: appreciation for the academic support they received but unhappiness at being labeled and segregated from their peers.[5] Some of our younger interviewees, like Jill Golding, were never diagnosed and went through school without any special education services or accommodations years after state and federal laws were enacted for their benefit.

Common sense explains the necessity of using a wheelchair, but definitions and explanations of "learning disability" have been debated throughout the brief history of the concept. A revised definition formulated by the National Joint Committee for Learning Disabilities appears to summarize the current consensus among experts:

> Learning disabilities is a general term that refers to a heterogeneous group of disorders manifested by significant difficulties in the acquisition and use of listening, speaking, reading, writing, reasoning, or mathematical abilities. These disorders are intrinsic to the individual, presumed to be due to central nervous system dysfunction, and may occur across the life span. Problems in self-regulatory behaviors, social perception, and social interaction may exist with learning disabilities but do not by themselves constitute

4. The federal statute is now known as the Individuals with Disabilities Education Act (IDEA), 20 U.S.C.A. §§1400–1491, but was originally entitled the Education for All Handicapped Children Act of 1975. Our brief summary is based on Torgesen 1998. The reference to Kirk appears in ibid., 13–14. See also the historical account of the concept of learning disability in Hooper and Willis 1989.

5. The rise in the 1980s and 1990s of the movement for "inclusion" signaled growing opposition to the routine use of segregated, self-contained classrooms for students with disabilities and a consensus that such students should be educated in typical classrooms whenever possible. To some extent, educational practices and placements have changed as a consequence. See, e.g., Biklen 1992; Pijl 1994; Speece and Keogh 1996.

a learning disability. Although learning disabilities may occur concomitantly with other handicapping conditions (for example, sensory impairment, mental retardation, serious emotional disturbance) or with extrinsic influences (such as cultural differences, insufficient or inappropriate instruction), they are not the result of those conditions or influences.[6]

As Sternberg (1999) notes, experts by the late 1990s reached a "broad consensus" on many aspects of learning disabilities, including their heterogeneity, their genetic component, their transmission within families, and their neurological origins. But Sternberg also observes that most experts agree that legal and political factors have distorted the concept of learning disability, leading to the use of inappropriate testing instruments and the classification of many children who do not actually have learning disabilities.[7] Overuse of the "LD" label, and the inappropriate diagnostic procedures used in many school districts, have prompted some critics to argue that "[t]here is no such thing as a learning disability" (Finlan 1994:1).[8] Other critics, such as Kelman and Lester (1997), acknowledge that learning disabilities may exist but contend that the line separating children with learning disabilities from those who have other academic difficulties is too uncertain to justify granting legal rights to the first group but not the second.

Debates and criticisms among the experts have their counterparts in the popular press[9] and in everyday discourse. The life experiences of individuals with learning disabilities teach them that their condition is widely misunderstood and is very often viewed with suspicion. The concept of learning disability is "fuzzy," unlike the sharp image of the wheelchair user. Persons with learning disabilities risk being perceived either as more cognitively impaired than they really are or as people who have no disability but are claiming a special status on the basis of "junk science" and poor policy (see Brown 1994:46). Studies of adults

6. The quote appears in Torgesen 1998:20 and is attributed to a 1988 letter from the National Joint Committee on Learning Disabilities to its member organizations.

7. Nearly twenty years ago, when definitions were inadequate and testing procedures reflected widespread conceptual confusion over "learning disability," James E. Ysseldyke and Bob Algozzine (1982:126) observed: "Whenever there is conceptual confusion regarding terminology, there is conceptual confusion in measurement. Diagnostic personnel have incredible difficulty demonstrating that a test is valid—that it measures what it says it measures—when they cannot define or describe what it is they are trying to measure. Hence, courts and legislatures have challenged diagnostic practices, and controversy and confusion reign supreme."

8. Other views dissenting from the prevailing paradigm are contained in Franklin 1987.

9. A tiny sample of hundreds of relevant articles, editorials, and letters to the editor will have to suffice: Rosemond 1994a; 1994b; Brown 1995; Shalit 1997; Wingert and Kantrowitz 1997; "Progress in Special Education" 2001; Morello-Frosch, Pastor, and Porras 2001.

with disabilities consistently report their fear that they will encounter negative judgments and discrimination if they make their disability known (Shapiro and Rich 1999:136–38; Brown and Gerber 1994:196; Engel and Munger 1996, 2001). The temptation to conceal their disability becomes stronger when they leave school, where diagnostic procedures had been mandated and familiar structures and routines were part of the landscape of American education. In the workplace, by contrast, the initiative rests with the employee or the job applicant to obtain a diagnosis and present a claim for accommodations to an employer who may know nothing about learning disabilities. Identity formation among adults with learning disabilities reflects two contending forces: the need to obtain on-the-job accommodations in order to perform their work successfully and the preference to pass as "normal" in order to avoid stigma and discrimination. In addition, they must continually wrestle with their own self-doubts, not just about their abilities and intelligence but about the disability itself.

One of our interviewees, Vicki Kennedy, conveys the ambivalence of her own identity in a striking statement comparing her invisible disability to one that can be seen. She suggests that invisibility makes her dyslexia questionable—in the minds of others and, perhaps, in her own mind as well:

> When you can't see it, it's like aliens. Do you believe in aliens or don't you believe in aliens? Well, if you saw a little green monster sitting on the table that told you that it was ET, you may believe it because you see it. . . . It's that visual perception. If we can see it, then therefore it is—most of the time, most of us. But when we definitely can't see it, they say where is it? Or is it just something that one had said to make up for an area that one may be deficient in, not as strong in? Has this one talked themselves into the fact that, yes, this is a problem for them and yes, there is a disability? Is there a disability or is there no disability?

Vicki's statement captures the elusiveness of the disability and the painful ambiguities surrounding it. Is there a disability, she asks, or is her true identity simply that of a less capable, less intelligent person? Has she simply talked herself into the belief that she is dyslexic? What would "they" say if she were more open about her disability? Her constantly shifting pronouns are especially revealing: Might Vicki herself be the "one" who could be fabricating a disability in order to conceal her own deficiencies?

Vicki is now in her mid-forties, having returned to college after working as an office assistant for a divorce attorney, as a hairdresser, and as a cosmetology instructor. She plans to become an educational psychologist or a social worker. Yet she has never sought or obtained a diagnosis as "learning disabled." She has never had accommodations of any kind, although she has actively pursued them on behalf of her teenage son, who is classified as dyslexic. Since Jill Golding's adult diagnosis was such a symbolically powerful event in her life, it is striking that Vicki resists getting herself diagnosed. Her son's psychologist has offered to run a battery of tests, and Vicki has no doubt that she is dyslexic. She does not, however, share Jill's conviction that a formal diagnosis will confirm her sense of self-worth and validate her perception of herself as an essentially capable person who has been misunderstood and deprived of appropriate accommodations. It is enough that she herself is now convinced that she has dyslexia, an insight that eluded her throughout her difficult childhood:

> I knew something was wrong, but I didn't know what it was. I didn't know why I didn't know my right from my left. I didn't know why I made threes backwards. I didn't know why I could not distinguish between a lower case "b" or a "d." Horizontal and vertical, you throw those two words at me, I don't know which is horizontal, which was upside down, which way is up and down, which way is sideways. . . . It was that bad, my right from my left, that my parents bought me a ring that I put on my right hand. . . . I literally would feel, I would take my thumbs and I would feel for the ring band to know that that was my right. And that's how I survived.

For Jill Golding, the formal diagnosis marked a turning point in her life. It helped her to objectify her learning disability and resist an earlier assumption that her disability was her self. Jill's view of the learning disability reinforces her insistence on a self that is essentially capable and worthy of respect—and a disability that is deserving of appropriate accommodations. Although Vicki has no doubt that she, too, has a learning disability, the boundaries between disability and self are less clear. Her life history to this point has not clarified these boundaries, and Vicki expresses no desire to achieve further clarity through a formal diagnosis and an open presentation of herself as a person with a learning disability. When boundaries and self-concepts remain fuzzy, and when disabilities are concealed, there is little opportunity for rights to become active.

Neither Jill nor Vicki experienced the process of identity formation as a child who was diagnosed with a learning disability and placed in the special education system. We conclude this section by contrasting their life stories with that of William Heinz, who was diagnosed in the first grade and transferred immediately from a typical classroom to a small, self-contained class for children with "special needs."[10] Although some of our interviewees flourished in the special education system, William's life story narrative dwells on the profoundly negative effects this watershed event had on his identity. William spent four years in segregated classrooms with children who were also classified as "handicapped" under state and federal law but had disabilities much different from his own. His description of the "physically and mentally retarded" children in his class includes a boy who thought he was an airplane: "You're walking in the line, and you got with the one guy, oh he was brutal! He thought he was an airplane. He'd make airplane noises, hold his arms out like they were wings everywhere he went. And he said, 'I'm an airplane.' And he wanted to be an airplane when he grew up. I just didn't feel I needed to be in there."

By the time his peers had entered sixth grade, William's mother forced the school district to remove him from his self-contained class and reinstate him in an integrated setting. Apparently the school district resisted. William observes grimly of self-contained classes, "It's like jail or something—once you get in, it's hard to get out." William had, by his own account, learned nothing during his four years apart from his peers, and he had to enroll in the fourth rather than the sixth grade when he returned. He lacked basic skills in math and reading, and he claims that he spent the remainder of his public school education trying unsuccessfully to catch up. His task was all the more difficult because he was two years older than his classmates and did not fit in socially.

William's childhood identity developed during a series of frustrating and humiliating experiences in the public schools. William knew early in his life that he was considered "learning disabled." The formal classification did not, however, enable him to achieve a distanced, objective view of his disability. Educators were inconsistent in their approach to his schooling, and his special education experiences tended to disrupt rather than facilitate his learning. His support services were inconsistent—by his own account, he received help from special education teachers during some years but not others. He skipped around from one grade and academic setting to another, and he had disciplinary problems because he was bigger than his classmates and tended to attract the attention of his teachers when there was trouble. He describes

10. Routine assignments of classified children to segregated, self-contained classrooms may be less common now than when William Heinz was a child. See the discussion of "inclusion" in note 5.

himself as an "outcast" and recalls that "in high school, people were afraid of me." It was not until the end of seventh grade that a special education teacher made a determined effort to teach William the fundamentals of math and reading that he had missed in the second and third grades. In high school, he combined vocational classes with out-of-sequence academic studies. His record was spotty and disjointed; his greatest fulfillment came from mechanical work, and he recalls that he achieved considerable success and respect for his skills in this area. When he finished high school, he got a job working on high-powered racing automobiles.

According to William, other events in his life also contributed to his sense of frustration and failure during his school years. His father, unemployed and alcoholic, treated William poorly and continually criticized his efforts: "No matter what I did to try to please him, it just didn't work." William now suspects that his father also had a learning disability, for he was unable to help William with homework even in the early primary grades. William describes how his mother, on the other hand, intervened frequently on his behalf, and she encouraged him to continue his studies and get help if he needed it. By the time we interviewed William, he had returned to college and was making steady progress toward his degree. Initially, he had great difficulty with his classes, but his mother learned about the disability support services offered at his college and told William, "When you're ready to grow up, there's help." Despite his embarrassment about asking for assistance, he eventually enrolled in a course that taught him college success skills. This was a turning point in his life story narrative. He claims that he finally learned how to be a student and to achieve academically despite his disability. Since taking that course, he has had straight A's in all of his classes— an indication, he believes, of his true intelligence and ability. He now feels that it is realistic to pursue a career as a teacher, a goal that he first formulated during his unfortunate experience in a self-contained elementary school classroom: "Actually, I first started thinking about teaching the first couple of years that I was in the BOCES classes, when I was real young. I'm like, my God, I can teach better than this. That is when I started thinking about it."

Despite these identity-transforming events in his early adult life, William still lacks self-confidence and regards his disability as an embarrassment: "I still don't really admit it [that he has a learning disability]. Like people I'll meet and stuff, I never bring it up, because in a way I still kind of am ashamed of it." In the past, when he entered and left the college disability services office, he would look both ways to be sure no one saw him. Now he is less fearful, but it is clear that his disability still strongly colors his sense of self. He lacks a distanced, objectified view of his disability. Indeed, he does not have a clear understanding of what it means to have a learning disability or what his specific condition is: "I still don't really know what it is. . . . Someday I'll know, but I don't even know what my learning disability is. I should go over there and get my records. I don't know if they'd give them to me, though, would they?" Ironically, although William Heinz knew his diagnosis much earlier in his life than Jill or Vicki, that information appears to have played no useful role until he returned to college. Instead, the early diagnosis permitted powerful cultural perceptions and institutional forces to enter the process of identity formation at a very early stage and created negative consequences with which William must still deal.

We do not suggest that William's story is typical of adults with learning disabilities who had childhood exposure to the special education system. Some of our interviewees gave more positive descriptions of their experiences with special education. Rather, our purpose is to present one of the patterns by which the symbols and social institutions associated with learning disabilities can affect identity formation at a very early age. Although one might expect that early diagnosis and intervention would help an individual to view his learning disability in a more distanced and objective fashion, William's story demonstrates that this is not necessarily the case. William was no more able than Jill or Vicki to separate his sense of self from his disability as a child, and as an adult he and Vicki—unlike Jill—still tend to blur their disability and their identity. Even now, William lacks a clear understanding of his disability and is not sure how he can learn more about it. Nevertheless, as a young adult, he can now tell a story about himself that aims toward a professional career in a mainstream occupational setting.

Because both Vicki and William tend to conflate their identity with their learning disability, it is not surprising to discover a similarity in their orientation toward employment rights under the ADA. Unlike Jill, neither Vicki nor William perceives a significant space in which rights might become active. Vicki, unlike Jill, is reluctant to tell others that she has a learning disability, although she must constantly guard against its effects. If she lowers her guard, the disability will "pop its nasty little head." She believes that it is up to her to compensate for the effects of her dyslexia. If her employer is unsympathetic, she will have to rely on herself or her coworkers to do the work. If an employer is "jerky," that is the employer's prerogative. Vicki does not analyze the problem in terms of her own rights, but in terms of the employer's lack of empathy. An employer can choose without constraint to be either "jerky" or empathetic, and there is little the employee can do in the face of uncaring behavior except to devise her own accommodations, like the ring Vicki wore as a child and rubbed with both thumbs to remind her which was her right hand. Vicki does not view confrontation or an insistence on legal rights as a viable option: "Forced empathy is not the answer." Whereas Jill views rights as consistent with caring relationships, Vicki rejects this possibility. If her employer is uncaring, and denies her the accommodations necessary to perform her job, then Vicki anticipates that she will simply resign or be fired while thinking to herself, "You have lost yourself a good employee."

William's assumptions about the prerogatives of the employer resemble Vicki's. He has little sense of the accommodations to which he is legally entitled; and, unlike Jill, he does not think in terms of rule violation or injustice when excluded from the social mainstream by those who ignore disability rights. When asked how he might respond to an employer who is unwilling to provide reasonable accommodations, William answers that the only possible response he could imagine would be to ask his college mentors for advice. If a school, for example, refused to hire him as a teacher because of his disability, his response would be similar to Vicki's: "It is your loss. See you later. And I wouldn't think twice about getting up and leaving then." He would not respond to discriminatory treatment by asserting rights, except in extreme circumstances: "I don't want to cause problems for anybody, so I don't think I'd go down that road. . . . Unless it was something that really violated my rights or something, then, it would have to be really bad though." Like Vicki, William essentially defers to the employer's right to discriminate on the basis of disability.

In a revealing statement, William explains that the employer's refusal to hire him might be justified by an inability to distinguish between William and the boy in his BOCES class who thought he was an airplane: "[Employers] have their reasons. Maybe it's somebody that was in normal classes and saw the BOCES classes where the learning disabled students were, where the kids thought they were airplanes, and you know what I mean. And maybe they [thought], well, if he's learning disabled, he was in those classes, he's one of them." Here, William's identity merges with that of the boy in his self-contained classroom, and the employer's identity becomes that of the "normal" student who saw William as part of this stigmatized class. Others could not distinguish William from the boy who thought he was an airplane. Perhaps William himself is not sure there is a difference. The uncertainty about identity and disability translates into deference toward the employer's discriminatory decision. The likelihood that William would ever respond to such a situation by asserting rights appears very small.

Conclusion

In this chapter, we have argued that identity is the appropriate starting point for an inquiry into the effects of rights under the ADA. Rights do not automatically spring into action each time an employer violates the ADA by unfairly refusing to hire an individual with a disability or by refusing to provide reasonable accommodations. As we have seen, even in cases when an objective observer might conclude that a legal violation has occurred, the individual herself may not perceive that she has been treated improperly. Both the "objective observer" and the individual with a disability are influenced in their perceptions by culturally conditioned ideas about the meaning of disability and the appropriate place for those who are considered to have disabilities. Before the question of statutory violation can be raised, there must be a perception that the individual has been relegated to the wrong side of a social boundary. For a person who is assumed to be unable to work, her exclusion from employment appears "natural" rather than improper. When the individual herself shares this perception, there is no space within which rights could become active.

We begin, therefore, with a consideration of identity in relation to rights. The question of who one is and where one belongs must be addressed before the issue of rights can be considered. We have discussed identity in terms of two elements: its "distributed" or interactive quality and the narrative process through which a coherent sense of self emerges from efforts to tell a story of past experiences. Our life story interviews with individuals who have disabilities allow us to see identity enacted in the very course of our conversations. As they speak with us, individuals like Sara Lane and Jill Golding, Rick Evans, Vicki Kennedy, and William Heinz offer an interpretation of their past. Sometimes they narrate more than one version of their own life story, changing their accounts of behavior and motive, making the stories darker or lighter. The narrative process itself is a key to identity, since the telling of life stories creates a protagonist—the self—who will engage in future experiences and perhaps in a career. The capacity to create an identity that lends itself to productive involvement in the social mainstream is extraordinarily important for men and women with disabilities. An individual whose identity does not appear consistent with inclusion in the workplace is unlikely to perceive the relevance of rights when he or she is denied employment or on-the-job accommodations.

The interactive quality of identity is also of great importance. Both physical and learning disabilities, despite their physiological and neurological foundations, have implications that are socially constructed.

Individuals like Sara, Jill, Rick, Vicki, and William must contend with the social meanings of their disabilities as they interact with others. Their sense of who they are emerges in large part from these interactions. Their identity, in Bruner's terms, is "distributed" among family, friends, classmates, coworkers, supervisors, and others. Social interactions involving individuals with physical and learning disabilities are affected by powerful influences that can produce stigma, aversion, misunderstanding, and overly pessimistic assumptions about the individual's capacity to work. When distributed identities are affected by these negative factors, they may seem inconsistent with the likelihood of a productive career in the social mainstream. When individuals and those around them assume that their identity is inconsistent with inclusion in the workplace, the guarantee of rights under the ADA may appear irrelevant.

As we have suggested in this chapter, individuals vary in the extent to which they differentiate their sense of self from their sense of disability. Some, like Sara Lane, resist the notion that their disability is their identity; although they would never deny that it is a significant part of who they are. Others, like Jill Golding during childhood and adolescence, find the process of differentiation more difficult. Jill did not begin to clarify the distinction between disability and self until her mid-twenties, and some interviewees, such as Rick Evans, Vicki Kennedy, and William Heinz, find the task difficult even in their adult years.

We believe that individuals like Sara and Jill as adults, who tend to draw clear distinctions between their disabilities and their selves, hold equally clear conceptions of their entitlement to participate in mainstream social settings. Because their disabilities do not dominate their understandings of who they are, they see themselves as essentially similar to others who attend school and pursue employment. Although their disability might be a factor at school or on the job, it can be handled through reasonable accommodations and should never be an excuse for total exclusion. Both Sara and Jill might expect to provide some of the accommodations themselves before asking an employer to assist, but they nevertheless retain a clear sense that they are entitled to full participation and that the employer under the ADA bears certain clearly defined responsibilities to ensure their inclusion. Others, like Rick, Vicki, and William, are uncertain about the employer's obligations in this regard, for the boundaries between their capabilities and their disabilities are far less clearly defined in their own minds.

For the person who clearly distinguishes between disability and self, social boundaries that exclude or stigmatize seem irrational, unjust— and, potentially at least, illegal. In this sense, identity connects directly to a sense of justice, for the unfairness of exclusion is apparent only to the person who assumes that inclusion is her natural and expected status. If individual capability in the workplace is assumed, then nondiscriminatory hiring practices and reasonable on-the-job accommodations appear to be natural entitlements. Individuals, however, who tend to blur the lines between identity and disability, and who are consequently less certain about their capabilities, tend also to question their right to participate fully in mainstream settings and to receive reasonable accommodations that would make such participation possible. For both groups of individuals, identity and disability are inextricably linked to the role of rights guaranteed by the ADA.

two

Life Story: Raymond Militello

[We contacted each subject of these life stories to schedule a reinterview, during which we shared what we had written and invited comments that could be added to our text. Raymond Militello did not return our calls, read our version of his life story, or participate further in our research.]

In Raymond Militello's life story, family and friendship connections count for a lot; but laws and the institutions that administer them appear misguided, confusing, and even corrupt. Raymond refers often to his parents and cousins, his Italian American neighborhood, and his childhood friends. As a young man with a learning disability, Raymond has struggled to succeed in school and college, and he still bears the scars of painful academic experiences. At times, he speaks cynically about his instructors and educational administrators but never about his friends and family. Raymond has thought a great deal about how to manipulate the system, enter through the "back door," and get ahead, but he does not worry much about accommodating his disability once he begins his professional career. He expects to continue in the family business, where personal connections will provide him with the arrangements he needs to work effectively.

Raymond describes himself as "five-five, Italian, about twenty pounds over-weight, and going bald." At twenty-six, he works in his father's business as a contractor and real estate developer, but he is also completing his undergraduate degree in business school. He is, by his own description, "easy-going, not short-tempered, mild unless you hit the right button. . . . I like to voice my opinion, whether people like to hear it or not. Especially, like the political stuff now, you shouldn't use this phrase, that phrase—that doesn't bother me. I'll say what's on my mind."

Raymond grew up in a suburban neighborhood in which, as he recalls, ev-eryone on his street was Italian American. Cousins lived nearby, and the children became lifelong friends. His memories of early childhood, however, are tainted by what he remembers as educators' damaging responses to his learning disability. After Raymond failed second grade, he was tested, diagnosed, and bused to a school outside his neighborhood to participate in special education classes. He recalls his two years at that school with some anguish:

> I hated it, because they would come and pick me up on one of those little buses, you know everybody calls them the retarded buses, however you want to phrase it. So all your other friends are getting on the regular bus, you're on that. But the worst thing about it was the kids in the class. . . . Some of the kids in the class were, they were just off the deep end. . . . The people who were in the learning disability classes, I didn't associate with them at all. I basically tried to stay away from most of them. I don't know if they were, I characterized them like mildly retarded or mentally retarded, some of them, I mean just the way they acted. . . . I knew I needed help, but I wasn't that bad.

Raymond was miserably unhappy during these early years in elementary school, but he remembers finding consolation playing with his cousins and the other neighborhood friends from whom he had been separated by the special education system. Within a few years his parents had him transferred back to his local school. He is not certain how they accomplished this change, but he is quite sure that he received no accommodations or special education services after he returned. Instead, his family hired a series of private tutors for Raymond, a practice that continues for his college education. Surprisingly, Raymond had to do the best he could during all of his school years without any provision being made for his disability in the classroom or during tests. It was only after flunking out of the first college he attended, and studying at a community college, that Raymond began to receive extra time for assignments and exams.

As a result of his experiences in the public school system, Raymond developed a strong dislike for education: "I still hate school. I mean, there's not one thing I like about it. The social aspect is fine; but as far as doing papers, projects, reading, I hate it. I've always hated it." Nevertheless, when Raymond completed high school he chose to go on to college rather than join the military or get a job, a decision that his parents strongly supported. Although his parents place a high value on a college degree, Raymond himself describes his decision to attend a small Catholic college, St. Jerome, in terms of personal relationships and good times rather than academic or professional goals:

> My cousin started dating this guy who became one of my best friends. He went to St. Jerome, and I started hanging around with a couple of his friends. . . . I started going down there like my junior year of high school. A few people thought I went there, because Friday I'd go down there, and sometimes I'd stay the weekend. Between going out to the bars, and the parties, and stuff, and then maybe once during the week I'd take a ride down there. And then a girl I dated in high school, she went there with them, too. So I figured I'd been having such a good time there, why not go there.

Without any accommodations for his learning disability, Raymond's first year in college was not very successful. He took a reduced load during his second and third years, but his grades got worse and he was obliged to leave. He transferred directly to the local community college, where his performance improved with the provision of extended time on all his exams. He then transferred to the management program at a nearby university, where he was enrolled at the time of our interview and where he expects to receive his college degree as soon as he completes eight more courses.

For a person who hates school and talks more about partying then academic goals, Raymond Militello has demonstrated a remarkable persistence in his studies. He has studied year-round, including summer school, since he turned nineteen. Often, after he selects a new course, he hires a tutor to teach him the entire course before the first day of class. The tutor then works with him throughout the semester, and Raymond finds he must often reread material two or three times before he can understand it. When he studied calculus, a particularly difficult course for Raymond, he began taking it at St. Jerome College, withdrew from the course, enrolled a second time and failed, hired a private tutor to teach him the course outside of school, and, at the time of the interview, had elected the course for the third time at the public university he attended. In effect, he has studied calculus four times.

Rather than perceiving himself as a persistent and determined student, Raymond describes himself as lazy: "You know, I'm a lazy student, that's part of my problem. . . . Like this calculus course, I can put more effort into it if I wanted to. There's no question in my mind. It's how much time do I want to devote to it?" In response to Raymond's self-description as lazy, which seems strikingly at odds with the time and effort he has actually devoted to learning calculus over the years, we asked him if he thought that he studied less than the other students in the class. He answered: "I don't know. Well, not in this calculus class, you know. I've surpassed everybody by probably threefold." In his mind, a lazy self-image exists alongside the realization that he works extremely hard on his academics.

Perhaps Raymond's self-characterization as "lazy" is merely a flippant response to a more troubling question: Why is it that a bright student who works extraordinarily hard nevertheless finds it difficult to achieve good grades in college? The same offhand attitude is apparent when Raymond discusses the reasons that he wants to complete his undergraduate degree after many years of difficult struggle. He claims that his college studies will have little practical benefit. Few if any courses will actually help him in his father's real estate and development business. Yet, he observes, college does broaden one's mind. But he immediately undercuts this philosophical observation with the sardonic aside: "That's what I was told, at least."

Raymond Militello's narrative alternates between stories of pain, effort, and humiliation on the one hand, and hard-boiled cynicism and ironic detachment on the other. This same pattern of alternation appears in his discussion of disability and accommodation under the law. At one point, we asked Raymond when he first thought of himself as having a learning disability. Unexpectedly, he answered: "I probably started using it a lot a few years ago, and I found out it really works good for you now (laughs). You know, it's to your advantage to have something wrong with you." Although we intended in our question to invite Raymond to discuss his disability in terms of its subjective significance, its place in his self-image, he instead described the disability as a tool that he recently learned how to manipulate in order to talk his way into advantageous situations. Throughout the interview, he returned to this theme. Every institution or bureaucracy has a back door. Only a fool tries to get in through the front door. People who are "in the know" always use the back door, and Raymond's learning disability, he has discovered, gives him access:

> The bigger the institution is, the harder it is to get in, because it's a bureaucracy. So there's always a back door somewhere, and it's just a matter of getting in that back door. . . . The front door is the worst spot to go, because you're just going to get shot down, because they treat you like everybody else and you're just a number. . . . To go in the front door, if you have to, it's miserable. . . . There's always a way to get in. There's always a way to do something.

Having a learning disability can be an asset, if you understand how to use it properly. As Raymond observes with some exaggeration: "It's a smaller group. They treat you a lot better. They pull up with the limo, and they take you there."

At these moments in the interview, Raymond presents himself as a deal maker, as someone who is streetwise rather than vulnerable. By his own account, he has discovered over the past few years that he has been handed a valuable bargaining chip, and he would be foolish not to use it: "Do I deserve it? I don't know. I'm sure there's other people who deserve it more than me. Like I said, I've learned to use it to my advantage. The older I've got, the smarter I've gotten with it. It's like, this is actually a good thing here." At this point in his narrative, Raymond has transformed his learning disability from a source of unhappiness, social isolation, and academic challenge to "a good thing" that gives him a leg up on others. Raymond mistakenly believes that having a disability confers "points" in affirmative action quota programs, and that his dyslexia entitles him to preferential admissions over an equally qualified individual who has no disability. He compares these imagined points to those that are awarded military veterans in the civil service system. He cannot believe that veterans would decline their points and withhold the documentation that would give them a "bump ahead" on the civil service list. Similarly, whether he deserves it or not, Raymond sees no reason why he should not claim the points that he believes he has accrued by virtue of his disability: "I think I use it more for its advantage now, because I'm privy to what you can do with it. You know, it opens up a lot of doors. If I wanted a government job, it would probably work great." It is ironic that Raymond, who claims he is perfectly willing to use what he conceives to be his disability rights, has availed himself of very few of the academic accommodations to which the law actually entitles him.

Raymond's self-portrayal as a hardheaded negotiator, seeking whatever advantage the system offers, appears most vividly in his description of discussions with the St. Jerome College administrators. While he was still a student there, he had problems registering for some of his college classes. Raymond discovered that he could use his family connections to his advantage: a friend of his father's worked in the registrar's office and got him into any class he wanted. After he flunked out of St. Jerome and completed his associate's degree at the local community college, Raymond returned to St. Jerome and made them an offer that he thought would get him reinstated through the back door:

> I basically told them, I need another year and a half to graduate from here. If you want my money, okay, take me back in, and can we do something with the low cumulative. Wipe some of the Fs off. . . . I said, if you want me to come back here and spend another $30,000, $35,000, okay, because my cumulative is low, I'm going to have to get As or Bs. I know I physically can't do that in most of my classes, I told them. I said, if you want to

go behind closed doors and pump that up to a 1.9 or a 2.0 or a 1.8 or whatever, I'll come back here. Well, they didn't want to do that. So I said, okay, I'll go to [the local university]. . . . They did discuss it. He didn't give a "no" right there, like this is ridiculous, we can't do this. . . . They called in a week, and they said, we just can't do that, blah blah blah. You know, they gave all their standards and all that. I said, okay, fine. . . . I learned after a few years that St. Jerome is a business. They tout that Jesuit education and all that, well they're giving you a lot of baloney over there. It's a good bait and switch operation.

Raymond's discourse transforms his learning disability, a stigmatizing and frustrating aspect of his youth, into a bargaining chip that he, as a shrewd poker player, has learned to use to his advantage. Raymond's ambivalence about his identity, however, surfaces throughout his life story narrative. At times, after asserting that he would be a fool not to take advantage of his disability "points," Raymond then admits that he despises the entire system that, as he imagines, awards such points to people like himself:

I really hate those kind of systems. I mean, that you should favor a certain group like me because of this, over a person who's normal. Well, I shouldn't say I hate it. It seems that in some instances you are favored more, you're not on an equal level. One person's up here, you're over here because of your disability, race, color, or creed. And because of this, some government law, boom, you're up here, you're way past them. That's the way I perceive some of it. That I don't like.

The statement expresses a great deal about Raymond's perception of disabilities and disability rights. On the one hand, there are "normal" people who have no special advantage. On the other hand, there are people "like me" who are not normal, whose "disability, race, color, or creed" sets them apart from the rest of society in some significant way. Raymond groups himself with those who are not normal and questions whether it is right for the government to step in and grant them preferential treatment. By this description, Raymond is both a shrewd person, someone in the know, and an abnormal person whose identity is marginal—not an insider at all, but a prototypical outsider, just as he was when he rode on the "retarded buses" instead of attending the neighborhood school. He enthusiastically utilizes what he understands to be a preferential system, but he simultaneously condemns the system's unfairness.

Despite his many struggles in academic settings, Raymond does not express much concern about on-the-job accommodations in his anticipated professional career. He expects that his family and friendship connections will make possible the arrangements and work routines he needs in order to succeed. Raymond decided years before that he would continue in his father's business, and for this reason he does not worry about the difficulty his learning disability may present for a future employer. The secretaries who work for Raymond's father currently provide him with substantial support in preparing term papers for his college classes. Thus, he has already developed many of the accommodations he will need for the writing he must do in his father's business, and he knows exactly how he will overcome prospective obstacles connected with his disability on the job.

Raymond assumes that, as an employee in the family business, he will readily obtain any accommodations he needs. But Raymond also expects to be an employer and eventually a business owner. His ambivalent perspective becomes even more pronounced when we ask how he would deal with a hypothetical employee with a disability like his own. Even if providing accommodations for such an employee were to cost Raymond a little more, he assures us that he would attempt to make the job accessible: "I'd be a hypocrite if I didn't. Because of what I went through, I would help them out. I wouldn't even think twice about that. I wouldn't shut anybody else down, because I know what I went through. So I'll always listen to somebody else, try and help somebody else out who's in the same boat." Yet Raymond admits that if the accommodations became too expensive and threatened to hurt his business, then he would have to refuse them: "If it's going to hurt your business, you can't do it. You're in business to make money. If, because you're spending an extra thousands of dollars because you have one or two or three people that do this, and it's hurting you rather than helping you, or keeping you at status quo, you have no choice. It's not a charitable organization."

At the personal level, Raymond feels great empathy for the employee who, like himself, has a disability that requires some accommodation in the workplace. As a personal matter, he is aware that it would be hypocritical if he failed to offer the kind of support that he himself struggled to obtain over the years. From a subjective vantage point, he can see the hardship, frustration, and unfairness experienced by those whom society deems abnormal. At the business level, however, Raymond has a firm sense of the limits of altruism. His vantage point is also that of the hardheaded business person who remains competitive by limiting costs and maximizing profits and who must make the most efficient use of a pool of prospective employees. Sympathy and support are one thing, but if the cost gets too high, then no business owner should be expected to jeopardize profits to the point where the business itself would suffer. No law should require him to do so.

In conclusion, Raymond tells us explicitly that he opposes the Americans with Disabilities Act (ADA). His position is not necessarily based on considerations of fairness—what Raymond assumes is the preferential treatment accorded persons with disabilities under the ADA. Rather, he believes that the ADA is just another unwelcome intrusion by the government into matters that properly are the prerogative of individual employers:

Q: Would we be better off if we didn't have a law like that, or do you think it's important to keep it?

RM: Probably wouldn't matter a hill of beans if the law wasn't there, because it's such a small amount of people. Who's it going to affect?

Q: Forty-three million people is what Congress found when they passed the law.

RM: Yeah, but hold up. That's like the welfare law. How many people are on welfare, how many people really don't need it. You know, do I really need it? I don't know. . . .

Q: So, your congressional representative comes out to talk to you and says the ADA is up for reconsideration, how should I vote?

RM: Depending on what it was costing? Probably say kill it . . . because there's too much government regulation in business.

For Raymond Militello, the law has offered little in comparison to the support he has found from family and friends and from his own ability to maneuver and make deals. He assumes that without the ADA his life would not have been much different. He suffered as a child because of the meddlesome interventions of the special education system. He continued his studies without many of the academic accommodations to which he was legally entitled. He anticipates a professional career in the family business where he will continue to make his own arrangements rather than rely on his rights. Rights have, he believes, provided a "back door" through which he has sometimes gained an advantage; but if the ADA did not exist, there would be other back doors and other ways to circumvent obstacles and come out ahead. Raymond looks forward to the time when he will be the person in charge and will have to make decisions that affect his employees. At that point, he hopes to display compassion to others with learning disabilities like his own, but he will not allow them to take advantage of him. As a businessman, his responsibility is not to run a "charitable organization" but to make sure that the family business continues to turn a profit. His ultimate obligation is to the business, his family, and his friends.

Reinterpreting the Effects of Rights

We have suggested that identity is the appropriate starting point for understanding how rights become active, because the question of who one is and where one belongs precedes the question of the rights one might choose to assert. Our discussion has emphasized the effects of identity on the role of rights, but the relationship between rights and identity runs in both directions. Rights can shape identities as well as be shaped by them. When we say that rights can constitute identity, we refer to the effect of rights on the two aspects of identity discussed in chapter 1: its intersubjective formation and the narrative process that plays a key role in the development of a sense of self. Scholars sometimes refer to the two-way relationship between law and society as "mutually constitutive," which means that law both affects and is affected by those for whom it is intended and by society in general. We use the term in this book to denote the specific effects that rights and identity exert on one another—recursively—over an extended period of time. We argue that the recursive relationship between rights and identity provides the foundation for a new conception of how rights under the Americans with Disabilities Act (ADA) become active in the lives of their intended beneficiaries.

The constitutive effects of rights on identity are often intended or assumed by legislators or judges. We can infer that this was the case with the ADA, whose drafters recognized that persons with disabilities had historically been excluded from the social mainstream because their identity and assumptions about their ability to work were distorted by stereotype and prejudice: "[I]ndividuals with disabilities are a discrete and insular minority who have been faced with restrictions and limitations, subjected to a history of purposeful unequal treatment, and relegated to a position of political powerlessness in our society, based on characteristics that are beyond the control of such individuals and

resulting from stereotypic assumptions not truly indicative of the individual ability of such individuals to participate in, and contribute to,
society" (ADA §12101(a)(7)). By granting broad-ranging civil rights to
those who had been labeled abnormal or deviant, the drafters intended
to ameliorate "the major areas of discrimination faced day-to-day by
people with disabilities." In turn, such rights-induced changes would
counter "stereotypic assumptions" about persons with disabilities and
replace them with perceptions "truly indicative of individual ability."
In short, the ADA treats rights as the answer to exclusion. It assumes
that new forms of legal protection can correct the distortion of identity
caused by fear and prejudice.

In this chapter, we present evidence from our life story interviews
suggesting that the constitutive effects of rights on identity are more
problematic than the drafters of the ADA imagined. Our interviewees
have taught us that rights do not typically have a direct, legally empow-
ering effect on their intended beneficiaries, but that rights nonetheless
can change both dimensions of identity that we discussed in the preceding chapter: social interactions and the construction of a narrative
of self. For example, rights affected Sara Lane's work relationships and
interactions at several points in her life story. Awareness of the disability rights movement influenced the editor of the *Ardmore Gazette*
to hire Sara; and passage of the ADA made the editor of the *Midwest
Tribune* "extremely accommodating" and led her colleagues to inter-
vene on her behalf, although Sara herself never invoked her rights. Jill
Golding's awareness of disability rights fundamentally changed her
self-perception and her narrative depiction of formative childhood
experiences. Because she now views herself as an intelligent and capable person with special needs that must be accommodated as a matter of right, she has transformed her career plans, developed a new
relationship with her parents, and engaged in debates with her boss
and coworkers about the inclusion of people with disabilities in the
workplace.

Even Raymond Militello, who expresses far greater skepticism about
the fairness and effectiveness of the ADA, provides evidence that rights
affect identity in ways that the ADA's drafters never anticipated. Raymond, the subject of our third life story narrative, believes that the constitutive effects of rights throughout his life have been stigmatizing and
have tended to undermine his identity as a full and equal participant
in mainstream social institutions. Raymond contends that ADA rights
are intrusive, that they breed resentment and social isolation because
they give some people an unfair advantage over others. Nevertheless,

he acknowledges that rights have enabled him to achieve some of his career goals by opening the "back door" to a college education and allowing him to manipulate the system to succeed as a student. Like Sara and Jill, Raymond never mobilizes his rights as the drafters of the ADA envisioned, yet rights have powerfully affected his identity, both positively and negatively.

After listening to the narrative accounts of our interviewees, we have concluded that it is important to develop new understandings of how rights influence the lives and identities of rights holders. Although express invocations of ADA rights prove to be rare and atypical, rights constitute identities in other ways. As McCann (1994:6) observes, law is "constitutive of practical interactions among citizens"; and, as we have suggested, it is within the everyday interactions among people with disabilities and their friends, family, coworkers, supervisors, and government officials that "distributed identities" evolve. McCann cites Galanter's (1983a:127, quoted in McCann 1994:6) emphasis on the communicative function of law: "[I]t affects us primarily through communication of symbols—by providing threats, promises, models, persuasion, legitimacy, stigma" and other kinds of meaning to the broader public. Through its symbolic and communicative capacity, McCann concludes, law—and legal rights—"shape the very terms of citizen understanding, aspiration, and interaction with others" (1994:6).

Building on the approach suggested by McCann, Galanter, and others, and drawing on the insights provided by the life story narratives of our interviewees, we present in this chapter a new framework for understanding the constitutive effects of rights on identities. We begin with an analysis of three prevailing theories: classical rights theory, the rights versus relationships model, and critical rights theory. We explore the assumptions and shortcomings of these theories and then present an alternative framework for understanding the constitutive effects of rights on identity that is more attentive to the role rights actually play in the everyday lives of people with disabilities. Drawing on the life stories of two of our interviewees, Raymond Militello and Barry Swygert, we conclude with the argument that rights and identity should be viewed in terms of their recursive effects over an extended period of time. Rights shape identities in a variety of ways throughout the life of the rights holder; and the identities thus constituted determine how and when rights holders turn to rights as a framework for interpreting perceived experiences of unfairness.

Constitutive Theories of Rights

Passage of the ADA illustrates a distinctive American faith in the power of rights to transform the lives and identities of those who have suffered injustice (compare Scheingold 1974). As we have seen, the ADA promises to bring about equal treatment and social inclusion—changes that will end stereotyping and discrimination and will change the demeaning perceptions of men and women with disabilities. The ADA thus reflects long-standing assumptions about the constitutive effects of rights on identity; but these assumptions are not universally accepted in contemporary American society. In this section, we outline the three theories about the constitutive effects of rights that have tended to dominate public debates. We follow this brief discussion with examples from our own research that suggest an alternative perspective on the role and consequences of rights.

Classical Rights Theory

The theory that rights constitute and protect the identity of Americans as citizens is deeply embedded in our democratic history and traditions. The Declaration of Independence and the Bill of Rights placed the rights of citizens at the center of the new American democracy. Every free and independent person could demand that the government respect certain fundamental rights and, conversely, the capacity to invoke such rights defined the identity of a citizen, as contrasted with those who could not and were considered less than citizens: slaves, women, children, prisoners, and insane persons. The constitutive effect of rights on the identity of citizens in a democracy seemed obvious to de Tocqueville (1945:255) and essential for governance:

> I do not say it is easy to teach men how to exercise political rights, but I maintain that, when it is possible, the effects which result from it are highly important; and I add that, if there ever was a time at which such an attempt ought to be made, that time is now. Do you not see that religious belief is shaken and the divine notion of right is declining, that morality is debased and the notion of moral right is therefore fading away? Argument is substituted for faith, and calculation for the impulses of sentiment. If, in the midst of this general disruption, you do not succeed in connecting the notion of right with that of private interest, which is the only immutable point in the human heart, what means will you have of governing the world except by fear?

Throughout American history, key social issues have consistently been framed in terms of rights. Legislators and judges have assumed that the enactment of civil rights can profoundly change the lives and social status of African Americans, women, workers, religious adherents, children, gays and lesbians, and others. This assumption explains the identity transformations anticipated after the post—Civil War civil rights legislation, the Civil Rights Acts of 1964 and 1968, the unsuccessful Equal Rights Amendment, and the ADA itself. The drafters of such legislation did not always make explicit their goal of identity transformation, but their assumptions about the constitutive effects of rights can usually be inferred. In the landmark Supreme Court decision in *Brown v. Board of Education* (1954:493), Chief Justice Warren spoke directly about the right of African American children to attend integrated public schools and its constitutive effects on their social interactions and sense of self:

> [Education] is the very foundation of good citizenship. Today it is a principal instrument in awakening the child to cultural values, in preparing him for later professional training, and in helping him to adjust normally to his environment. In these days, it is doubtful that any child may reasonably be expected to succeed in life if he is denied the opportunity of an education. Such an opportunity, where the state has undertaken to provide it, is a right which must be made available to all on equal terms. . . . To separate [African American children] from others of similar age and qualifications solely because of their race generates a feeling of inferiority as to their status in the community that may affect their hearts and minds in a way unlikely ever to be undone.

Justice Thurgood Marshall, the great exponent of civil rights, drew similar conclusions about the constitutive effect of rights on the identities of persons with developmental disabilities. In his dissent in *City of Cleburne v. Cleburne Living Center* (1985:467, 473), decided five years before passage of the ADA, Marshall wrote:

> For the retarded, just as for Negroes and women, much has changed in recent years, but much remains the same; out-dated statutes are still on the books, and irrational fears or ignorance, traceable to the prolonged social and cultural isolation of the retarded, continue to stymie recognition of the dignity and individuality of retarded people. . . . As the history of discrimination against the retarded and its continuing legacy amply attest, the mentally retarded have been, and in some areas may still be, the

targets of action the Equal Protection Clause condemns. With respect to a liberty so valued as the right to establish a home in the community, and so likely to be denied on the basis of irrational fears and outright hostility, heightened scrutiny is surely appropriate.

In the classic conception, rights do not merely entitle an individual to *do something*—vote, attend an integrated school, receive due process, worship, or marry. They also entitle each individual to *be someone*—to be recognized by others as a citizen, as a member of society, as an autonomous individual within the American democracy. Rights can make citizens out of those who were formerly slaves, chattels, dependents, or patients. The ADA is a recent manifestation of a theory as old as our Republic, that rights can change society and transform the identities of individuals who have been excluded and oppressed. Viewed from this perspective, the constitutive effect of rights is an article of faith, an assumption deeply embedded in American political ideology.

It is widely recognized, however, that social, economic, ideological, and political barriers may obstruct the workings of rights and frustrate their intended constitutive effects on identity. Scholarship on the mobilization of law acknowledges the existence of such obstacles and documents their impact on the actual effect of rights (see, e.g., Black 1973; Silberman 1985; Burstein and Monaghan 1986; Milner 1986). As Zemans (1983:695) writes: "Whatever rights are conferred are thus contingent upon the factors that promote or inhibit decisions to mobilize the law." Inquiry into factors affecting the mobilization of law is entirely consistent with classical rights theory, since it assumes the constitutive effects of rights in circumstances where barriers do not interfere with their operation. Indeed, the implicit and sometimes explicit policy goal of such scholarship is to identify social barriers and mitigate their influence so that rights can exert their intended effects. By contrast, some scholars have questioned the effectiveness of rights theory itself as a means to achieve progressive social change (see, e.g., Mayhew 1968; Rosenberg 1991). We consider two of the most prominent challenges to classical rights theory in the discussion that follows.

The Rights versus Relationships Model

A contrary perspective on the constitutive effect of rights assumes that rights erode social relationships and sense of self. In contemporary American society, a great deal of writing about rights deemphasizes their role in creating free and autonomous citizens and instead warns that the price we pay for rights is the weakening or destruction of relationships among family, friends, neighbors, coworkers, social networks, consociations, and business enterprises. Conversely, when relationships are strong and enduring, the participants are unlikely to invoke rights against one another, because they value intimacy and cooperation over adversarial legalism. Since identity, as we and others define it, is "distributed" within social relationships, the theorized opposition of rights and relationships implies significant limitations for the constitutive effects of the ADA. Viewed from this perspective, statutes like the ADA may actually undermine identity by damaging the network of relationships within which identity develops.

Classical rights theory focuses on positive identity changes thought to result from the *advantages rights confer,* such as the opportunity to vote, attend integrated schools, serve in the military, live where one chooses, claim protection against interference with free speech or religious worship or against cruel and unusual punishment. By contrast, the rights versus relationships model focuses on undesirable identity changes thought to result from *being one who uses rights.* Because it tends to view these changes in negative terms, the rights versus relationships model challenges the assumptions underlying classical rights theory. It assumes that relationships can be irreparably harmed when social interactions rest on the coercion of law rather than choice or affinity—a consideration that it sees as missing from classical rights theory, which overlooks the problematic social consequences for a person whose identity rests on rights.

Many strands of contemporary thought reflect the presumed opposition of rights and relationships. For example, sociolegal scholars in the 1960s and 1970s argued that every society contains a continuum of mechanisms regulating social interactions, imposing sanctions, and enforcing norms (see, e.g., Macaulay 1963; Pospisil 1971; Abel 1973; Galanter 1974). At the formal end of the continuum is the official legal system, which relies on courts and lawyers, statutes and caselaw. At the informal end are the "appended" systems of law and lawlike structures (Galanter 1974), which rely on continuing relationships and interactions, group norms, and interpersonal or charismatic authority. Rights are associated with the formal or official end of this continuum. Their effects at the more informal ranges are always in doubt, since law has a limited capacity to penetrate into "semi-autonomous social fields" (Moore 1978). These scholars suggest that, where social relationships are stronger, more interconnected, and intimate, law and legal rights play a less important role (see also Gluckman 1955). Conversely, where relationships are weak or attenuated, law becomes more active. Black (1976:41), for example, observes that "[l]aw is inactive among intimates, increasing as the distance between people increases but decreasing as this reaches the point at which people live in entirely separate worlds." According to these theorists, the constitutive effects of rights should be relatively weak for individuals and interactions within dense relational networks, where official legal norms and institutions have limited influence.[1]

Sociolegal scholars discuss the theorized opposition of rights and relationships in terms of its empirical validity, but other writers argue essentially the same proposition in normative terms. That is, many critics maintain that rights tend to destroy valuable social relationships and should therefore be avoided or curtailed.[2] Although these commentators do not necessarily phrase their arguments in terms of the negative constitutive effects of rights on identity, such a conclusion is often implicit in their arguments. They express skepticism toward rights not only because rights are difficult and expensive to mobilize but because of what rights do. Advocates of alternative dispute resolution (ADR), for example, contend that formal rights claims in adversarial settings can destroy valued relationships and cut off the possibility of mutually beneficial interactions in the future.[3] Political conservatives argue that rights are selfish and destructive of social consensus and civic responsibility.[4] Communitarians view the constitutive effects of rights in terms of their tendency to disrupt cooperative social relationships and create opposition and hostility rather than a sense of obligation toward the community.[5]

In sum, the diverse theorists who view rights in opposition to relationships would agree, despite their differences, that the ADA poses risks for Americans with disabilities. Since identity is "distributed"

---

1. A thoughtful reexamination of the "rights versus relationships" model in sociolegal scholarship appears in Yngvesson 1985 and in the related commentary by Galanter (1985).

2. See critical discussion of this position in Greenhouse, Yngvesson, and Engel 1994.

3. See descriptions of the ADR movement in Tomasic and Feeley 1982; Harrington 1985; Hofrichter 1987.

4. See, e.g., Glendon 1991:14: "Our rights talk, in its absoluteness, promotes unrealistic expectations, heightens social conflict, and inhibits dialogue that might lead toward consensus, accommodation, or at least the discovery of common ground. In its silence concerning responsibilities, it seems to condone acceptance of the benefits of living in a democratic social welfare state, without accepting the corresponding personal and civic obligations. In its relentless individualism, it fosters a climate that is inhospitable to society's losers, and that systematically disadvantages caretakers and dependents, young and old. In its neglect of civil society, it undermines the principal seedbeds of civic and personal virtue."

5. "[T]he expression of ever more wants, many quite legitimate, in the language of rights makes it difficult to achieve compromises and reach consensus, processes that lie at the heart of democracy. . . . A return to a language of social virtues, interests, and, above all, social responsibilities will reduce contentiousness and enhance social cooperation" (Etzioni 1993:6–7). See also Etzioni 1995, 1996, 1998.

within one's network of social relationships, disrupting such relationships through the assertion of rights could have negative effects on one's identity. For these theorists, then, the ADA could harm the identities of those it was intended to help and its adversarial effects could place people with disabilities outside the social mainstream rather than integrating them into the social settings from which they have been historically excluded.

The rights versus relationships model leads to predominantly negative conclusions about the effects of rights on identity. Some scholars have suggested that these pessimistic conclusions are not supported by fieldwork studies of law in everyday life. White (2002) and McCann (1994), for example, demonstrate that rights sometimes have highly beneficial effects on relationships and on the identity of those who participate in them. On the basis of our own interviews, we agree that the positive as well as the negative effects of rights on relationships vary from one context to another. We will suggest that it is overly simplistic to assume that rights always damage identity by undermining social relationships.

Critical Rights Theory

Critical legal theorists offer another widely cited challenge to classical rights theory. The critique of rights by critical legal studies (CLS) scholars in the 1970s and 1980s emphasized the indeterminacy of rights and their paradoxical tendency to legitimate oppression by creating a false sense of formal neutrality and equality. These scholars argued that the "myth of rights," endorsed by classical rights theory, is essentially a sham that provides a protective cover for entrenched forces of racism, sexism, and class domination in society. The consequence of rights in a regime of liberal legalism is to reproduce inequality and oppress those who purportedly benefit from them. Thus, Freeman (1998:286) argued that the Supreme Court's antidiscrimination law "normalizes the existing patterns of inequality and hierarchy;" and Tushnet (1984:1386) wrote, "It is not just that rights-talk does not do much good. In the contemporary United States, it is positively harmful."

Although the original CLS critique did not examine the constitutive effect of rights on identity as such, it had a great deal to say about the effects of law on consciousness and action. According to CLS scholars, classical rights theory is a cornerstone of liberal legalism, which tells individuals they have power and autonomy as citizens of the modern state but in fact denies them the capacity to exert control over others who have greater power. From our perspective, then, the CLS critique of rights has important, if unstated, implications for identity. CLS scholars suggest that liberal legalism uses rights to create a sense of self that is illusory and ultimately destructive, because ordinary citizens often discover that they lack the very capacities that the myth of rights claims to safeguard. Unlike classical rights theory or the rights versus relationships model, the CLS critique of rights concerns itself with *what happens to the identity of individuals who come to see themselves as rights bearers.* According to the critique, harmful consequences flow from the individual's illusory belief that he or she has gained something important from rights.

This highly skeptical view of rights was at times modified, even by some of its original proponents,[6] and has been challenged and revised by feminists and critical race theorists, who have, nonetheless, accepted some of the key premises of the CLS critique. Feminist and critical race scholars tend to address more explicitly the constitutive effect of rights on identity and are less inclined to reject rights categorically. Instead, they point to the beneficial role rights can play when rights holders, who thoroughly understand the social conditions and needs of disadvantaged minorities, participate in the creation and implementation of rights. The constitutive effects of rights, according to these commentators, vary substantially depending on how they evolve and the social and political context in which they are used. For example, the effect of the civil rights movement for the identity of African Americans was positive to the extent that rights were associated with a "powerful combination of direct action, mass protest, and individual acts of resistance, along with appeals to public opinion and the courts" (Crenshaw 1988:1382).[7] The variable effects of rights are apparent, according to many feminist and critical race theorists, when one listens to the evidence of personal narratives and the actual experiences of individuals and groups.[8] Because we share their interest in how rights influence the lives of rights holders, and because we agree that narrative accounts

6. See, e.g., Kennedy 1997. Our use of the term "modified" may be unfair. The author himself characterizes this discussion as "an attempt to dispel some common misunderstandings of the nature and implications of rights critique" (315).

7. For feminist responses to the CLS critique of rights see, e.g., the essays in Bartlett and Kennedy 1991; and Weisberg 1993. For responses by critical race theorists, see the essays in Crenshaw, Gotanda, Peller, and Thomas 1995; and Delgado and Stefancic 2000. The categories of "feminist" and "critical race" theorist overlap substantially, and some of the most influential writers have been identified with both schools. One manifestation of this overlap is the collection edited by Wing (1997).

8. Schneider, for example, argues that the CLS critique achieved a limited view of the constitutive effects of rights on identity because it failed to recognize the dialectical relationship between rights and political practices and experiences: "Admittedly, rights discourse can reinforce alienation and individualism, and can constrict political vision and debate. But, at the same time, it can help to affirm human values, enhance political growth, and assist in the development of collective identity" (Schneider 1993:509). Similarly, we

by rights holders are invaluable for understanding the effect of rights on identity, we concur with those critical theorists who call for a more grounded and contextualized inquiry. Our own research, which relies primarily on the life stories of persons with disabilities, illustrates one response to this call.

Critical rights theory, in its original form, could lead to pessimistic conclusions about the capacity of rights under the ADA to transform the identities of people with disabilities;[9] but a perspective that emphasizes context and the role and position of rights holders may lead to different conclusions. To date, the most important effort to explore these varying critical perspectives on rights and apply them to issues of disability and identity—albeit one that relies primarily on the analysis of caselaw rather than personal narrative accounts—is Minow's (1990) influential book, *Making All the Difference: Inclusion, Exclusion, and American Law.* Minow agrees with critical scholars who contend that classical rights theory can actually reinforce myths and stereotypes about social difference. Under classical rights theory, disability rights are granted to a category of individuals who can establish their entitlement to statutory protection by virtue of significant differences between themselves and persons without disabilities. Proving such differences opens the way for legally mandated accommodations that are not required for individuals who have no disabilities. Paradoxically, rights analysis is premised on an assumption of equality yet its methodology operates by proving difference and according special treatment only to those identified as rights holders. People who avail themselves of their rights are thus caught on

---

discern a link to our interest in the identity-constitutive effects of rights in essays such as the introduction to Crenshaw, Gotanda, Peller, and Thomas 1995 (xxiii), where the editors point to the "social and transformative value" of rights that CLS scholarship, in their view, tends to overlook:

> Crits tended to view the idea of legal "rights" as one of the ways that law helps to legitimize the social world by representing it as rationally mediated by the rule of law. . . . Crits of color agreed to varying degrees with some dimensions of the critique—for instance, that rights discourse was indeterminate. Yet we sharply differed with critics over the normative implications of this observation. To the emerging race crits, rights discourse held a social and transformative value in the context of racial subordination that transcended the narrower question of whether reliance on rights could alone bring about any determinate results.

9. Cole (2000), for example, explores the possibility of a "critical disability theory" that would expose the indeterminacy of the concept of "disability" itself. She notes some of the ways in which the concept has been appropriated and "medicalized" by employers to serve their own purposes rather than to eliminate stigmatization and discrimination in society. She argues that the prevailing understanding of rights under the ADA focuses on an "unnatural ability-disability binarism" rather than on the unjustified exclusion of some Americans from employment. Thus, "as currently applied, the ADA minoritizes the people it is intended to protect" (555).

the horns of a dilemma: rights are the vehicle for achieving equality, but to invoke rights one must first identify oneself as unequal—in the sense that one's abilities fall short of an imagined "norm." The constitutive effect of rights on identity is thus to take away in the very act of giving: attaining the right to inclusion in mainstream settings and activities is accompanied by a demonstration that one is marked indelibly by one's disability.

Minow argues that the dilemma of rights arises from a perception that "locates the problem in the person who does not fit in rather than in relationships between people and social institutions" that, for example, create a workplace designed to meet the needs of some but not all potential employees (111). She posits an alternative, "social relations" approach, which begins with a different perception, namely, that the problem is located in workplaces that arbitrarily accommodate one segment of society but not another. "Disability" has no inherent meaning. What constitutes a "disability" in one setting may have no significance, or even be an advantage, in another setting, invalidating any attempt to define the term categorically. " 'Difference,' " Minow contends, "is meaningful only as a comparison. . . . As a relational notion, difference is reciprocal: I am no more different from you than you are from me" (111). "Disability," in this latter conceptualization, is not an immutable quality of the individual but is society's problem. Exclusion associated with disability is a signal that an individual has not been provided for as others have been and that there is a shared responsibility for changing the social relations and institutions that create the disadvantage. An appropriate legal response is to empower the rights bearer to participate in making decisions that will change relationships in the school or workplace and promote inclusion.[10] When rights are conceptualized in terms of social relations, their constitutive effects on identity are, in theory, no longer stigmatizing.

10. Provisions for accommodations in the Individuals with Disabilities Education Act (IDEA) and the ADA, for example, reject rigid guidelines for implementing rights and instead specify procedures intended to encourage dialogue and mutual decisionmaking to mitigate the consequences of difference by creating social environments with greater flexibility. The IDEA requires that school districts establish a multidisciplinary committee to meet with parents of children with disabilities and create an individualized educational plan tailored to the needs of each child. Regulations enacted by the Equal Employment Opportunity Commission (EEOC) to implement the ADA envision a dialogue between employer and employee when necessary to devise reasonable accommodations (29 C.F.R. §1630.2(o)(3)). Yet even these mechanisms are available only to students or employees who can first prove that they have a disability, and thus they still contain many of the shortcomings of classical rights theory. In prior published work, we have discussed the potential and the pitfalls of such approaches when viewed from the perspective of the rights bearers themselves. See Engel 1991; Engel and Munger 1996; Munger and Engel 1998; Engel and Munger 2001.

Minow's analysis suggests that different conceptualizations of rights can have different effects on identity, and our own interviews with the intended beneficiaries of disability rights tend to support many of her conclusions.[11] Minow's work has influenced our research, but our methodology differs from hers. The life story narratives of our interviewees lead us to conclude that the sharp differences Minow perceives between different formal approaches to rights may be less meaningful in practice than at the doctrinal level. Minow, like most of the theorists we have discussed in this section, focuses on rights that have been explicitly invoked, typically in the context of a formal legal proceeding. The negative consequences of rights are, for the most part, associated with these formal claims. Our interviewees, however, describe a number of less explicit ways in which rights exert their effects on the identities of people with disabilities. In order to draw meaningful conclusions about the constitutive effect of rights on identities, we think it essential to consider the actual life experiences of the intended beneficiaries of the ADA, even when they take no formal legal action.

Toward a New Theory of Rights

In the preceding discussion, we outlined three widely cited theoretical frameworks for interpreting the constitutive effects of rights on identity: classical rights theory, the rights versus relationships model, and critical rights theory. All three frameworks resonate at times in the life story narratives of our interviewees. Yet much of the commentary associated with these theoretical perspectives appears limited or irrelevant when considered in light of the actual life experiences of people with disabilities. Many writers who associate themselves with these three perspectives assume that the formal qualities of rights—doctrinal classification systems or technical legal modes of analysis[12]—are most important in determining their effects. They further assume that rights typically become active only when they are invoked in formal legal proceedings. The life stories of our interviewees belie both of these assumptions. The formal qualities of rights under the ADA—the doctrinal features that occupy the attention of most judges and legal academic writers—made

11. For a discussion of the dilemma of special education rights, as experienced by the families of children with disabilities, see Engel 1991.

12. By "technical legal modes of analysis," we refer, for example, to debates over "suspect" or "quasi-suspect" classes of individuals and levels of judicial scrutiny under equal protection analysis, as well as debates concerning principles of statutory construction applied to the ADA and the interpretation of its legislative history.

little difference to our interviewees, since none of them experienced the law in a formal legal setting. Rather, the narratives of our interviewees suggest that rights become active far more often in informal, nonadversarial contexts, sometimes without the effort or even the knowledge of the rights holder. Our interviewees present us with a challenge: to construct new understandings of the constitutive effect of rights on identity based on the important finding that none of the sixty interviewees participated in a formal rights claim or even consulted a lawyer about the ADA, although all who had disabilities experienced what they perceived as unfair or illegal treatment. Despite the notable absence of formal legal activity in these life stories, it is evident that rights significantly influenced the lives of our interviewees, sometimes in dramatic fashion.

In one sense, it is not surprising to find that none of our interviewees resorted to ADA rights to make a formal claim. Sociolegal scholars have observed for many years that formal mobilization of the law is a relatively rare phenomenon in America, popular beliefs to the contrary notwithstanding,[13] and civil rights infractions and employment conflicts are among the legal problems least likely to be pursued by aggrieved individuals.[14] Although our sixty interviewees were not a predictive sample and were not intended to be statistically representative of all Americans with disabilities, we see nothing unusual or atypical in their avoidance of formal rights claims. The ADA's rights and protections are now available to nearly 50 million Americans with disabilities,[15] yet a

13. See generally Kritzer 1980–81; Felstiner 1974 (noting that "avoidance" rather than adjudication or mediation tends to characterize dispute behavior in "technologically complex rich societies" such as the United States).

14. Mayhew and Reiss 1969; Miller and Sarat 1980–81. Curran (1977:143–46), in her landmark study of the use of lawyers, reports a 4 percent rate of lawyer consultation per employment problem, a rate lower than for other problem types, such as consumer problems (12 percent), constitutional problems (12 percent), and personal injuries (34 percent).

Of course, consultation with a lawyer does not necessarily lead to the assertion of a legal claim or a determination on the merits, for which rates are presumably lower. In a careful analysis of research concerning medical malpractice, for example, Michael Saks (1992:1178–79, 1225) describes a study by the RAND corporation which found that only 4 percent of injuries caused by negligent doctors led to consultation with a lawyer (a rate comparable to lawyer use for employment problems in the Curran study), and subsequently only 2 percent led to the filing of a lawsuit, and only 0.3 percent resulted in the commencement of a trial. Even this seemingly low rate of litigation per lawyer consultation was actually inflated by an unusual aspect of the study. All of the cases that constitute the 4 percent figure for lawyer consultations were determined by an independent panel of medical experts to have involved injuries caused by a doctor's negligence, yet even in this group of malpractice cases whose merits had been vouchsafed by neutral medical experts, lawyers filed a formal claim in only half of the cases brought to them for advice.

15. See the introduction, note 3, concerning the difficulty of estimating the number of Americans with disabilities.

majority of adults with disabilities remains unemployed,[16] and remarkably few rights holders[17] have filed formal complaints of ADA violations with federal, state, and local agencies since the act's inception.[18]

Some might conclude that the reluctance of ADA rights holders to bring formal claims merely substantiates the CLS critique of rights as illusory and ineffective. The testimony of our interviewees does not support such a conclusion. Listening to their life stories, we find ample support for the growing number of sociolegal scholars who contend that the role of law in everyday life—and its effect on identity—cannot be measured only by the frequency of recourse to lawyers and official legal institutions or remedy systems. Recent research on law in everyday life has deepened our understanding of law's subtle and sometimes powerful effect on behavior and consciousness.[19] Some of the most important

16. See, e.g., N.O.D./Harris 1998:7: "Among the adults with disabilities of working age (18 to 64), three out of ten (29%) work full or part-time, compared to eight out of ten (79%) of those without disabilities, a gap of fifty percentage points."

The Census Bureau Survey of Income and Program Participation (SIPP) adds depth to a complex picture of employment among persons with disabilities. SIPP survey data for 1994 show that unemployment rates vary widely among persons with disabilities depending on the severity and type of disability. For example, the unemployment rate among young adults (age twenty to twenty-four) with a "moderate" disability is relatively low—20.4 percent. Unemployment rates rise among groups of persons with more severe disabilities and may exceed 80 percent depending on age and years of education. See Hale, Hayghe, and McNeil 1998:5.

17. Between July 26, 1992, when Title I of the ADA became effective, and March 31, 1998, only 175,226 charges of discrimination under the ADA were filed in all federal, state, and local enforcement agencies combined (Moss, Ullman, Johnsen, Starrett, and Burris 1999:34). This figure represents an average of only 30,904 charges per year at all enforcement levels among the approximately 29 million Americans with disabilities who are of working age.

18. Our conclusion that formal rights claims are relatively "few" in number is based in part, but not entirely, on a rough comparison of the limited number of complaints, the large number of Americans with disabilities who work or want to work, and the frequent allegations of unfair treatment that we and other researchers encounter in our interviews. Other indirect measures also suggest that relatively few rights violations lead to formal claims under the ADA. A 1993 survey, for example, found that although 27 percent of all American employees experienced some form of employment discrimination, only 10 percent of that number (2.7 percent of all employees) filed a formal claim. See Slonaker and Wendt 1995:21. There is no reason to think that employees with disabilities exceed that 10 percent figure for complaints per experiences of employment discrimination. Indeed, data described by Blanck (1998:56) from 1996 suggests that employees with disabilities may be more reluctant than other victims of discrimination to bring formal charges. In that year, only 23 percent of all employment discrimination charges filed with the EEOC alleged a violation of ADA rights as compared with 47 percent that alleged racial discrimination and 41 percent that alleged gender discrimination. See Blanck 1998:56. Although these statistical measures are far from precise, one might be justified in drawing the preliminary inference that 10 percent, and possibly substantially fewer, is a fair estimate for the number of individuals with disabilities who file complaints when they believe their ADA rights have been violated.

19. See literature summaries in McCann and March 1995; Sarat and Kearns 1995. Both of us have engaged in other studies identitifed with this research tradition; see, e.g., Engel 1984, 1993, 1995; Munger 2002.

of these studies, moreover, have demonstrated the value of narrative accounts by ordinary citizens in exploring the constitutive effects of law. Yngvesson (1997), for example, presents the narratives of adoptive and birth parents and their children to examine (among other things) the effect of closed and open adoption laws on the construction of motherhood, family, and self.[20] Ewick and Silbey (1998:249) collected stories of everyday experiences from a sample of New Jersey residents, and conclude that "legality is a durable and powerful structure of American society because it is ordinary and has a common place in daily life." Gilliom (2001) solicited narrative accounts of women welfare recipients in order to document the system's oppressive effects on their lives and consciousness as well as their sometimes effective efforts to subvert the system's rules. White (1991) discusses the narrative of a legal services client facing termination of her welfare benefits, who responds with a story that proves surprisingly effective. Bumiller (1988) traces the effects of antidiscrimination laws by listening to the accounts of ordinary people who experienced discrimination in their everyday lives.

These narrative-based studies provide a perspective that we find missing from most of the theoretical literature on rights discussed above. The three constitutive theories of rights we described in the preceding section tend to ignore the subtle, contextual factors that emerge more clearly in research that listens carefully as ordinary people talk about their neighborhoods, their coworkers, their families, and the varying and volatile quality of social interactions. We have found in our own research that such factors are crucially important in determining the role rights play. Our own research, however, differs from some of these narrative-based sociolegal studies of everyday life in that we focus on identity as it emerges and changes over a long sweep of time.

Our inquiry into the constitutive effects of disability rights, then, resembles sociolegal studies of law in everyday life that attempt to discern the role law plays even when its formal institutions and procedures are not set in motion. Yet our approach, which relies on life story narratives, provides a perspective different from research on legal rights that draws on temporally limited accounts of particular conflicts or encounters and from studies that aim to produce a static set of categories or ideal types. Since our interviewees describe relationships, aspirations, and events from early childhood to adulthood, we are able to see with heightened clarity the continual transformations and "alternations" of

20. In an earlier work, Yngvesson (1993) uses complaint narratives by residents of two New England communities to explore the role of lower level criminal court officials in the construction of identities, relationships, norms, and meanings in the everyday life of those communities.

identity (Rosenwald 1992:272–73) that are less obvious in narratives confined to a limited time frame. The temporal depth of the narratives we collected, along with our focus on the effects of a specific civil rights statute, the ADA, provide us with a distinctive view of law in everyday life.[21]

We seek, then, an alternative perspective on the constitutive effects of rights on identity, and the narratives of our interviewees suggest the importance of reconceptualizing the three prevailing theories that have dominated public debates. The life story interviews we have collected provide us with a foundation for understanding more precisely how rights become active in the lives of rights holders. Our analysis of these rich and varied accounts has led us to conclude that a new theory must take into account at least four ways in which rights affect identity:

1. *Formal legal proceedings.* As we have already observed, our interviewees' accounts are notable for the complete absence of any attempt to invoke rights by lodging a formal claim or even by consulting a lawyer when confronted with behavior they perceived as unfair. The absence of formal rights claims among our interviewees is particularly striking in light of the fact that our call for research subjects inevitably brought us into contact with a group of men and women who tend to be more engaged and attentive to outside resources than many of their peers. Our interview sample was, if anything, biased in the direction of activism rather than passivity. Yet the use—or even the threatened use— of formal legal proceedings by our interviewees played a minimal role in their life experience. Rights under the ADA simply did not become active or exercise constitutive effects on identity in this direct, unmediated way. Of course, rights could become active in our interviewees' lives through formal legal proceedings initiated by someone else. We found no evidence, however, that any of our interviewees benefited directly from ADA proceedings brought by another worker against their employer, for example, or as a member of a class action lawsuit. To the extent that formal legal proceedings by others indirectly or symbolically affected our interviewees, we would group such effects in the three categories that follow.

2. *Transformation of self-perceptions.* The life stories of interviewees like Jill Golding suggest the extent to which rights can change the self-image of individuals with disabilities, enabling them to reassess their

21. Bumiller, for example, concludes that antidiscrimination law is largely ineffective and that "people who have experienced discriminatory treatment resist engagement in legal tactics because they stand in awe of the power of the law to disrupt their daily lives" (1988:109). We suspect that she might have reached different conclusions about the role of rights in her interviewees' lives if she had elicited life story narratives rather than simply asked for accounts of specific incidents of discrimination.

own capabilities and envision more ambitious career paths by incorporating in their plans the reasonable accommodations and the nondiscriminatory treatment guaranteed by the ADA. In chapter 1, we suggested that a key component of identity is the narrative of self that one continuously composes, revises, and retells in different circumstances. These narratives not only bring order and meaning to past events, they also make possible "new living action" by the self they portray. Rights can play a crucial role in the construction of these narratives without ever being formally invoked. Jill Golding, for example, formerly told the story of her childhood in terms of her own shortcomings, but her later awareness of rights contributed to a *transformation of her self-perception*. Reinterpreting events of the past, Jill now tells her life story in terms of the denial of her legal right to educational accommodations. Armed with a new perception of her past and her current rights and capabilities, Jill plans a career in nursing that would have been impossible in the absence of rights. The obstacles that she faces—like those she faced during childhood—are now identified as the product of discrimination or illegality rather than personal shortcomings. Rights have made a great difference for Jill's identity and have contributed to a dramatic transformation of her narrative of self.

3. *Cultural and discursive shifts.* In a number of the life stories we collected, it was clear that rights, even when they are not formally invoked, can affect identities by contributing to paradigmatic shifts in everyday thoughts, speech, and actions. Cultural and discursive shifts derive from many sources, including media reporting of the ADA and the relatively rare and atypical acts of enforcement it has spawned. These shifts affect the interactional and intersubjective dimension of identity as well as its narrative dimension. They may manifest themselves in many ways, from casual conversation and everyday description or persuasion to negotiating or bargaining in the shadow of the law. For Jill Golding, rights become active around the coffee pot at work. There Jill confronts her coworkers and even her supervisor when their conversation fails to acknowledge the rights of persons with disabilities. Jill inscribes ADA rights into her everyday conversations at work in an effort to transform her own identity and produce new cultural images of the identities of persons with learning disabilities. In this way, she attempts to change the thoughts and speech of her coworkers and supervisor to conform more closely to the ADA.

Cultural and discursive shifts may occur in many other ways. For Sara Lane, rights affected her identity even before enactment of the ADA. The disability rights movement had, through its public advocacy, created a perception within the Gannett newspaper chain that it was "cool" to hire people like Sara with visible physical disabilities. The subsequent enactment of rights under the ADA apparently affected her female coworkers' perceptions of Sara as a journalist. According to Sara, they view her in terms of her capabilities and her entitlement to professional advancement, and their support at key moments has proved crucial to Sara's success.

4. *Context-creating role of rights.* As a result of cultural and discursive shifts, as well as the fear of legal enforcement, rights are sometimes implemented unilaterally by third parties rather than through advocacy by the rights bearers themselves. Sara Lane's employers at the *Midwest Tribune,* for example, provided accommodations without prompting when they finally realized that the ADA required them to do so. Other interviewees benefited from broad institutional changes that occurred when universities or corporations responded to the mandates of the ADA. These institutional, context-creating shifts are not usually directed at any individual rights holder but represent an effort to change the environment in which all persons with disabilities pursue their studies or employment. For Raymond Militello, special education rights became active in this way at an early age, with profound consequences for his identity, many of which Raymond deeply resented. The context-creating role of rights in the public schools caused him such distress as a child that his parents eventually withdrew him from special education entirely. On the other hand, the institutional arrangements provided in college, in conformity to the requirements of the ADA, have actually helped Raymond to succeed academically. Rights affected Raymond's life because these institutions changed their routines to implement the legal requirement of nondiscrimination and provision of reasonable accommodation. Rights were silent partners in the formation of Raymond's identity, exerting both positive and negative effects over a period of many years.

In sum, we suggest that a new theory of the constitutive effect of rights on identity must take into account the variety of ways in which rights become active in the lives of their intended beneficiaries. Rather than assuming that rights exert their effects only when they are explicitly invoked in formal legal proceedings, commentators must recognize that rights usually affect identities in other ways: through the transformation of self-perception, through cultural and discursive shifts, and through their context-creating role. When the effects of rights are viewed in this way, the inadequacies of prevailing theories become apparent. Classical rights theory may have had some indirect or symbolic relevance for our sixty interviewees because of its mythic significance, but they never mobilized their rights in ways that proponents of this theory usually envision. None of our interviewees engaged in litigation, despite the assumption of classical rights theorists that the best way to study rights is through appellate court opinions.

The rights versus relationships model also proves an inadequate framework for interpreting the life experiences of our interviewees. Since none of them has brought a formal rights claim, none has placed relationships at risk in quite the way these theorists imagine. When rights become active in other ways, their effects on relationships are not necessarily negative, as the life stories of Sara Lane, Jill Golding, and even Raymond Militello convincingly demonstrate.

Finally, the original CLS critique of rights provides an inadequate framework for understanding what these life story interviews tell us about the effect of rights on identity. Although ADA rights have indeed fallen short of creating an inclusive, accessible, nondiscriminatory workplace for all Americans with disabilities, the CLS critique of rights fails to capture the ambivalence toward rights felt by many of our interviewees or their recognition that rights offer both risk and reward. By emphasizing our interviewees' own views on the value of rights, we are perhaps exposing ourselves to the criticism that we have ignored the power of false consciousness. A critical theorist might contend that the power of liberal legalism resides precisely in its capacity to fool ordinary people into thinking rights have value when in fact they do not. To this, we can only respond that, as a general matter, we tend to give great weight to the opinions of the rights holders themselves. We think the false consciousness argument fails to recognize the conflicted feelings people really have about their rights. Moreover, we think people's ambivalent views of rights are often warranted, because the effects of rights on their lives are indeed quite complicated. For our interviewees who are deeply ambivalent, like Raymond Militello, as well as for others who hold more positive views of rights, the original CLS critique of rights provides little understanding of how rights have affected their identities.

We conclude that the role of rights apparent in our interviewees' stories demonstrates the shortcomings of the three most widely cited theories of the constitutive effects of rights on identity. In the section that follows, we draw on this understanding of rights and present a perspective that emphasizes the interactive relationship between rights and identity over time. We view the impact of rights on identity as "recursive," by which we mean that when rights change identity, one consequence of the change may be a new orientation toward rights themselves, because they may now appear more (or less) relevant to one's life than they did before the identity shift. In short, we posit a dynamic relationship between rights and identity. As rights change individuals' sense of who they are and where they belong, their readiness to embrace rights may also change. Rights and identity exist in a continual feedback loop. They are mutually constitutive. We illustrate this interactive effect of rights and identity by comparing the life story narratives of Raymond Militello and Barry Swygert.

The Recursive Effects of Rights and Identity: Two Examples

We illustrate the interactive relationship between identity and rights in two sharply contrasting life stories. The first story is Raymond Militello's. The identity-constituting effects of rights in his narrative are largely, but not exclusively, negative; as a consequence, he expresses caution and cynicism about his own readiness to use rights. The second story is Barry Swygert's. Barry's physical disability occurred relatively late in his life, and rights played a key role in helping him to construct an identity that permitted him to go forward with a productive and fulfilling career. Unlike Raymond, Barry speaks positively of his rights and readily embraces them as a means to project a new sense of self that integrates key components of the person he was before the onset of his disability.

Raymond Militello's life story illustrates both the constitutive effects of rights on identity and the role of identity in shaping an individual's orientation toward rights. Rights have woven a particularly complex pattern in Raymond's life story, seeming at times to have worked to his disadvantage while at other times to have provided important educational benefits. His early experiences with accommodations for his learning disability contributed to his lasting skepticism about the legitimacy and effectiveness of rights. Raymond's more recent experiences as a beneficiary of disability rights have been positive: he acknowledges their benefits but resists being perceived as a rights holder.

Disability rights became active early in Raymond's life, both through their context-creating and their cultural and discursive effects. In elementary school, he was diagnosed as dyslexic and placed in a program that separated him from his peers. The stigmatizing effects of this experience made a deep impression on him and caused Raymond later to view disability rights as unfair in educational settings and inappropriate in the workplace. Raymond learned at an early age that rights' constitutive effects can alter the identity of the rights bearer. He saw, moreover, that rights can be intrusive; "his" rights were imposed on him by the school. The lesson of this unfortunate experience was reinforced by his parents, who eventually rejected all special educational accommodations the school offered Raymond and instead employed tutors to work with him at home.

Yet Raymond's grade school experience and his lingering fear of stigmatization still contribute to his profound ambivalence toward the accommodations he has received in college. Rights and identity continue to interact and shape one another in an ongoing dynamic process. Raymond now attempts to blur the connection between his special accommodations and his identity-threatening disability by asserting that he obtained the benefits because he possesses what he considers a universally admired quality, namely, savvy in finding the "back door" to opportunities that many others seek but only a few are clever enough to obtain.

Notwithstanding the positive effects of accommodations he has received in college, Raymond's role as an employee and manager in his family's business has reinforced his resistance to rights. Raymond's only experience as an employee has occurred within his family's construction business. His perceptions of rights in the employment setting are, not surprisingly, those of the manager of a successful business. Thus, he argues that accommodations for employees can be costly, and, he concludes, "If it's going to hurt your business, you can't do it. . . . It's not a charitable organization." Raymond is reluctant to affirm a role for legal rights in the employment setting for another reason as well. "I mean, it's not that the law is a bad thing either," he says, but "it depends on the person a lot. . . . I mean, if someone's going to stand up and fight for something, they're going to go far." Raymond believes that rights will not change the fortunes of someone who is not going to fight for himself, and he views himself as a fighter above all else. Of course, Raymond has not needed rights to succeed as his father's understudy in the family business. Just as his family obtained private tutoring for him as a student, so the family business has easily accommodated his learning disability. Raymond has relied on a secretary employed by his father to correct his grammar in business letters and even in school assignments. He has not hesitated to ask others to check his math. With the increasing availability of computers to help with his writing and arithmetic, he contends that his dyslexia has less and less bearing on his performance in the workplace.

When asked about rights for employees with disabilities who have not received accommodations, Raymond confronts his ambivalence about rights in settings outside his family business and, in the last analysis, his ambivalence about his own identity. He resists the mandate of rights for persons with disabilities, in part because they are an unwanted burden on business, but also because he still believes that rights

can stigmatize the people they are supposed to benefit. In a highly revealing statement, Raymond equates being a rights bearer with having
an abnormal identity: "I don't know if I deserve [accommodations] or
not. I really hate those kind of systems. I mean, that you should favor
a certain group like me because of this, *over a person who's normal*" (our
emphasis). Ironically, although Raymond rejects rights as a means for
obtaining accommodations, in part because of the negative constitutive
effects that he perceives, he enjoys perfect accommodations within his
family's business. Because he will probably spend much of his career in
this business, he may never be required to reconcile the contradictory
perceptions of accommodations engendered by the interplay of rights
and identity in his life.

Barry Swygert's life story, which we have yet to relate, contrasts
sharply with that of Raymond Militello in its depiction of the effect
of rights on identity; like Raymond's story, however, it reinforces our
argument that rights and identity mutually constitute one another over
time. It is difficult to imagine anyone who has benefited more from
the ADA than Barry Swygert. Unlike Raymond Militello, who blames
rights for turning his otherwise invisible disability into a problematic
identity, Barry believes that rights have helped him adjust to a deteriorating physical condition resulting in paraplegia. Doctors discovered
his spinal tumor just after Barry turned thirty. He had been a physically
active and vigorous young man. Within eight years after diagnosis, he
lost much of the strength on the left side of his body as well as some
sensation on the right, and he could no longer walk or dress himself
without assistance. At each stage of his transition from full physical
capacity to severe physical impairment, he resisted the idea that he was
"disabled." Eventually, however, he came to recognize that his disability was a key component of his identity: "It's the most important thing
that happened in my life because it's formed me, it's guided me, it's
instructed me as to who I am and how to be. It's given me my rules
and my regulations and my parameters, but at the same time it's, it's
humiliated me. And it's the thing by which I've learned the most about
myself, the tool that I've used to learn the most about myself, although
I still, I'd have to say that it's a constant struggle."

The emergence of a radically transformed identity required Barry to
reorient himself toward many aspects of his social environment, including the legal rights that were available to him because of his disability.
The process was gradual, and at times Barry resisted the changes it en-
tailed. Following his second surgery, Barry says his life was in "limbo"
because he had not fully accepted his disability. His deteriorating physical condition forced him to alter his living and working arrangements,

and he became increasingly dependent on others to perform everyday tasks such as dressing, bathing, and eating. He still thought he was "going to wake up from the dream. . . . I was going to be healthy again." As he looks back he understands that "there was a reality; I was not dealing with it. I was trying to go about life normally. I was not saying, 'OK. I'm disabled.'" Yet Barry has "a great support network of friends . . . that knew me for as long as I've been normal through this whole thing." Barry's friends helped him as he struggled to accept the transformation of his body. A friend told Barry about a program of the New York State Office of Vocational Rehabilitation (OVR)[22] that offered employers a partial salary subsidy for hiring persons with disabilities. In order to apply, Barry would have to acknowledge that he had a disability as defined by law and that he qualified for support as a matter of right. His friend urged him to accept his condition—and the rights associated with it—saying, "You know, you're legitimate." Barry did apply and received assistance that has enabled him to work.

Disability rights became an important component of Barry's life, enabling him to reconstitute his identity as a capable and active person. They made it possible for him to receive support services and accommodations and to resume employment and serve as an advocate for others with disabilities. At the same time—recursively—Barry's transformed identity created a new orientation toward rights, a readiness to talk about and use the ADA in highly persuasive ways. Rights helped Barry to integrate his current circumstances with elements of his preonset identity. Using his experience as a fundraiser and public relations manager, Barry "sold" himself as an employee to a nonprofit human services provider. Working as a public relations representative, Barry has begun to make a name for himself as an advocate for the rights of persons with disabilities: "And slowly but surely my life and my lifestyle and my situation and my brain and my intellect and my innate ability to articulate got me more and more involved in the world of people with disabilities and I became an advocate."

Barry's perception of disability rights—his "rights consciousness"—has provided an important resource for the successful reconstruction of his identity. He sees himself as a new person, but one who possesses many of the same qualities that he had before his disability. Moreover, he views his disability as an asset in his advocacy work: "So when I first came out of the hospital like this, I thought I was going to be a burden and I found that I'm a benefit, that people have really learned a

22. Now known as VESID, an acronym for New York State's Office of Vocational and Educational Services for Individuals with Disabilities.

lot from me and are really enlightened by interacting with me because they don't have the opportunity to interact with somebody who's this disabled. But because I'm cognitively on the ball, you know, I'm able to communicate and I understand."

Barry firmly believes that the constitutive effects of the ADA have enabled him to play this unique role and to be a "benefit" rather than a "burden." Yet Barry rejects formal legal proceedings as a means to make ADA rights active. He refers to the coercive effects of the law as a "wedge" or "sledgehammer" and argues that use of the law in this way tends to breed resentment and resistance. The proper way to achieve access or accommodations is through mutual agreement:

BS: It's like a match game. How do you meet your partner? How do two people that get along meet and become friends? . . . You can only mix certain chemicals.

Q: But what about your analogy to racial discrimination and the employers that say, "I don't have good chemistry with black people so I won't hire any?"

BS: Well, I think that certain minds can only be opened up by certain situations and certain people. And I might be somebody who might be able to sit down with somebody who's never had to deal one-on-one with somebody who is disabled. And by the time they've spent a week with me, they don't see the disability anymore, they only see me as a person. . . . You have to experience spending time with a black person to realize that the majority of them are good. You have to spend time with a person with a disability before you don't see the skin color and the disability anymore.

Drawing on the constitutive effects the ADA has had on his own identity, Barry thinks he can help to create "good chemistry" for other individuals with disabilities in their dealings with employers.

Barry's life story illustrates several of the ways in which rights become active. First, as we have seen, the ADA contributed to the transformation of his self-perception and enabled him to reconstitute his identity and go forward with an ambitious career plan. Second, the ADA has become active in Barry's life through the cultural and discursive shifts it has engendered. Barry himself draws on these discursive shifts when he uses rights to persuade employers to accept employees and customers like himself. He uses his charm and persuasive skills, rather than explicitly invoking the law, to make others appreciate the benefits of having a person with a disability as an employee or associate. Third, the ADA became active through its context-creating effects, shaping the organization of New York's Office of VESID and encouraging Barry's employer to change his hiring practices and work routines to include an employee with a severe physical disability. Barry's employer has provided every needed accommodation, adjusted his work assignments as his physical capacities have changed, and tailored his work to his special talents in order to make it possible for Barry to flourish by doing what he does best. In this way, Barry has developed his specialization as a mediator for persons with disabilities in politically visible settings.

Barry explicitly endorses the view that the ADA's most important effects have occurred through its broad and pervasive impact on our culture rather than through the adversarial rights claims it makes possible:

> I think the ADA is more of a statement of civil rights—that people with disabilities are human beings. It's like the ERA [Equal Rights Amendment]. It never passed. . . . I think that it's nice to have the laws, but the individuals are the ones that are going to have to go out and make the difference themselves on their own. So, the ERA was never passed, and women still are working on an uneven thing. But they still have every right, and they're more and more powerful and they're influential and they've joined together. I think people with disabilities are doing the same exact thing. The ADA passed, the ERA didn't pass. The ADA makes a big statement that you can use, and you can point things out. . . . But you can't use it as a, putting pressure on people, because that's negative and negativity doesn't work with people.

Barry suggests that the ERA also had identity-constituting effects despite the fact that it failed to become law. The ADA's effects are perhaps more powerful—it "makes a big statement that you can use"—but not necessarily because it, unlike the ERA, provides the basis for formal legal action. Efforts to apply the ADA in adversarial proceedings are "negative" and counterproductive. Rather, Barry asserts that the ADA's most important effects are paradigm shifts, changes in the ways employers and employees think and talk about the inclusion of individuals with disabilities in the workplace.

Barry Swygert's views, and his life story narrative, support the concept that identity and rights are interactive. The identity-constituting effects of the ADA facilitated Barry's reentry into employment and shaped his role as an effective advocate and mediator. As an employee, recursively, Barry deploys rights on behalf of himself and others and thus enhances the ADA's constitutive effects. Barry's life story provides a counterpoint to Raymond Militello's. For Raymond, the interaction over time between rights and identity leads to an escape from law, a philosophical rejection of its role in his career despite the occasional assistance it has provided him. For Barry, the interaction between rights and identity leads to an embrace of the law, an endorsement of its positive symbolic effects on culture and society. Although these two life stories are, in some ways, mirror images, both illustrate the mutually constitutive relationship between rights and identity that becomes all the more apparent when viewed across the broad temporal field provided by life story narratives.

Conclusion

In this chapter, we have attempted to reinterpret the effects rights have on identity. We began with a discussion of three highly influential views of the constitutive effects of rights: classical rights theory, the rights versus relationship model, and critical rights theory. We described the first of these as an axiomatic framework for understanding the historic relationship between rights and the identity of citizens in our society. The second and third theories challenge the assumptions underlying classical rights theory and point to the undesirable, negative effects rights can have. The value of each of these theories for understanding the history and role of rights in America cannot be doubted, yet when we place them alongside the insights obtained from our interviewees' life story narratives, they prove inadequate to explain the subtle, complex, dynamic, and often contradictory qualities of the life story accounts. We conclude that new theories of rights are needed, theories that derive from the words and experiences of rights holders themselves and view rights in terms of their everyday consequences and not just their formal or institutional manifestations. Critical race and feminist theory and recent studies of law in everyday life have provided us with invaluable models and research tools for attempting this kind of reformulation.

The life story accounts of our interviewees point us toward a variety of ways in which rights become active in the lives of their intended beneficiaries. First, rights can become active when a formal claim is lodged with a governmental official. Although this is the one way in which rights *never* became active for any of our interviewees, it is the *only* way that is usually considered by most legal scholars, judges, legislators, and policymakers. Second, rights can become active when they transform the self-perceptions of potential rights holders. That is, rights may cause individuals with disabilities to think differently about who they are and where they belong and may encourage individuals to differentiate between their disability and their sense of self. These changed self-perceptions can have powerfully enabling effects on some individuals, such as Jill Golding, who came to view herself as a capable professional who had been the victim of unfair treatment rather than as an unintelligent person who lacked the ability to pursue a career. Third, rights can produce cultural and discursive shifts that transform the identities of individuals with disabilities because of new ways in which people—including the individuals themselves—think and talk about the self. Jill, Sara Lane, and Barry Swygert all provide examples of this sort of effect of rights on identity. Finally, rights can play a context-creating role that changes identities by altering the physical and social environments in which people with disabilities live. A number of our interviewees found that their educations and their careers were advanced by the impact of ADA rights on the institutions and organizations in which they studied and worked; but some, like Raymond Militello, discovered that institutional responses to rights could also produce stigma and isolation.

Mindful of the various ways in which rights can become active even when no formal legal claim is asserted, we then suggest that rights and identity can be understood in terms of a dynamic interaction over time. The temporal depth of our interviewees' life story narratives provides us with some insight into the recursive nature of the relationship between rights and identity. In chapter 1, we suggested that rights do not come into play, do not even appear relevant, until the identity of the potential rights holder gives rise to the perception that he or she has been treated inappropriately. In this chapter, we suggest that the relationship between identity and rights runs in both directions—that identity and rights are mutually constitutive. Thus, perceptions of disability and self can indeed determine whether rights become active; but rights in turn can affect and change identity, making it appear that an unfair act of exclusion has occurred when previously—before rights played their role—the same act might be perceived as natural and appropriate. When rights transform identity, the identity thus transformed may in turn lead to a greater role for rights.

We do not suggest that the recursive relationship between rights and identity inevitably leads to a greater role for rights and a more positive identity consistent with inclusion in mainstream occupations. On the contrary, we acknowledge that rights can at times prove harmful to those they are intended to benefit and can actually limit rather than facilitate their careers. But we do not share the view of those critics of rights who assert that these harmful effects are inherent in the nature of rights themselves. Rather, we think it essential to listen carefully to the hesitations and the ambivalent perceptions of individuals like Raymond Militello and others whose life stories we present in later chapters. From them we may come to understand not only how rights become active but also how—and why—they succeed or fail in their intended purpose.

three

Life Story: Sid Tegler

Sid Tegler lives in an old house on a tree-lined street in one of the dozens of picturesque small towns in western New York. Having grown up in this house, Sid has known many of his neighbors since childhood. The house next door has been in his neighbor's family since the original owners built it two generations ago. Other neighbors have lived on the street for at least a generation. Sid's parents bought the house when they moved to the town years ago and remained there throughout Sid's childhood. After leaving home to attend college and graduate school and to work for several firms in New York City, Sid returned to his childhood home, which he now shares with his widowed father. Here he has a network of personal friends and is part of the local business community, whose values and culture he shares.

Through his junior high school years, Sid planned to attend West Point and pursue a military career. In the ninth grade, while skiing deep powder after a heavy snowfall, Sid hit a piece of equipment concealed by the snow and suffered a spinal injury. If the injury occurred today, he observes, medical advances would have enabled him to walk again. If the injury had occurred five years earlier than it did, he probably would have died. Because he was injured at that particular time and place, he recovered his health but has been unable to use his legs for the past thirty years. Sid abandoned his plans to attend West Point, but he remained committed to the ideals of strength, self-sufficiency, and personal excellence.

Sid spent the next three years hospitalized. He kept up with his schoolwork through individual tutoring, which had its advantages despite his social isolation: "In a way, it was good, because I could take a subject that normally takes ten months and get it done in about five weeks. And just go through and take the exams or whatever, and it would be all gone. And then go on to the next subject." Sid was clearly a gifted student, and his return to high school in his senior year proved academically successful. His parents always assumed that he would continue his education at least to the graduate school level, and his teachers were generally encouraging about his college prospects. A few teachers, nevertheless, shared the assumption that higher education was not for people who used wheelchairs: "There were always a few that said, 'Well, maybe get a job at Goodwill or whatever, because that's what crippled people do.' And so the teachers and I would have a meaningful exchange of views and that would be the end of our correspondence."

I ran into that teacher a couple of years ago, and he asked, "What's new?" And I told him I was just elected to the Board of Trustees of Goodwill. And he said, "That's good, you'll teach the people things that you know."

After high school, Sid chose to spend several years in a therapy program hundreds of miles from home, but he then applied to, and was accepted by, an exclusive college on the East Coast. Part of the attraction of this college was the flexibility of the administrators in providing accommodations, unlike other colleges that Sid found either resistant or paternalistic. He recalls his college years, in the late 1960s and early 1970s, with obvious pleasure. They were a time of intellectual growth and social enjoyment. He majored in an esoteric liberal arts field and had close contact with professors and fellow students. He also enjoyed the parties and bull sessions. Because many of the buildings were quite old, accessibility for wheelchair users was a problem, but Sid, along with college administrators and fellow students, improvised successfully. The college installed ramps in some locations and relocated classes to accessible rooms. Football and hockey players carried Sid into buildings when necessary. For parties on the upper floors of dormitory buildings, extraordinary measures were sometimes required: "Some of my friends were mountain climbers. So they'd say, 'You want to go up to the party up on the fifth floor?' And I'd say, 'Yeah, sure.' So they'd throw a rope down and I'd climb up and party and then climb back down. . . . It helped if you had been partying before you got to the building."

During the winter, snow blocked the sidewalks and made it difficult to get from building to building: "The feeling there is, at least it seemed to be, from the part of the city fathers was that it was God's will that the snow fell, let Him take care of it." Although he must have experienced frustration at times, Sid scarcely mentions it in his narration. Instead, he makes it clear that his college experience was memorable and rewarding.

Because of Sid's interest in statistics, his college department chair encouraged him to study accounting rather than law or medicine after graduation, and Sid followed this advice. He chose to attend the M.B.A. program of a prominent university in New York City. Once again, he and the university administrators approached accessibility issues in a casual fashion: "They said, 'Do you think you'd have any problem getting around here?' And one of the deans and I walked around and looked at the structure, and I said, 'Nah, I don't think so.' They said, 'Where would you live?' 'Well, probably out by the Square.' And they said, 'Okay,' and that was it. It just wasn't an issue." Sid spent more time studying than partying in graduate school, and focused on his goal to "go out and start making some money."

During his search for a job, Sid frequently encountered skepticism about his employability. Like some of the colleges he had considered, many employers perceived his use of a wheelchair to be an insurmountable obstacle: "They said, 'How would we send you off on an audit of an oil refinery in Jersey?' It's just a real concern. How are you going to climb up there and check the contents of that big tank. That, someone has to do. I wasn't about to tell the guy who was interviewing me I climbed up to the fifth floor but I was three sheets to the wind . . . that didn't seem like the thing to say to the stuffy interviewing department."

As graduation approached, his instructor introduced him to a small firm nearby, where he was employed in the tax department. This firm did not consider his disability an issue when he was hired, but their attitude was exceptional. "Mobility was a serious concern in most of the other firms. Just because that's the nature of the job, that you either are shut-in doing taxes, or you're out looking at someone else's records wherever they happen to be. . . . So that part of it just was precluded. . . . I hated auditing, loved the tax stuff but I hated the auditing."

Sid's employer considered the skills he could contribute rather than the tasks that might be difficult because of his disability: "My guess is that they saw that background in statistics and said, 'Well, someone's got to stay back and crunch the numbers in the home office. And whether the numbers come from across the street or the far side of the world, someone's got to crunch them here. Tegler, that's you.' 'Okay.' Someone had to do it, so I did it." Sid stayed with the firm until the point when they expected employees in the tax department to return to school for a J.D. or a Ph.D. At that time in his life, Sid did not want to become a student again.

For the next few years, Sid stayed in the city and moved from job to job. At one point he returned to the business school as an assistant dean, but he realized that this career path, too, would eventually require a Ph.D.

One of the faculty took me aside and said, "You recognize you really should be taking your doctorate courses now?" I didn't really want to be a student again, and they asked, "Then why are you here?" . . . It was kind of tough to work with them on the same level during the day, and then be their understudy in the evening. I tried it. It was tough. Especially if I told one guy he couldn't have the office, then one hour later I was in his class. . . . "Can I have that office? How badly do you want to complete this course?" I found him an office.

After leaving his position at the business school, Sid interviewed with a number of firms. Some of them, like the first firm that employed Sid, considered his disability a nonissue in the hiring process, while others viewed it as an insuperable obstacle. One prospective employer expressed concern not only about Sid's ability to fit into the organization but also about their clients' reactions to an accountant with a disability. Sid's approach to these incidents was to express his disdain and move on. "I really couldn't lose an awful lot of sleep about their concerns. In part because it was difficult enough just moving from point *A* to point *B*. I had enough to take care of me. If that was important enough to [the employer], and how I really didn't fit into the little mold, all right. There are other companies in town."

Sid was aware of the early stirrings of the disability rights movement, and he participated in one demonstration by sitting in front of a bus. But he had little patience with the political approach to problems of discrimination and preferred to deal with prejudice by brushing it aside and achieving success through his own efforts: "I thought, gee, this is a terrible waste of time. Why not just make some money and hire these people to have them work for you?"

There were some people, real go-getters, who said, "We're going to change the world." I thought, "I'm too busy in school. I don't have time for this." And they said, "Wouldn't it be cheaper to take a bus than to have to drive that expensive car?" And I had to admit it would be. They said, "Can you get on the bus?" And I'd never thought about it, because it wasn't an option open to me. . . . And I said, "Yeah, let's give it a try." So about twenty of us sat in front of the bus, and one person actually chained herself to the wheel of the bus. . . .

The guy said, "Hey, you've got to be one of the team." I'll play the game once. And then I thought, "This is stupid. If you're really serious, run for public office." It took me twenty years to [run a political campaign], but if you're really serious, go out and actually do it. . . . A lot of the people who talk about political activism, whether it's standing in front of a bus to make sure it's wheelchair accessible, or at universities for that matter, if they had to really go out and do the political stuff that I did, door to door, I don't think most of them would do it, because it's an awful lot of work. And a lot of time, a great deal of expense.

Sid decided to leave the city after a particularly unpleasant job with an insurance company, where his boss required him to implement the company's downsizing policy by firing a number of his fellow employees. Although he had a job offer with an attractive firm in Florida, Sid chose instead to return to his hometown in western New York: "I guess it was in part just coming back to my roots and thinking about things. And there was really no rush to do anything at the time." He still had friends in his hometown, and they offered to put him in touch with some local businesses. He set up his own practice as an accountant, management advisor, and part-time investment advisor and has enjoyed being self-employed for the past fourteen years.

I talked with my father, and he said, "Please come back." He was strongly encouraging, almost insisting on it. He was very strong against Philadelphia or one of the other cities, I guess because my mother had just recently died and he wanted to have me back here. He said, "Let's give it a try and see if it works."

The contrast between big-city and small-town life was dramatic. After returning home, Sid fit in readily with the local network of friends and fellow small business owners. His work involves a great deal of personal contact. Mobility is not a major issue. If his clients are located in accessible buildings and the weather is good, Sid goes to their offices. Otherwise, they visit him. He belongs to the Rotary Club. He has worked as a consultant for the local Republican Party, and he is an active college alumnus who has interviewed and helped to screen prospective students. He knows his neighbors and many others in the local community, and at this point in his life prefers these close-knit relationships to the anonymity and excitement of the big city. Self-employment also has its advantages for an individual who enjoys the challenges of self-reliance: "I really liked being on my own. I liked the freedom that was there, recognized that there are times when, if you're on your own, you haven't got someone to work for or a client or a job to work on, come Friday there ain't no paycheck at all. And so you have to budget things accordingly, but I liked the freedom. I really liked it." He remained in contact with the firm in Florida and still wonders occasionally if he should follow up on their job offer. But as time passes, Sid appears more and more rooted in the town and neighborhood to which he has returned.

At that particular time, that was a "lost opportunity, wish-I'd-taken-it" kind of thing. That would have been with a major firm down in Tampa. It would have been great, but I didn't take it. I had to let it go. And I was always thinking, "Gee, maybe I should have." I kept hearing every other year or so about someone else who was looking for someone. . . . That still comes up from time to time. . . . My roots are here now, and I've been to Florida a few times, and it's fun to visit. In time, it might be fun to just retire there, but my roots are here.

Sid remains skeptical about political activism on behalf of individuals with disabilities, and he questions the policy assumptions underlying the Americans with Disabilities Act (ADA). At one time, he was recruited by a leading Democratic political figure, but Sid shrugged off the approach by disclosing that he was a Republican. Disability rights are not central to Sid's view of how the world should work: "I am disabled, and I'm sensitive to it, but that's not foremost in my thinking." He has urged that political functions be moved to wheelchair accessible settings, but otherwise he has not been vocal about disability rights. As a general matter, he opposes the intervention of big government: "I really don't feel that the government or any large, organized group, whether it's the employer or the government or anything, owes me something unless I can make them, like a profit, or further their cause in some way. So that, in many ways, I think the answer to your question is, no, it [the ADA] hasn't affected me at all. Or if it has, it's only indirectly, like those curb cuts." Sid sees curb cuts as a valuable sign of progress, since they benefit a number of citizens, including seniors and children. But broader disability rights under the ADA are questionable because they distort the appropriate cost-benefit calculation any employer should make for any employee.

Q: Is there a role for law to make sure [employees with disabilities have opportunities]?
ST: Yeah, but it may be as much of a threat as anything else. That is, if you make sure that this individual at least has a reasonably fair shot, that's all that they can really ask. . . . But the employer, if you're going to preclude someone from having that fair shot, we can make your life a living hell.

The ADA may promote some superficial attitudinal changes, but it does not affect deeper underlying perceptions and beliefs about people with disabilities. Those perceptions will evolve over a much longer period of time, with or without the ADA:

> I think for a generation or two, it's just going to paint a veneer. Maybe in two or three or four generations there will be some changes, but, say twenty years or so, that's a reasonable time horizon for looking forward. There's just going to be a nice coat on the surface. . . . I think there's been a minor shift, in that people are a little bit more open with their feelings, whether it is prejudice or hesitancy than there was before; but then people are more open about a lot of things than they were a generation ago. I don't know if that's good or bad, and that's almost a personal judgment.

Throughout his life, Sid has made ad hoc accessibility arrangements with educators, employers, and clients. When he encounters irrationality or ill will, he expresses his disagreement and gets on with his life. As a businessman, he has used the law on occasion to handle conflicts, but he would never sue an employer for violation of his rights under the ADA. His approach is to deal with each individual or situation in a forthright manner, use reason to deal with irrationality, cut losses when reason fails, and hope that attitudes will change over time. Sid explained that, even in the Rotary Club, he encounters some older members who don't know how to interact with a person in a wheelchair: "About half their numbers are retired or close to it, and they still recall things that were done when they were in their twenties. And they say, 'Well, crippled people didn't get around.' I said, 'Yeah, but since then they've invented things like wheels and fire and so on.' So then we trade insults, and that's the end of it. So it's the feeling of the individuals, not the group." Through these offhand exchanges, Sid speaks up for himself and opposes discriminatory attitudes while avoiding invocation of the framework of rights and big government that he opposes. Believing it important to eschew self-pity or the victim mentality, Sid remains true to the culture and political philosophy of the small town to which he has returned and the business community of which he has become a part.

[Our reinterview with Sid Tegler came five years later. Much had changed in his life. He had married and had moved out of his father's home to a new house he built on the outskirts of town. His business had expanded. He had served as president of the local Rotary Club and had run, unsuccessfully, for a position in the town government. Although his life circumstances had changed, his personal philosophy was much the same as it had been during our first interview.]

I think you've got the tone just fine. The philosophy I thought was pretty much there, and it's the way I think about the idea of the ADA. Great concept, noble undertaking, doesn't really have that much of an effect on me. . . . I don't think that I have certain rights you don't have just because I'm burning up tire rubber. I admit, I would take advantage of ramps that someone put in so I could be gainfully employed or provide a service for them. . . . If [someone] didn't put a ramp in or made some accommodation, but the guy down the street has, I'm going to go do business with him. I'm not going to beat my head against the wall. It's a waste of time. I don't have the motivation to try to prove you wrong because you're not going to make accommodations for me. Life is too short.

As far as the disability rights thing, I guess that's one of the disagreements I have with some of my sisters and brothers who are of the "lame persuasion." I don't see it as a major issue. It's an inconvenience. It does limit some things, like mountain climbing . . . and I probably won't be a forest ranger jumping out of airplanes to put out forest fires. but I don't want to do that anyway.

I think you're antagonizing the people as a group that you may want to befriend, or at least keep on neutral terms. And it's true for a number of other groups, whether it's folks who are disabled or folks who may be of a different racial or ethnic or religious persuasion, for that matter. If you recognize that the other side is at least interested, potential marketplace customers, employers, whatever, are interested in talking to you in part because you might have some-thing to sell them, a service, or a good, or whatever. And if you can convince that customer or group of customers that it's in their best interest to at least hear you out . . . they won't really care whether you're in a wheelchair or not. . . . They won't care. They're indifferent. They're not hostile, they're indifferent.

Work and Identity

For Sid Tegler, as for virtually all of our interviewees, issues of identity are inseparable from employment. Sid's success in creating an identity that distinguished between self and disability facilitated the professional career he was able to construct after returning to his small town roots. To continue our discussion of identity and rights, we now turn to the centrality of work in shaping the sense of self and the very meaning of "disability." The emphasis of the Americans with Disabilites Act (ADA) on employment rights in achieving inclusion for persons with disabilities acknowledges the relationship between identity and work for all Americans. In this chapter, we explore connections between ADA employment rights and the efforts of adults with disabilities to transform their identities by participating more fully as members of the American workforce.

To achieve inclusion, persons with disabilities—Sid Tegler is but one example—must overcome deeply rooted practices and perceptions that contribute to their exclusion from employment. The identities of persons with disabilities have historically been "spoiled" (Goffman 1963) by the presumption that they are incapable of work. Yet work—and being perceived as able to work—is fundamental to adult identity in American society. Jobs create an identity in an immediate and direct way. When a person becomes an accountant, a journalist, a taxi driver, or a short-order cook, her social identity is influenced by daily interactions connected with her work and also by societal images and expectations connected with the job. Employees are often selected on the basis of stereotyped assumptions about the appropriate identity of jobholders. Understandings about employment filter back into the earliest stages of socialization, education, and identity formation. A disability that is perceived to limit or preclude employment fundamentally affects identity formation and preparation for adult life from an early age. In such cases, disability may indeed seem to overpower or taint other aspects of the self.

Thus, the culture of work in American society shapes the very practices of employment and perceptions of identity that the ADA seeks to change. Our observations in chapters 1 and 2 about the constitutive effects of rights have suggested a number of ways that ADA employment rights might change these practices and perceptions. But the evidence provided by our interviewees suggests that the prospects for fundamental change in the workplace are highly problematic, even when one takes into account the often subtle and indirect effects of rights. The culture of work in our society is resistant to change and capable of constraining the very processes of employer-employee interaction on which the ADA depends to achieve its goals. Moreover, as we show, the historically rooted perception that disability and employment are incompatible has subtly influenced the ADA's definitions of employment rights, limiting and conditioning them in ways that render their constitutive effects more ambiguous and problematic. We suggest that the effects of the ADA on the workplace and on the lives of its intended beneficiaries cannot be understood without considering the connections between work and identity in American society.

In the first part of this chapter, we describe the fundamental problem confronting persons with disabilities, namely, the presumption that disability and work are incompatible. We discuss the historical interconnections—constructed in part by the law—between disability, dependency, and unemployment and their implications for the constitutive role of ADA rights in reshaping workplaces and identities. In the second part of this chapter, we describe the constitutive role that rights have played in the employment experiences of three of our interviewees. Chapters 1 and 2 provide us with the framework we need to identify and understand the constitutive effects of rights in relationship to work. We consider employment and the role of rights for Sara Lane and Sid Tegler, whose life stories have already been given, and for Jim Vargas, a young physical therapist with a learning disability. In the concluding section, we return to our initial questions about civil rights and social change as we discuss the implications of our research for strategies of inclusion in the workplace.

The ADA and the Dilemma of Work, Identity, and Disability

Qualities of intellect, attitude, and physical skill associated with adult employability and self-sufficiency are, to use Bruner's term, "canonical" expectations for the adult self (1997:147–48). In virtually all of the life stories we have presented, the centrality of work in the formation of identity is apparent from the earliest memories of parental guidance, peer interaction, schooling, and job seeking. The experiences and teachings of childhood and adolescence prepare us for employment, and our early sense of self is greatly influenced by this goal. During adolescence, educational institutions emphasize fundamental skills that prepare the individual for work or further education leading to work.[1] The experiences of childhood and adolescence help create a framework of values, goals, and options for work and career and at the same time locate us in that framework by evaluating our likelihood of future success. Thus, the self seen through the lens of future employment emerges long before employment is a possibility.

The link between identity and work is fundamental. In our culture, the very fact of being employed in itself confers moral citizenship.[2] The reverse is also true: those who do not or cannot work are typically viewed as persons who are not entitled to the full respect due an adult citizen and instead are seen as marginal and dependent on others (see Karst 1989; Handler and Hasenfeld 1991). The chronically unemployed not only suffer loss of income, they risk losing the respect of peers and pay an even heavier price through diminished self-respect. Thus, a disability that limits or prevents employability also threatens social standing and self-respect as well as practical self-sufficiency. For persons with disabilities, the relationship between identity and employment marks treacherous terrain. The very term "disability" is often used to describe a condition that prevents an individual from working. The identity thus created for persons with disabilities is widely perceived as incompatible with the assumption that they, like others, should work and pursue a

1. For example, a leading text on the economics of education states: "The presumed goal of educational planning is to promote productivity by matching expected demand for skills with the supply. The chief purpose of the approach is to forecast manpower needs by skill categories and then to transform manpower requirements into educational requirements. The educational system can then adapt itself to these forecasts" (Cohen and Geske 1990:212). The role of schools in socialization for work derives from the belief that schools should prepare children for smooth integration into adult life as productive citizens. That this goal dominates all others, such as personal development, is the result of historical factors that have narrowed the broader goals of education to serve society's most powerful institutional forces—namely, the engines of the economy. See Bowles and Gintes 1976.

2. Shklar (1991:84, 91–94) notes that the "intimate bond between earning and citizenship" is not surprising. The freedom to be gainfully employed has been an important element in the demands for full citizenship by those historically excluded—minorities and women. The moral underpinning of work arises from social and economic institutions that value individual labor and devalue dependency. See Handler and Hasenfeld 1991.

career.[3] For persons with disabilities, therefore, attaining employment is a crucial step in the quest to achieve recognition as independent and worthy participants in society.

The identity that one must acquire to be perceived as employable is largely predetermined in our culture by the existing practices of work and by assumptions about the employees who perform them. Unlike employment prevalent during earlier historical periods in which the family or extended family was the unit of production, wage labor has long been standard in our economy. While a family work unit might have great flexibility in assigning roles to family members based on individual capabilities or talents, wage labor offers little flexibility of this sort. Further, most people still take for granted that wage labor is work outside the home and consists of jobs—"ready-made packages of paid employment" (Kahn 1981:1). Wage labor does not create a place for the abilities of a particular worker. The worker without ability to perform a "job," as the employer predefines it, has no place to work and no chance to attain independence and self-sufficiency.

Workplace practices create expectations about the characteristics of an employable adult: a physical appearance and social skills acceptable to coworkers, basic motor skills, ability to use common facilities (such as a bathroom or a parking lot) and appliances (such as a telephone or a computer keyboard), self-discipline, and cognitive skills such as reading and writing, reciting, interpreting, and working with information in compact units over defined time spans. Workers are not expected to have identical abilities, but all are expected to meet minimum physical and cognitive standards required for a particular form of work and workplace. Persons with a disability often have qualities that misleadingly appear to place them outside the expected parameters.[4] Of course, if one were to imagine a different way of organizing production of the same output, different abilities and skills might be more important and many of the seemingly neutral criteria that currently keep people with disabilities from working might no longer be considered absolute requirements.[5]

3. See H.R. Rep. No. 485, 101st Cong., 2nd Sess., pt. 2, 1990 at 7 ("According to a recent Louis Harris poll 'not working' is perhaps the truest definition of what it means to be disabled in America.").

4. Employers frequently misjudge the appearance of persons with disabilities, overestimating the costs of accommodating their disabilities and underestimating their productivity. See Blanck and Marti 1997:375–80, 405. Hahn (1994:108–10) suggests that physical appearance may create anxiety and even fear in the "abled" and, thus, become an even more subtle barrier to employment.

5. As Wright (1983:420–21) observes, "It must also be remembered that employability is not related in a simple way to degree of disability, that many unforeseen social, as

The boundary between the able and the disabled is determined by existing social practices that distinguish and valorize certain qualities or types of "ability." For all persons in our society, ability is relative, varying significantly with the activity in question. Most people have greater ability in some activities and lesser ability in others. Yet the term "disability" is often applied categorically to divide individuals into two distinct social groups, those who are "able" to exist self-sufficiently in society and those with a disability who irrevocably lack something essential that only an "able" person has. For this reason, as Funk (1987:7) has observed: "The general public does not associate the word 'discrimination' with the segregation and exclusion of disabled people. . . . [T]he absence of the disabled coworkers is simply considered confirmation of the obvious fact that disabled people can't work."

The identity-related assumption that persons with disabilities cannot work has deep roots in our culture and our laws. This assumption was manifested as early as the sixteenth-century in English precursors of American law regulating labor and relief of the poor, and it extends to current American laws concerning social welfare benefits (Stone 1984; Greenwood 1996). Stone argues that "the very notion of disability is fundamental to the architecture of the welfare state." Throughout our history, she notes, the concept of disability has been used to determine "when people are so poorly off that the normal rules of distribution should be suspended and some form of social aid . . . should take over." The earliest laws reflected suspicion of beggars claiming to be disabled and unable to work and adopted a very limited view of disability in order to encourage work (Stone 1984:12–13).[6] As Stone observes, the definition of "disability" was the "the mirror image of the concept of work" (55). Anyone not in one of the excused categories was deemed able to work, a "strategy by default" that, as Stone comments, "remains at the core of current disability programs" (40). Many modern laws continue

---

well as personal, forces may combine to open up opportunities for even those with the most severe disabilities. . . . The enormous potential for widening opportunities by using enabling technology, by modifying tasks to meet functional limitations, and by eliminating unjustified barriers, including architectural, legal, and attitudinal barriers, also enters vocational outcome."

6. Early English law supported the emergence of a free labor market by denying public support to those persons deemed able to work. Begging appeared to violate the principles of the free labor market, which required self-sufficient laborers to work rather than surviving on the largesse of a wealthier social class. By 1834, the law limited "deserving" paupers to five categorically defined conditions—youth, sickness, insanity, "defective" (i.e., physically disabled), and age or infirmity. "Defectives" initially were the "blind, deaf, and dumb"; later the "lame" and "deformed" were included; and by 1899 epileptics were also included under this rubric (Stone 1984:47–48). The inclusion of epileptics under the restrictive English poor laws is particularly ironic in view of a recent holding by an American court excluding a person with epilepsy from coverage by the ADA. *Deas v. River West* (1998).

to define disability in ways that suggest that work is problematic or impossible for persons with a disability. These laws rely on a categorical medical or clinical diagnosis of a disability that simultaneously declares an individual incapable of self-sufficiency and qualifies the individual for benefits.[7] Although the current definition of disability relies on medical and clinical knowledge, the implication of abnormality and presumed exclusion from activity leading to economic self-sufficiency survives from centuries past.

Alternative perceptions of the relationship between disability and employment—and consequently identity—have emerged from contemporary movements for more benefits and broader rights for persons with disabilities.[8] The perspective that inspired the ADA, termed the "socio-political" model by Richard Scotch (2000) and others, rejects the medical/clinical presumption that a disability is an individual failing (see also Scotch 1984; Hahn 1985). Instead, "disability is viewed not as a physical or mental impairment, but as a social construction shaped by environmental factors, including physical characteristics built into the environment, cultural attitudes and organizations" (Scotch 2000:214). Accordingly, persons with a disability are recognized as the victims of social stereotypes and unfair treatment, and civil rights are perceived as an appropriate remedy to protect members of this minority from discrimination. The commitment of the ADA to an inclusionary workplace reflects such an understanding, and its provisions potentially create a new identity for persons with disabilities as capable employees who face discriminatory physical and social barriers.

7. Stone (1984:4) notes that "medical certification [of a disability] has become the core administrative mechanism for a variety of redistributive policies." In the United States, medical certification qualifies individuals for, among other "benefits," pensions, accident insurance, poverty relief, debt relief, special treatment by the criminal justice system and tax systems, medical care, public housing, and special educational benefits (6).

8. Berg (1999:6–12) has identified four contemporary theories of disability: the *moral view* that a disability is a sign of impurity or immorality, the *biomedical paradigm* that suggests a disability is a "defect, deficiency, dysfunction, abnormality, failing or medical problem" (quoting Bickenbach 1993:61), an *economic model* that interprets disability as a condition evaluated by weighing worker productivity against the costs of accommodation, and the *social/political theory* that holds that the responsibility for burdens associated with biological and cognitive differences are not the responsibility of the individual but are caused by "society's stigmatizing attitudes and biased structures." Disability rights advocates, who sponsored the inclusionary employment rights articulated by the ADA, embraced a social and political understanding of disability and placed responsibility for nonemployment on work environments that limited the use of an employee's abilities rather than on individual differences. Yet other views of disability remain powerful and have influenced the formulation of the ADA's disability rights. For example, Berg observes that a moral theory of disability underlies the "express exclusion of an assortment of historically stigmatized differences such as transvestism, transsexualism, and kleptomania from the ADA's definition of disability," sustaining their construction as "personal moral failings."

To realize the new identity-creating potential of the ADA, the employment provisions of Title I require equal treatment for all individuals "with a disability who, with or without reasonable accommodation, can perform the essential functions of the employment position" (ADA §12111(8)). This definition of a "qualified" person presumes that the "essential functions" of many prepackaged jobs could potentially be performed in several different ways. The particular way a job has been defined or organized may create a discriminatory barrier to employment, and if so found, the law requires that the work be restructured to accommodate the employable person with a disability. Thus, the drafters of the ADA envisioned a radical transformation of the culture of work, requiring workplaces to adapt to the individual capacities of qualified workers rather than the reverse. The implications for identity are no less radical because the law presumes that employment and disability are mutually compatible rather than incompatible.

Yet in other respects, as some critics of the ADA have pointed out, the act may reinforce the deeply ingrained identity that both stigmatizes persons with disabilities and suggests that disability and work are incompatible (see Berg 1999; Cole 2000). Employment rights granted by the act, including accommodations, are reserved for those claimants who fall within the ADA's medically informed categories of impairment (ADA §12102(2)(A) and 29 C.F.R. §1630.2(h)). Rights claimants must demonstrate that their disability, so defined, also "substantially limits one or more of the major life activities" that "the average person in the general population can perform" (ADA §12102(2)(A)). Thus, an employee who wishes to invoke the ADA's provisions must establish an identity, at least for purposes of the law, that sets him or her apart from coworkers as both abnormal and deficient in performing major life activities (compare Minow 1990). Such a categorization is potentially stigmatizing because it perpetuates—rather than erases—the social distinction between people identified as rights bearers and their coworkers, a distinction with a long history of stereotyping. Further, because the very definition of rights bearers incorporates a presumption of substandard ability, accommodations offered to the employee with a disability may appear to coworkers to be a form of affirmative action that unfairly advantages the less capable worker. To some, this perception may be reinforced by similar perceptions of affirmative action in other civil rights contexts.[9]

9. See chapter 4, where we discuss the discourse of racial rights in connection with our interviewees' perceptions of the ADA.

Perhaps most ironic is the potentially limiting construction of identity that may be inferred from the ADA's requirement of "reasonable accommodations" (§12112(b)(5)(A), (B)). The requirement that an employer provide reasonable accommodations reflects the sociopolitical understanding that inflexible workplace practices create unnecessary barriers to employment of persons with disabilities who might otherwise perform the "essential functions" of work (see Berg 1999). Yet the right of "qualified" employees to have barriers to work removed exists only if such measures are not too costly to the employer.[10] This limited right to accommodations potentially conveys a more mixed message about identity than disability advocates might have wished. The right to accommodations does not ultimately depend on whether the workplace excludes some persons because it was poorly designed, or whether productivity might in the long run be enhanced by a larger pool of candidates for employment, or even whether exclusion from the workplace would be unjust. Rather, the reasonableness requirement turns on whether a disability renders a person so unlike other workers—that is, so abnormal—that alteration of the existing workplace, even if its design is flawed and exclusionary, would be too costly or disruptive and would impose an "undue hardship" on the employer (§12112(b)(5)(A)). Although the provision for accommodations was intended to change workplaces, and ultimately to transform identities, its emphasis on preserving the short-term efficiency of existing workplaces may in practice reinforce the assumption that the identity of the individual with a significant disability is potentially incompatible with employment.

Although the ADA's construction of disability in some ways perpetuates the assumptions that exclude persons with disabilities from the workplace (O'Brien 2001), the law's constitutive effects also depend on what individuals perceive to be true about themselves. The law may reinforce perceptions of unemployability if individuals are predisposed to accept them, but it may have different constitutive effects when rights contribute positively to patterns of interaction with others or the creation of forward-looking narratives of the self. Since multiple theories informed the language of the ADA, different narratives could readily be built from its rights provisions. Sid Tegler's life story is consistent with the act's underlying commitment to identities based on autonomy and

10. The right to reasonable accommodations is limited by the requirement that the cost of accommodations not impose an "undue hardship" on the employer. See ADA §12111(10). Berg (1999:13) notes that this requirement is consistent with economic theory's "core premise that inequality is acceptable if it would be economically inefficient to eliminate it."

full citizenship. Yet Sid deliberately rejects rights because they would set him apart and would, in his view, be inconsistent with independence and self-sufficiency. By contrast, Sara Lane perceives the ADA to have both stigmatizing *and* inclusionary effects, depending on the context, and she assumes that rights may be deployed strategically to promote inclusion while avoiding the risk of stigma. Throughout our research we have been struck by the range of the ADA's constitutive effects, depending on contingency and context. In the following sections, we examine three life story narratives to see how these varying constitutive effects manifest themselves in the employment setting.

Working with Rights

The drafters of the ADA created rights in order to change the workplace, to reverse the presumption that all workers must adapt to "ready-made jobs," and to combat the perception that the "disabled" cannot work. In order to understand the capacity of rights to bring about this change, we now consider the role that rights have played in reconciling work and identity in the life stories of three interviewees. We begin with two individuals whose life stories have already been presented—Sara Lane and Sid Tegler. Both Sara and Sid are successful professionals who have used wheelchairs since childhood. We then compare Sara's and Sid's stories with that of another interviewee, Jim Vargas, who has a learning disability and has had more difficulty than Sara and Sid in reconciling his sense of self with the requirements of his job. Our discussion of their stories focuses on how their employment experiences and concepts of self have affected one another, and on the constitutive—and recursive— effects of rights in this process.

The three life stories each describe the deep dilemma of maintaining one's identity *as an employee.* Throughout their employment experiences, Sara Lane, Sid Tegler, and Jim Vargas have confronted a disparity between the assumptions employers make about the identity of the "normal" employee and the socially constructed identities of persons with disabilities. We suggest that this disparity—and the manner in which it is handled—is important for the role of rights. As they recount experiences that shaped their identities and employment opportunities, each of the three describes the self who became employed, who interpreted and responded to employers' and coworkers' treatment, and who decided whether and how to seek accommodations, to invoke rights, or to leave the job and seek other work. Because identity is the linchpin of the dilemmas they describe, Sara, Sid, and Jim have been particularly sensitive to the potentially powerful constitutive effects that rights might have on perceptions of their identities. Their concerns touch on both elements that shape identity: interaction with others and a narrative of the self. In their stories, Sara, Sid, and Jim each talk about the role of rights in the workplace very differently. We think their distinct orientations to accommodations and rights derive from their self-concepts and their different ways of managing the tensions between identity and employment.

Sara Lane and Sid Tegler

Although they have similar disabilities and quite similar backgrounds, Sara Lane and Sid Tegler developed different self-concepts and sharply divergent responses to employment, the need for accommodations, and rights. Both grew up with ambitious career aspirations and the encouragement of supportive parents. Typically, the culture of employment contributes to the development of expectations and career choices by young persons approaching adulthood, and Sara and Sid both expected since childhood to be employable because of their positive view of their own capabilities. They considered their disabilities marginal to their identities and distinct from their sense of self. Each acquired a belief in self-sufficiency, and neither expected employers to change the nature of work for them. Indeed, too much attention to their disabilities threatened the identity they wanted to maintain as an employee. Identity as an "able" professional, for which they had prepared all their life, included conformity to the expectations of the workplace. Challenging the rules of the workplace in order to gain full access to employment opportunities would have required them to challenge their employers' and fellow employees' expectations and might also have undermined their own self-concepts.

Notwithstanding these similarities of upbringing and orientation toward disability and work, they responded to the dilemmas created by their identities within the employment setting in different ways—Sara by adapting and slowly building an image as a professional that she treated as "capital" to help her achieve accommodations and Sid by withdrawing from employment in a large firm in order to avoid the limiting expectations of an employer or coworkers. Significantly, both Sara's and Sid's first jobs involved back-office employment with little prospect for advancement. Sara was able to maneuver within her job to form friendship networks, gain experience, and eventually rise to a position of much greater responsibility. Sid was not able to create similar opportunities for advancement. Although his first employer suggested he might advance by completing a Ph.D. program in tax, Sid chose not to do so because he did not like being in school. Although we cannot say what would have happened had Sid used his opportunities differently, he differs from Sara in his unwillingness to employ strategies of maneuver or compromise within an organization. While Sara's approach to seeking accommodations has been more pragmatic, balancing her requests for accommodations against the cost to her professional identity, Sid has a more heightened—even an exclusive—concern with pride and principle. It is difficult to imagine Sid suffering the humiliation Sara experienced while working at the *Midwest Tribune* without an accessible bathroom or quietly attempting to increase the range of his assignments.

These dilemmas of identity and employment reveal great differences between Sara's and Sid's self-concepts that, in turn, alter the constitutive effects of rights on their relationships and self-perceptions. Sara's pragmatic orientation toward the reconciliation of identity and employment has made her particularly attentive to the potential influence of rights on her employers' and coworkers' perception of her as an employee. She avoided seeking more costly accommodations at the *Ardmore Gazette* because she thought they might be viewed as inconsistent with her role as a member of the editorial team, even though the newspaper's support for the growing disability rights movement suggested that such a claim might have been successful. Later in her career, after passage of the ADA, she avoided invoking the law because doing so would have depleted the "capital" she had accumulated as a valued employee. Sara places a low value on invoking the ADA, not because she lacks knowledge about her rights nor because she believes that the legally mandated changes in the workplace would not be beneficial, but because she thinks the law lacks power to alter the relationships that constitute the workplace. She fears that obtaining the benefits mandated by the ADA would disrupt the workplace and diminish her status as an employee.

Sara's hesitancy to invoke her rights to accommodations, such as accessible bathrooms or special parking, is partly a product of concerns about the relational effects of rights on her identity, namely, the cost of trading off the professional respect she has earned over the years as a reporter. But relational considerations do not entirely account for her refusal to invoke the ADA. For example, Sara does not use a relational frame of reference when she discusses the possibility of seeking extraordinary accommodations, such as permission to work at home or lengthy medical leaves. These are accommodations Sara would actually welcome, but not if they were granted to her alone as the result of an individual claim of rights. Sara thinks the ADA might entitle her to such accommodations but fears they would set her working conditions apart from those of other workers. She would like to see such benefits conferred collectively through demands made by the newspaper guild on behalf of all employees. Since the guild is unlikely to press such demands, however, Sara hesitates to assert them despite their pragmatic importance to her work. These accommodations might threaten even her *own* sense of professional identity quite apart from their fairness or utility or her employer's willingness to grant them. Thus her concerns about the negative effects of rights extend to their impact on the narrative of self that anchors her sense of who she is.

Although Sara has avoided the express invocation of rights in the workplace, her pragmatic and persistent employment strategies are sometimes indirectly linked to the ADA, and her life story suggests some of the ways the law's constitutive effects have worked in her favor. Sara never confronted her employers over her right to have accommodations, but she placed herself in favorable situations where, with the help of supportive colleagues, she effectively changed her employers' perceptions of her so that receiving accommodations became consistent with her identity as a professional journalist. The exception in her life story that proves the rule, and the only example of confrontation she describes, is the claim for an accessible bathroom at the *Midwest Tribune* made *by others* on her behalf. The actions of her coworkers demonstrated to the employer that having this accommodation was reconcileable with Sara's role as a "normal" employee. Probably the ADA and the great public awareness it produced made her peers more sensitive to her needs and more supportive of the expectation that she should receive such an accommodation.

Sid Tegler views his employment dilemmas in terms of an identity quite different from Sara's, and he understands rights to have a more profoundly subversive constitutive role. Unlike Sara, Sid links his identity not to ability alone but to a narrative of citizenship, which requires autonomy without special accommodations. In contrast to Sara, he eventually became reluctant to seek employment, and he has chosen self-employment rather than tolerate, or attempt to change, the "disabled" identity that employers tried to impose. The decision to exclude himself, rather than be excluded, from the workplace seems closely related to the relationship between self and disability on which he bases his self-respect. Unlike Sara, whose self-concept as an able person was unaffected for most of her career by her struggle for accommodations, Sid Tegler now takes a negative view of accommodations because he thinks they would undermine his identity as an independent and

autonomous individual. Sid strongly rejects dependency, and his concept of identity is not linked to ability alone but to the value he attaches
to full citizenship.

Sid Tegler's hostility to the ADA extends beyond the employment setting, encompassing all special benefits or protections linked to disability
alone. For Sid, legal rights should not become active in the employment
setting—or elsewhere. He particularly resents what he perceives as the
presumption underlying the ADA, that persons with disabilities require
special rights in order to be fully included as citizens: "I don't think
that I have certain rights you don't have just because I'm burning up
tire rubber." Sid attaches more importance to his identity as a person capable of full inclusion without special rights. Ironically, his attraction to
a model of citizenship that rejects reliance on others resonates strongly
with the cultural and legal tradition that separates disability and work
by limiting the scope of protective legislation to those few individuals
judged abnormal and truly dependent. Sid resists any implication that
his disability places him within that class.

Jim Vargas

Jim Vargas differs from Sara Lane and Sid Tegler in many ways. Perhaps
the most obvious is that his learning disability is invisible to employers. Unlike Sara and Sid, Jim must consider in each job or employment
application whether and how to disclose his disability in order to perform like the ideal employee the employer may have envisioned. Jim
therefore faces a rather different dilemma of employment and identity,
and his approach to rights reflects the uniqueness of his quandary.

Jim is a licensed physical therapist in his late twenties. His learning
disability was diagnosed in elementary school, and he still has difficulty
with both reading and writing. His parents and teachers did not push
him to achieve academically, and he drifted toward courses in manual
arts in high school until a biology teacher inspired him and transformed
his career plans. Jim applied successfully to a number of colleges with
programs in physical therapy and chose a university where he benefited from accommodations for his learning disability. He eventually
received his degree and passed the state examination on his second
attempt. He has confidence in his ability as a physical therapist and
believes that his "hands on" skills give him a significant advantage in
his work.

Jim likes his work, but he has discovered that the work environment
offers him less flexibility than college did to accommodate his working
style. Jim describes the increasing work load that he and other physical
therapists carry, and he now sees as many as twenty patients a day in

half-hour time blocks. All procedures must be carefully documented. Because he cannot keep up with the paper work, he voluntarily works through his lunch hour and stays late. His inability to handle the record-keeping requirements inevitably affects the quality of his work. He finds himself cutting treatment time in order to work on his notes, and thus he cannot provide his patients with all of the treatment he is capable of giving. He reluctantly acknowledges that he suffers great frustration and changes jobs frequently because he is unable to perform at the high level of which he knows he is capable.

Jim faces a further dilemma in seeking employment and requesting accommodations. Because learning disabilities are invisible, the disability is usually not "in play," even though it may affect his job performance, unless the employee chooses to reveal its existence. Jim's personal strategy is to wait until the conclusion of a job interview before deciding whether to mention his learning disability. Is it preferable to reveal or conceal the disability? Choosing to *reveal* that one has a learning disability may prevent employers and colleagues from misinterpreting its effects on work performance, because symptoms of a learning disability could otherwise be perceived as lack of discipline, aptitude, or intelligence. Yet disclosure may be met with disbelief rather than understanding, and it is far more difficult to explain the nature and effects of a learning disability and the accommodations needed than is the case for many physical disabilities. If, on the other hand, Jim *conceals* his disability, he will have no access to legally mandated accommodations that may enable him to perform work successfully. He must assume the entire burden of making adjustments, must obtain assistance without the employer's knowledge or help, and must assume the risk that the effects of his disability will be misinterpreted as professional incompetence.

Thus, the employment dilemma Jim experiences is different from the dilemmas experienced by Sara and Sid. Rights cannot play a role in Jim's employment, other than in Jim's own mind, until he chooses to reveal his disability. He is strongly disinclined to do this. He believes his employers would not spend money on costly conveniences such as stenographers and transcribing equipment, since they would probably not perceive such expenditures as contributing to the bottom line. Even more importantly, Jim thinks that employers are likely to be skeptical of an employee's claim that a learning disability exists at all (see Reiff 1997 and Fike 1997 for discussion of the dilemma of disclosure faced by employees with learning disabilities). Sara and Sid, by contrast, can at least assume that the existence of their disabilities is beyond dispute. Jim has concluded that he can resolve this dilemma by proving his worth to an employer before he can even consider a discussion of his learning disability. He thinks that an employer will be more inclined to help an employee who has already demonstrated his value to the company, but this means paradoxically that to obtain accommodations an employee must first prove himself without the accommodations he actually requires. Thus, when Jim interviews for a job he does not mention his learning disability, if at all, until he has convinced the prospective employer that he is qualified. "And then I say, 'Well, by the way. . . .'" The fact that Jim might even consider discussing his disability with a prospective employer, despite all his misgivings, suggests how deeply he fears that nondisclosure might affect his job performance and jeopardize his employment.

Jim's description of his approach to accommodations suggests the magnitude of his concerns about the constitutive effects of rights on relationships within the employment setting. Yet he makes it clear that, even if he should decide to request accommodations, he holds very low expectations for meaningful assistance from an employer. By telling his employer about his learning disability, he would bring a potential problem to the employer's attention, but Jim assumes that the benefits to be obtained from the revelation will be minimal and probably inadequate. Jim knows that he is legally entitled to accommodations. He received them at the university he attended; but universities and other educational institutions are among the leaders in adapting, however imperfectly, to the needs of persons with disabilities, and therefore constitute a unique environment for requesting accommodations. At the university, a special office existed to accept and manage Jim's identity as someone with a learning disability; ideally, his learning disability would have been perceived as distinct from and marginal to his basic intellectual, cognitive, emotional, and other personal qualities. That is, his disability in an academic setting would more likely be regarded as distinct from his self. By contrast, his employers have little knowledge of learning disabilities, and the routine practices in his employment settings appeared to Jim to provide no leeway for managing the potentially disastrous consequences of his self-revelation. Jim has most often decided, therefore, that requesting accommodations would be counterproductive. Indeed, he believes that adaptation of work to the needs of persons with learning disabilities is an idea whose time has not yet come.

Jim's attitudes toward accommodation are deeply ambivalent and may only partly be based on pragmatic concerns about the constitutive effects of rights on his employer's or coworkers' perceptions. He acknowledges the desirability of civil rights for employees with learning disabilities, and he believes in his own ability, yet he seems committed to accepting the burden of making accommodations on his own. Jim's ambivalence about rights may arise from a lack of clarity in his mind about the distinction between his concept of self and his disability. In this sense, Jim differs from Sara and Sid, whose sense of identity is based on a completely capable self who happens to have a disability. For Jim, identity and disability blur in ways that call into question his *own* view of his qualifications for employment and thus his entitlement to on-the-job accommodations.

Jim is a professional with a graduate degree in a "hot" field, where there is plenty of work and the pay is good, yet he has already left three jobs of his own accord. In our group discussion, another interviewee asked Jim whether his job-hopping might be related to his learning disability. Jim's response is revealing: "No, no I don't leave because, I, I try to think that I'm not leaving because of my learning disability, and I really think that I'm not, because I have a lot of other things going on in my life as far as I like to travel. And photography, I'm trying to get into that. So, I think that that's part of it. But I do find that I get burnt, very quick." Jim's ambivalent answer suggests an uncertainty about his identity. On the one hand, he is aware that his disability affects his work. On the other hand, he is reluctant to see his career as anything but the product of his own ability and volition, a view that fails to acknowledge the role his disability plays and that blurs the boundary between self and disability. Asserting rights is inconsistent with the narrative of self that he has constructed to reconcile his superior skills with his frequent job changes.

Perhaps because of the blurring of his identity and disability, Jim finds it difficult to look to rules outside the workplace for validation of his competence. Other interviewees are able to separate a learning disability from self-concept and look to rights to reaffirm a view of the self as capable—Jill Golding, the subject of an earlier life story, is a case in point. Jill eventually viewed her rights as confirmation that she was capable, and she thought it obvious that an employer who denied her an opportunity to work would be in the wrong. Jim Vargas has no such view of himself or of his rights. Unlike Jill, and unlike Sara Lane and Sid Tegler, Jim tends to view his professional ability exclusively within the framework of the job as it is predefined by his employer and to consider his disability a frustrating but unavoidable limitation on his ability to do the work. In the group discussion, another interviewee observed that Jim's job as a physical therapist is not *essentially* about writing or paperwork and might be defined differently so as to allow Jim—and his coworkers—to dictate their reports into a tape recorder. It is clear that this possible redefinition of the job never occurred to Jim. Jim does not assume that rights could validate his competence by requiring alteration of an inappropriately designed job, nor that rights might permit him to serve his employer's most important goal: providing superior service to his customers. Rather, his identity validates the employer's preexisting view of the job, thereby making it highly unlikely that Jim would view rights as relevant to him or his work.

Jim's reluctance to invoke the ADA on his own behalf is not merely a reflection of his pragmatic concerns about the effects of rights on his identity and on relationships within the workplace. Jim accepts the need for the ADA but has difficulty placing himself within its ambit, not only for the pragmatic reasons we have just described, but also because he believes that he is partly to blame for his problems at work and that he bears the moral and cultural burden of adapting to the job. In a sense, Jim would like to achieve, without accommodations, the professional status and respect Sara now enjoys. He believes that once he is perceived as a skilled therapist and a valued employee, he might then be in a position to invoke his rights under the ADA. Once an employee is "in" and has gained an employer's good will, then the employer's view of him may change and may accord requests for accommodations greater legitimacy. Yet Jim seems to lack the self-assurance required for Sara's brand of self-help. His identity confusion results in a strikingly ambivalent attitude toward moral responsibility for the disparity between "normal" work routines and the adjustments that would enable him to succeed in his profession. Jim's blurred self-concept makes him unable to attempt the strategic maneuvers in the workplace that Sara successfully deploys. Sara's strategic approach results in situations in which the ADA can exert an indirect influence on arrangements in the workplace. For Jim, the influence of the ADA is far more remote. If disability rights eventually affect his job at all, it will be the result of some process wholly unrelated to his own efforts.

Conclusion

The ADA was intended to change the workplace for persons with disabilities by requiring greater flexibility in the organization of jobs as well as an end to discriminatory hiring based on stereotypes and misperceptions about the capabilities of individuals or the costs of accommodation. Our research on how rights become active shows a more thorough blending of the law and its social context than the drafters of the ADA could have imagined. Our findings suggest that rights have rarely become active in the lives of our interviewees through formal processes.

The men and women with disabilities who participated in our study did not attempt to achieve the ADA's goals by formally invoking rights. Yet our research also shows that identity and rights interact in many other ways that offer untapped possibilities for the inclusion of persons with disabilities in the workplace.

Sara, Sid, and Jim exemplify different ways in which evolving concepts of self become associated with rights and rights consciousness. These differences have significant implications for the potential role of the ADA. While Sara has recently been more ready to seek change and encourage her employer to accept accommodations consistent with the ADA's requirements, Sid and Jim now appear unlikely ever to invoke the ADA. Sid expects to remain self-employed; and, unless Jim overcomes his deep ambivalence about his own self-concept, he is more likely to switch jobs than to seek change at his places of employment. For Jim, the law lacks power to help him redefine his identity so that he might become a more active advocate for his rights in the workplace. Likewise, for Sid—and for Sara when she contemplates requesting extraordinary accommodations such as the right to work at home—self-concept represents the most formidable barrier to the entry of the ADA into the workplace. Their concern is not just that legal rights might disrupt work relationships or cost them some friends, but that the greatest loss would be their own hard-earned sense of self. This nonpragmatic consciousness of rights presents a serious challenge to the power of the law to facilitate change in the workplace, since it posits a potentially irreconcilable conflict between self-concept and the identity that is seen to result from invoking rights under the ADA. When an employee perceives rights primarily in this way, he or she will be reluctant to invoke the law unless changes accompanying its implementation not only counter the material costs associated with disability rights but also counter the negative effects on the employee's self-concept.

Paradoxically, the ADA was originally intended to transform identities rather than run aground on them. As we have noted, the ADA challenges the traditional assumption that jobs must inevitably come "prepackaged" with their own implicit and explicit definitions of the personal capacities required of the employee who could fill each employment niche. Potentially, the ADA could subvert the tendency of these presumed definitions of the ideal worker to ripple back in society where they shape the attitudes of job trainers and educators from primary school onward, instilling stereotyped understandings about workers and the legitimacy of excluding those whose identities vary from this imagined norm. The ADA creates a new opportunity to negotiate the arrangements and routines associated with each job based on the particular abilities and needs of individual workers, rather than accepting the prepackaged job as an inflexible statement about the identity of the worker who belongs in the workplace. This new flexibility and expanded definition of the qualities and characteristics of the American worker should, at least in theory, have its own ripple effects. One of the most important consequences of the ADA should be its transformation of the identity of children and young adults with disabilities throughout the educational and social systems, so that "disability" and "worker" are no longer considered incompatible and inclusion becomes the norm throughout society.

In the next three chapters, we explore some of the implications of our research about rights and identity and attempt to clarify the circumstances under which inclusion can occur. One explanation for differences in the way our interviewees interpret their experiences can be found in popular discourses that influence how people talk and think about fairness and rights. We suggest in chapter 4 that discourses frame issues of inclusion and exclusion and shape orientations to rights. The choice of a discourse and the experiences that ground its application are influenced by other circumstances that determine an individual's access to cultural, social, and material resources. Family relationships, social class, and race are among the most significant of these circumstances, and their role in shaping identity and rights consciousness are examined in chapter 5. Finally, our interviewees' life stories make it clear that men as compared to women with disabilities must contend with rather different factors as they construct an identity and a career. Just as gender is fundamental to identity, so it is critical to the role of the ADA. Gender is the subject of chapter 6.

four

Life Story: Georgia Steeb

At the age of thirteen, exactly thirty-two years before the day of our interview, Georgia Steeb suffered an accident whose effects divided her life in two. Before the accident, according to the story she tells, she was an active, popular, and successful student: "I was involved in many things. Before my accident, I was a cheerleader. I was in student council. I had a lot of friends. I was very active, very active. I loved school. I loved going to school. I had perfect attendance from the fourth grade right on up until I had my accident." Her story of life after the accident, however, is one of struggle and anxiety. As soon as she returned to school, she discovered that she was, in many ways, an outsider. Her world had changed, and during the years that followed she found it difficult to cope with these changes as she attempted to reconcile her goals for a family, a career, and a satisfying social life. In her struggle, she turned primarily to a newly acquired religious faith and secondarily to a sense of legal entitlement.

Georgia Steeb speaks rapidly, jumping from one idea to the next. An initial invitation to describe herself produces this response:

> Okay, who am I. Well, a forty-five-year-old white, divorced female single parent, presently enrolled in Empire State College. I have twelve semester credit hours to finish for my bachelor's degree. It will be a B.S. degree in educational studies, concentrating in counseling and learning disabilities. . . . My daughter is nineteen. She's going to Bible school in Canada. She commutes and she works. I'm very involved with church functions. We live quite a kind of biblical life, and that takes up most of our time, actually. I am a part-time substitute teacher for our school district. Transportation is one of my biggest problems. . . . My mother, we live in a duplex here. My mother lives on the other side. And as it stands now, should I get a 5:30 call-in, it's usually, she's the one that takes me in.

The initial statement goes on at great length, touching on many additional concerns, from her mother's age (she is now seventy years old), to Georgia's increasingly serious health problems, to her daughter's transportation needs and her own wish to acquire a van. She then mentions her marriage and divorce and the dilemma she faced seventeen years ago as a single mother who had to choose between continuing her education and staying home with her young child. For Georgia Steeb, the events and challenges of the past are still present, still interconnected, and, at least in part, still unresolved. But now she lives as a single parent, her daughter is nearly an adult, and her mother's age raises questions of how to cope in the coming years.

Georgia was born in a small industrial town and grew up in a blue-collar family dominated by her maternal grandmother. Neither of her parents graduated from high school. Georgia recalls that they were hard working and loving parents, but her mother had "very low self-esteem" and her father tended to be passive: "What Mom said kind of went, and what Gram said went, and Dad just went along with it." Georgia felt that neither parent provided guidelines or standards for her when she was growing up, although both took pride in her achievements: "They were very proud of me. They encouraged me. I was the first one in the family, actually, to go on to college." Nevertheless, Georgia now associates the lack of parental structure and guidance with her persistent feelings of nervousness that later ripened into a debilitating condition.

When Georgia was thirteen years old, she fell from a tree and fractured her spine, which left her unable to walk. She was hospitalized for the next four months and then transferred to a rehab clinic for another six months. The following September, however, she rejoined her high school class in the tenth grade. Even before she returned, she discovered that her identity as a paraplegic was different from her identity before the accident as a student who could walk. The school administrators debated whether to allow her to reenroll. They did not know how to transport Georgia to and from school or how to include her in classes on the inaccessible second floor of the high school building. In the end, she was readmitted with the understanding that certain classes, such as business or typing courses, would simply be unavailable to her. A janitor was enlisted to carry Georgia up the steps and into the high school each morning. The administration, in a conspicuous display of flexibility, agreed to waive the rule requiring all girls to wear skirts, so that Georgia could more comfortably handle the physical demands of entering and leaving the building. She negotiated the corridors in a light-weight wheelchair donated by the Lion's Club.

Georgia recalls feeling "very hurt" by her exclusion from certain activities: "I did feel left out in a lot of areas." She was not only denied the opportunity to take some classes, but also her friends no longer invited her to concerts and parties: "The parents didn't want the responsibility of taking me. Everyone's afraid of being sued. So those were the kinds of things that bothered me." The school refused to allow her to travel to Washington, D.C., with the senior class. She remembers that, when two classmates copied her homework, the teacher accused only Georgia of plagiarism and implied that Georgia used her disability to elicit sympathy and to cover up her dishonesty. When she thinks back to her high school years, Georgia contrasts contemporary advocacy of disability rights with her own struggles and the school's attitude that Georgia was not a person who had rights, but was "privileged" to be allowed to attend school at all.

[When we met with her in November 2000, six years after our initial inter-view, Georgia Steeb disagreed with parts of the account of her life story we had written. She acknowledged that some of her views had changed, and we believe her recollections were somewhat different as well, empha-sizing more of the positive aspects of her early experiences. Georgia, and her mother (to whom she had showed our write-up), disputed some of our interpretations. These critical views are reflected in the italicized comments by Georgia that follow.]

I think, through what you've written here, you've neglected to bring to the surface . . . [that] back in 1962, whether it had been any nearby school district, none of the schools were accessible. I would have had the same difficulty, no matter. And this, as I read it, tends to leave out the time period. Anybody who was disabled in this area [rural western New York] would have run into the exact same problem. And as I read this write-up as if I didn't know the person, I would think, "Oh, how could a school system do that?"

That was the principal and vice-principal, how they wanted to help, but they were coming from the aspect of administrators. And it was, what were they going to do with me, and how were they going to work within the budget and work out something. They were willing to, but they did definitely make the statement to me that it was not a "right" or a law or anything that they had to meet my needs for education. That it was a privilege. But I think it was because my parents also were pushing: "Well, why isn't my daughter being, what's going on with her being able to go back to school?" And that's when they evoked the comment, "We're doing our best, and it's really a privilege we're giving her, to come back. You know, we don't have to." In other words, you could make arrangements to go to a special school or be sent away. . . . And when you're told that, that's frightening. . . . Physically, your life is changed, and then you are threatened with, well, you may not be with your friends. You may not be in the same environment that you've grown up with. . . . When I was totally vulnerable, I couldn't move. And I think that's when a lot of my separation anxiety began.

But there were adjustments that were made. Like the school nurse came up the first year I was back. She came up everyday at a particular time to come into the women's lavatory and pick me up and put me, because there were no accessible bathrooms. She picked me up and put me in the bathroom stall everyday. . . . Teachers were totally sympathetic and helpful. I was in dramatics club. I had teachers who got plays that called for a wheelchair person in it. Like my class night, they did a skit out of Cleopatra, where Cleopatra is carried in, and I got that part. So teachers overwhelmingly supported me.

And my friends remained the same. . . . The one incident with parents not wanting to take me to a concert [was an] exception to the rule. But reading your write-up made it seem like the rule. . . . I had a great social life in high school. I went to the prom every year. I had boyfriends every year. I mean we went to, when I look back I wish I hadn't done those things. But it would be your parties here and there and stuff like that.

As high school graduation approached, Georgia's parents were generally supportive but not actively encouraging or directive about Georgia's planning for the future: "If I didn't want to go [to college], I could stay home with Mom and Dad for the rest of my life." A guidance counselor took a different view, however, and helped Georgia conduct a search for a college that would welcome and provide for her. She eventually selected a large midwestern university nearly a thousand miles from home. Her parents drove her to school, but as soon as they left her in her dormitory she began to experience extreme anxiety. After only two days, she left the university and returned home. Her parents welcomed her decision to withdraw: "My mother was glad. She was sick all the way home. She didn't want me that far away."

The way that it is stated in this sentence sounds like your parents are jerks, but the magnificent guidance counselor jumped in. That wasn't it. My parents, I put down here, [reading from her notes written in the margin of our text] were inadequate in their ability to advise me due to their lack of knowledge in post-secondary education. There was no way that my mom and dad could advise me.

And it wasn't that the guidance counselor took a different view. He was simply in a position to provide me with the information. . . .

And as far as my returning back from when I went out to college. My parents wanted me to go to college. Mom just preferred that I be closer. She didn't like the idea of being states away, a thousand miles away, or whatever. She wanted me to go to school but just a little bit closer. . . . Then I did, I enrolled at a local college, and I wasn't home every weekend or anything. They were fine with that. Everything was okay with my father, and my mom was glad for that. She just wanted me to be [in college] locally.

Georgia subsequently enrolled in a local teacher's college, but withdrew after two years because the campus was physically inaccessible and she was unable to get into the classrooms in which her courses were held. She transferred to a local Catholic college near her home but began to experience severe anxiety attacks that eventually made it impossible for her to continue. At the beginning of her second semester, she moved out of the dormitory and returned home in a state of severe depression. After half a year of complete withdrawal and isolation, she began to go out socially with a friend, and she took her first job working as an administrative assistant at a hospital. She continued to receive treatment for her anxiety attacks, however, and her dependence on Valium became an addiction.

Georgia met and married her husband during this period, and gave birth to her daughter two years later. Frustrated by the physical inaccessibility of businesses in her home town, Georgia found it difficult to apply for jobs. She took in ironing, but was largely unemployed for a number of years. One winter, during a blizzard, she was stranded without her Valium and suffered a serious breakdown that led to her admission to the psychiatric ward of a hospital. There, she met an elderly Baptist minister who led her to be "born again" in her Christian faith; as a result, she weaned herself from her dependence on Valium and transformed her life to conform to her new religious commitment. At the same time, she and her husband divorced. She viewed the divorce from the perspective of her newly discovered faith: "I was young and I was learning about things, and I was understanding what bitterness can do to you—and the act of forgiving, and how feelings are involved within the act of forgiveness."

After her religious conversion and her divorce, Georgia learned how to manage her psychological ups and downs with a much more controlled and moderate use of medications. Eventually, her religion and her child-rearing responsibilities began to suggest to her a new career path. Georgia's daughter shared her mother's strong religious faith, and she found public school difficult for that reason. Acceding to her daughter's request, Georgia provided home schooling during the seventh and eighth grades. The next year, Georgia's daughter enrolled in a church school, where Georgia began to teach as a volunteer. This experience encouraged Georgia to work toward certification as a teacher. At the time of our initial interview, Georgia was attempting to attend the college classes required for teacher certification, but transportation was a problem and she also found herself limited by a deterioration in her physical condition, and by tendonitis and back spasms.

I [still] have three incomplete courses. Well, the courses are completed, but I need to do a major in each three. Now that's been that way since 1996, and I need to complete those. When those are completed, I have two remaining courses for my bachelor's degree. But things within my personal life have taken place since that time, not only medical. . . . So different things have made it difficult for me to just concentrate on that. [Getting my degree] took a back seat.

In the meantime, Georgia continues to live in a duplex with her mother, and she accepts frequent assignments as a substitute teacher. Her mother drives her to these jobs. She particularly enjoys working with children who have learning disabilities, and she is taking a college course that focuses on this topic. She also believes it important to take psychology courses, since she has been told that most special education students also need good counseling.

At that particular time, I was a part-time, call-in substitute teacher, and I no longer do that. Transportation became the major problem. I have developed some other medical problems . . . and my endurance level has decreased since the first interview. . . . For me to go in for either a half-time substitute or full-time, by the time I [take a taxi and] get home twenty-five dollars isn't worth it for half a day or fifty dollars for a full day.

Georgia Steeb is not particularly interested in working with children who have physical disabilities like her own. She admits that she does not like to associate herself with others who have physical disabilities, because the public has many false assumptions and stereotyped perceptions about people in wheelchairs. She often encounters negative attitudes when she goes out with her mother or daughter. Sales clerks will speak to them while ignoring her, even if she is the one making the purchase. "So I think that might be a reason that I try not to associate. And it's not a snobbishness, if you want to call it a 'disability snobbishness,' that I don't want to be associated with disabled people. But it's because I know that normal people have no idea what it's like being disabled, what they think, and what their preconceived notions are."

Georgia attended a church-sponsored seminar in which the participants were required to select a disability that they could pretend to experience for the evening. She was astonished that people readily chose to be blind, deaf, or to have developmental disabilities, but no one was willing to be a wheelchair user. Georgia believes that her disability is the most stigmatizing because the wheelchair user is more segregated, physically and psychologically, than a person with any other disability:

The wheelchair was the most helpless of them all and made you feel more self-conscious to the people around you. You're lower than everybody else around you. . . . It's something that brings attention to your disability. A person could say, well, so does a white cane for a blind person. . . . But it's not the same way as being stared at or looked upon or say, "No, you can't sit here, you're in the [way]. There's fire codes, you can't sit here." I've been turned out of restaurants, and lots of different kinds of things.

Georgia resents the prejudiced or discriminatory behavior of others, yet she feels ambivalent about the appropriate response. On the one hand, she is inclined to protest or retaliate; on the other hand, she is inclined to forgive. Georgia describes, for example, her experience at retail stores with cluttered or narrow aisles that are inaccessible to wheelchair users. Once, she actually protested to the manager of the local Montgomery Ward:

Oh, he says, we're getting in all the Christmas stuff, that's what it is, we've got so much Christmas stuff. And I says, that's malarkey, because it's the same way all year 'round. He says, well if you need any help, I can get our clerk, they can get, if you see something that you want to look at. That isn't the point. How can I see what I want to look at if I can't even get into the area to look? . . . I did tell the manager, I says, you realize this is against the law, that it has to be at least somewhat more accessible. . . . I'd like to get a whole list of disabled people and boycott. That's where the 1960s stage starts coming back. Because they don't figure that there's enough of us out there.

The store's inaccessibility triggered a perception that her rights had been violated. As a consequence, she protested to the manager and even imagined organizing a boycott in the spirit of 1960s protests. In this particular story, the law provides the framework for her perceptions and her responses. In other instances, however, her religious faith provides the framework and leads Georgia in a rather different direction: "My Christian knowledge and my heart knows that you don't take that attitude. I know in my heart that I'm always supposed to display what Christ would display when he was on earth. And he didn't take, I mean he did take a lot of garbage, but it can't be this attitude that you have to do what I say or I'm going to, you know. My demeanor should always reflect that in which I believe."

The same ambivalence is apparent when Georgia talks about hypothetical examples of employment discrimination based on her disability. Although she is inclined to perceive such behavior as a violation of her legal rights, her willingness to invoke the law, even in a hypothetical discussion, is always tempered by her belief that a Christian must be prepared to forgive and turn the other cheek. To some extent, she says, her response would depend on the degree of intentionality and bias displayed by the hypothetical employer who refused to hire a job applicant in a wheelchair. Ultimately, however, she concludes that the

Bible would not require her to be so meek that she could not work at all. If the job were the right one for her, she believes that it would be consistent with her faith to invoke the law in order to gain employment: "The Bible says you don't work, you don't eat. . . . I don't make a crusade out of something just for the point of it, but if it was a job I really wanted and knew that I could do, and I didn't have a problem, everything was all a-okay, go ahead [and use the law]." Nevertheless, Georgia, like other interviewees, expresses her reluctance to use rights to force her way into a work setting where she is not wanted: "I would not do that, even though I like the job and even though I knew that I could do it." In that case, she might file a formal complaint, and even pursue her claim to the end, but then refuse the job after it was made available to her. By doing this, she might at least create a better opportunity for the next applicant with a disability.

Georgia Steeb considers herself a child of the 1960s, and draws on her memories of social protests in the cause of justice. The era was one in which civil rights were often invoked, and she readily incorporates the rights paradigm of the Americans with Disabilities Act (ADA) into her conversation. At times, according to her narrative, she has asserted her rights in nonofficial contexts, such as her confrontation with the store manager at Montgomery Ward. She has never, however, consulted a lawyer or filed a formal complaint based on perceived discrimination against her as a person with a disability.

For Georgia, the 1960s were also the time of her religious awakening. Law and religion do not necessarily lead her to different conclusions about the appropriate response to discriminatory behavior. She believes that the Bible might condone her assertion of rights in some instances, especially where the law could provide her with employment necessary for her own survival. Law and religion, however, appear to provide Georgia with somewhat different frameworks for perceiving and interpreting social interactions that could fall within the ambit of the ADA. Her religious belief in the importance of forgiving unenlightened or sinful behavior is different from her rights-based conviction that discrimination is illegal and must be fought and eliminated. For Georgia, the two frameworks exist in a sometimes uneasy tension, and occasionally they pull her in different directions. The vestiges of the rebellious 1960s are still apparent in the discourse of a born-again Christian, whose rehabilitation and ability to pursue a career owe everything to the strength of her religious faith.

[During the previous interview] I was substitute teaching. That was very stressful. I mean I enjoyed it, but it was stressful. I think my outlook, I might have been a little more intense. I'm a little more laid back now. . . . I've got a grand-daughter now, she's going to be two in January. And my daughter is expecting her second child next month. . . . My mom just turned seventy-six, and mom's always been there for me. I've had friends pass away, and I'm going to be fifty-two this month.

And you start to reflect on what's important: my daughter and my grandchildren and what I instill in them and other people. . . .

I put down here just one note on this page, "We have become a rights-oriented society." We have gone so far into each individual's rights for everything that it's choking us. I mean, I'm so grateful for the Americans Disability Act [sic]. For many, many people it's opened many doors. It's done a lot for independence. But I don't expect some little tiny store someplace, who doesn't have a really good income, to expect that they are going to put in a ten thousand dollar ramp. . . . But I believe that there's a lot of people out there that don't have that attitude. They're just, you know, demanding, demanding, and it's not just in the physical disability area but a whole lot of other areas. . . .

When we had our other interview, I think I gave an impression that I would not legally take a route, if I was turned down for a job or if I felt there was some sort of discrimination, somehow battling between my religious beliefs and turning the other cheek. I think there are very definite times in which the law should be invoked and people should sue. Oh yes, most definitely. You know, just because I'm born again does not mean I'm a doormat, and you lay down and you roll all over me. . . .

Does the end always justify the means? I don't like people getting away with things, but my religious view, it says be anxious for nothing. God will always work something out. It doesn't matter what, but that doesn't mean that legally, when something is not done right to a person with a disability, that they should not sue for that. But some, I believe, can be very, very petty and insignificant to sue. We're sue happy. We're sue happy with everything. With the rights of people, it's gone well beyond what the Constitution intended for rights.

Discursive Frameworks and ADA Rights

To this point in the book, we have argued that the relationship between rights and identity holds the key to understanding how the employment provisions of the Americans with Disabilities Act (ADA) become active in the lives of their intended beneficiaries. We have suggested that perceptions of who one is and where one belongs play a critical role in determining whether rights are understood as relevant, and, further, that the law itself may help to shape such perceptions. In our discussion of the relationship between rights and identity, we have emphasized that the constitutive effects of law are not uniform, but arise in different ways for individual interviewees and with varying degrees of influence. We can understand these variations and differences by examining more closely the resources on which particular interviewees draw to construct a life story and interpret the role of rights. That is the purpose of the remaining chapters of this book. In them we consider personal attributes and circumstances that affect our interviewees' access to resources that they use to construct a career. The topics we explore in these chapters include family, religion, community, education, class, race, and gender. All of these contribute to the stories of the self in which rights play a more or less prominent role.

We begin our discussion of resources with an inquiry into the influence of interpretive frameworks that are available to many individuals as they attempt to assimilate social resources and experiences into coherent life stories. Of course, each individual may adopt highly idiosyncratic ways of thinking and speaking about his or her experiences. We use the term "discourse" to describe these patterns of thought and speech. In the course of conducting our interviews, however, we became aware of a small number of widely shared discourses that are familiar to many Americans and available to those who seek to use them—as a resource—to create order and meaning. In this chapter, we suggest that interviewees such as Georgia Steeb sometimes employ one or several of these discourses to talk about their life stories and, more particularly, to describe the disparity between the kind of treatment they consider fair and the treatment they actually receive.

In the discussion that follows, we focus on three such discourses: the discourse of racial justice, the discourse of the market, and the discourse of religion. Each is distinct in many of its features, yet they often overlap in a given narrative. Georgia Steeb, for example, deploys the discourse of religion as she measures the value of rights by the yardstick of her Christian faith; yet she also refers at times to the discourse of racial justice when she explores the analogy between disability rights and the civil rights of African Americans. Although these discourses are not the only ones available as a resource for creating order and meaning, they are very common modes of thinking and speaking in American society. They are closely connected to issues of rights and identity that we have already considered. The discourse of racial justice, for example, emerges from the historical experience of classic rights theory in the United States, which we discussed in chapter 2; the discourse of the market is associated with the social and economic forces we discussed in connection with employment and identity in chapter 3; the discourse of faith typically connects the individual to family, education, and childhood influences on identity formation, whose significance we emphasized in chapter 1.

In the preceding chapters of this book, we have emphasized the relationship between rights and identity, and we have discussed identity in terms of two important features: its interactive, intersubjective quality and its narrative component. The connection between discourses and identity should be obvious. A discourse is, by definition, interactive and intersubjective. It is the communicative medium through which the self interacts with and comes to be distributed among others, thereby establishing a sense of identity. Further, because a discourse is a way of thinking and talking about experiences, narrations of the self continually draw on available discourses to create and recreate identity. These connections between discourse and identity are central to our analysis. The three discourses we explore are intimately involved in the constitutive processes of identity formation as well as in the broader societal processes that enable law, at times, to become part of the common sense understandings of the world.

The use of any discourse carries with it a tendency to shape perceptions and constrain assumptions about the "of course" nature of the social world. As Foucault (1972:60) observes, discourse analysis "concerns, at a kind of *preconceptual* level, the field in which concepts can coexist and the rules to which this field is subjected." Each discourse thus contains its own implicit definitions of "the limits and forms of the *sayable*" (Foucault 1991:59). We explore how these three discourses enable our interviewees, and those with whom they interact, to think and speak in particular ways about the fairness or unfairness of the employment experiences of people with disabilities.[1] If potential rights holders cannot articulate a disparity between the treatment expected and the treatment actually received, they may come to accept as natural and appropriate what might otherwise be considered exclusion or discrimination. They can perceive no space within which ADA rights could become active. The three dominant discourses discussed in this chapter can serve as resources that enable persons with disabilities to conceptualize their everyday experiences as problematic or nonproblematic and rights as relevant or irrelevant. These discourses, in other words, profoundly influence valuations of rights and the role they should play in governing behavior and social interactions.[2]

The Discourse of Racial Justice

In American society, the most powerful symbolic expression of civil rights historically has been their association with race. Of course, civil rights have been deployed on behalf of many groups, including women, workers, religious and ethnic minorities, medical patients, children, gays and lesbians, and many others. Nevertheless, we suspect that if Americans were asked what group they principally associate with the struggle for civil rights, most would answer racial minorities in general and African Americans in particular. Moreover, in the late twentieth and early twenty-first centuries, popular discussion of racial rights has tended to connect them with the concept of affirmative action. Thus, when we refer to a "discourse of racial justice" we have in mind the use of concepts and language that are widely shared in our society as

1. It might be argued that the statutory language of the ADA is itself part of a discourse of disability rights, a way of talking and thinking about the inclusion of people with disabilities in the mainstream institutions of our society. While there is good reason to believe that such a discourse has begun to emerge, we do not make that claim in the discussion that follows. Instead, we examine perceptions of the ADA as they are filtered through other discourses—in particular, the three that are the subject of this chapter.

2. Habermas (1996:33) suggests that, as a general proposition, law exists in relation to interactive communities and thus law's role in society depends on the operation of discourses within those communities: "Modern law lives off a solidarity concentrated in the value orientations of citizens and ultimately issuing from communicative action and deliberation." We understand the problem facing the ADA in similar terms.

Americans talk—and sometimes heatedly disagree—about fairness and justice for racial minorities.

The discourse of racial justice, because of its historical importance, provides Americans with a familiar vocabulary for talking about civil rights, and it is hardly surprising that the same vocabulary would be applied to talk about civil rights that have nothing obvious to do with race. The passage of the ADA itself, and the form of the guarantees it provides, owed much to the history of racial justice in America. When disability could be characterized as a mere "skin-deep" difference and exclusion of workers with disabilities could be characterized as "employment discrimination," the ADA acquired greater moral force (see Tucker 2001:341–42). The rejection of workers with disabilities and the refusal to provide reasonable accommodations for them could then be portrayed as irrational and unjust—as a deprivation of rights—just like racial discrimination.

But the analogy between disability rights and racial justice can be a two-edged sword. Those who oppose the implementation of racial rights, or those who specifically object to affirmative action for racial minorities, may transfer their skepticism to the somewhat different arena of disability rights. They may ask with suspicion whether "reasonable accommodations" are simply another form of affirmative action. The discourse of racial justice provides a ready-made conceptual framework for thinking and talking about other civil rights, and its multivalent effects are at times apparent in the narratives of our interviewees. These effects are both profound and subtle. Sometimes the interviewees—whites as well as African Americans—view their sense of entitlement as legitimated by comparisons between disability and the history of racism and racial rights in American society. At other times, white interviewees, in particular, feel precluded from invoking civil rights because they see their own identities as fundamentally different from those of African Americans and their experience of disability-related unfairness as unique. In a sense, they view the category of rights as already filled by a social group to which they do not belong. Furthermore, some interviewees associate civil rights primarily with affirmative action, which they oppose. For these interviewees with disabilities, their opposition to affirmative action can create a dilemma, since it inhibits them from conceptualizing their own experience of unfairness in terms of rights.

The narrative accounts of two young white males—Raymond Militello and Ron Zander—illustrate the profound and sometimes divergent effects of the discourse of racial justice on persons with disabilities. Raymond, whose life story we have already presented, describes himself as "five-five, Italian, about twenty pounds overweight, and going bald." At twenty-six he works in his father's business as a contractor and real estate developer, but he is also completing his undergraduate degree in business administration. Raymond's life story narrative frequently alludes to family. He grew up in a suburban neighborhood in which everyone on his street was, like his family, Italian American. Cousins lived nearby, and the children became lifelong friends. Family connections have always provided security for Raymond as well as close social ties. He decided years before that he would continue in his father's business. He does not worry about the difficulty his learning disability may present for a future employer, because he expects to be self-employed in the family company. In cooperation with secretaries who work for Raymond's father, he has already developed effective accommodations for the writing he must do, and he knows exactly how he will overcome prospective obstacles connected with his disability on the job. Even as a student, family connections are important to Raymond. When he had problems registering for some of his college classes, Raymond discovered a friend of his father's in the registrar's office who got him into any class he wanted.

Family and family connections have been far more important to Raymond than rights. Even when he was a child, interventions and private tutors arranged by Raymond's parents took the place of legally mandated special education services. At no time in his life story does Raymond frame his experiences in terms of his legal rights. He thinks he was treated unfairly and unreasonably until his parents rescued him, but he does not tell us that his rights were violated. Later in the interview, when we speak explicitly about the new rights available under the ADA, Raymond views matters from the perspective of a small businessman rather than a potential rights holder. Congress should kill the ADA because it is too expensive and "there's too much government regulation in business."

Yet Raymond does perceive rights as relevant to his own experience in one sense, and here we see the connection between the discourse of racial justice and the perception of disability rights. Raymond equates civil rights with preferential treatment. He believes that employers are legally obligated to provide preferential hiring to racial minorities and, after enactment of the ADA, to persons with disabilities as well. Although the ADA contains no such requirement, Raymond believes that job applicants with disabilities must be hired ahead of similarly qualified applicants who have no disabilities. Because the ADA grants "civil rights" to its beneficiaries, Raymond simply assumes that it conforms to the pattern he and others associate with affirmative action and with stereotyped notions of the "advantages" enjoyed by African American job applicants.

Raymond's use of the discourse of race in his narrative produces inconsistencies and contradictions. He expresses ambivalence about the rights claims of racial minorities. He believes that such claims have caused people to assume that minority employees are unqualified and got the job because of their race: "If you fit into that class, black male, black female, Puerto Rican, Hispanic . . . and you get hired in an all white industry or office, first thing people think is he or she got hired because they're black or they're Puerto Rican. You know, they could have been the best qualified person for the job. Nobody really knows. So automatically everybody thinks you got the job just because of your color." Since Raymond believes that the ADA also creates preferential hiring requirements for persons with disabilities, he thinks the ADA could create the same dilemma for them: "You know, this person is classified as learning disabled. But it's a minority, and [hiring this person] makes us look good." Raymond believes that African American and Latino employees have been stigmatized by the very rights claims that have advanced their careers, and he fears that he may suffer the same kind of stigma if he invokes disability rights under the ADA.

Thus some of our interviewees, most of whom are white, express reluctance to invoke disability rights because of what they perceive as the racial connotations of rights discourse. Although in some sense they may view their own encounters with discrimination and exclusion as equivalent to the experiences of racial minorities, they find it impossible to associate themselves closely with the lives or the legal strategies of persons of other races. We perceive a deep ambivalence in our interviewees in this regard. They view themselves as victims of unfair treatment; they even recognize in some cases that this treatment is analogous to the treatment of racial minorities; but they avoid invoking the framework of rights to describe their treatment or to suggest a remedy, because to do so would equate them with a group they are unwilling to embrace as allies, a group toward which they themselves may even feel racial animosity.

Although Raymond Militello disapproves of what he views as preferential treatment for racial minorities, his view is more complex when it comes to the advantages he has derived from disability rights. Raymond's philosophy of life turns on his belief that in any situation or institution, "there's always a back door somewhere; and it's just a matter of getting in that back door. . . . The front door is the worst spot to go, because you're just going to get shot down." Raymond believes that he, like members of racial minorities, has gained access to the all-important "back door" because of his learning disability. He thinks his disability provides him with preferential treatment, in college and elsewhere, and that he would be a fool not to take advantage of it even if he thinks affirmative action for members of racial minorities is wrong. Thus, while acknowledging what he perceives as the drawbacks of rights, Raymond enthusiastically embraces any special advantages available to him. One would be naive to wait hopelessly at the front door, when the back door is wide open:

> That's part of life. I mean, if I was going out applying for a job and I knew I had a better, I knew I'd get bumped up for the first time on the list if I told them I was dyslexic and it's a $50,000 a year job, or whatever it is, I'd tell them. It's like people in the military. They go for civil service, they have points. "You were in the military, oh, we'll give you twenty extra points on the exam because you served." Are they not going to tell a civil service employer that they didn't serve in the armed forces, and get bumped ahead of the list?

Does Raymond feel this sort of preferential treatment is fair or that he deserves to be bumped ahead of other applicants? In general, he does not. In an observation we have quoted previously, Raymond states:

> I don't know if I deserve [those points] or not. I mean, I really hate those kind of systems. I mean, that you should favor a certain group like me because of this, *over a person who's normal*. Well, I shouldn't say I hate it. It seems that in some instances you are favored more, you're not on an equal level. One person's up here, you're over here because of your disability, race, color, or creed. And because of this, some government law, boom, you're up here, you're way past them. That's the way I perceive some of it. That I don't like. (our emphasis)

Raymond's deep ambivalence about rights reveals the complexity of his self-perceived identity. Because of his disability, he sees himself, in his own word, as not "normal." It is unfair to give abnormal people an automatic advantage over others. Yet he also feels intensely that he has been the victim of exclusionary treatment and social stigmatization. He has been treated unfairly. Furthermore, he is nobody's fool. People who do not know how to take advantage of opportunities in life, how to find the back door, are naive losers. Yet Raymond believes that if he takes advantage of the back door created by legal rights, he would associate himself with racial groups with whom he is not necessarily comfortable. And he recognizes that the invocation of rights can contribute to his social identity as abnormal at the same time that rights may give him access to mainstream social settings. He may get the job or be admitted to the college but, by succeeding through the invocation of legal rights, he may cause others to view him as an underqualified outsider, a special case rather than a regular employee or student.

Although Raymond's orientation toward the framework of rights is particularly complex and deeply ambivalent, we believe that he provides one example of a broader phenomenon. We suggest that the shadow of racial difference falls across civil rights generally in American society. When other kinds of rights—including disability rights—are created by statutes such as the ADA, the potential rights holders must speak of themselves in a language whose vocabulary and core concepts developed in large part through the historic struggles for racial justice. In this sense, rights holders under the ADA, like other rights holders in our society, must come to terms with issues of race even when race is not involved with their potential claim in any obvious way.

The history of racial justice in America has created a discourse about unfairness and oppression that is available to other victims of injustice and can expand the options for conceptualizing and communicating their experiences. But, as we have seen, the historic association of rights claims with African American claimants can also cause hesitation. This double effect is apparent in an interview with Ron Zander, a white high school senior with a learning disability, who would like to become a police officer. Consider how race weaves in and out of the following exchange about employment rights—and personal experiences—of persons with disabilities:

RZ: I'm sure if it came down to it and I got fired from the police force, I could go to court and my lawyer would say that the plaintiff . . . has a learning disability, or just a reading problem, and it never affected his job. And I don't think it's fair that he got fired. And hopefully I'd get my job back. . . . Like you hear sometimes someone got fired because they're black, because they're different. It's just, it's all prejudice, that's what it is. You know, prejudice means a lot of different things. It could mean race-wise. It can mean like, if people don't understand something, they're scared of it. . . . Like I told a girl I was seeing that I had a reading problem, and the next day I got dumped. And I asked her why, and she didn't tell me that was the reason why. I knew that was the reason.

Q: Then you're saying that you thought this girl's behavior, or people that treat black people in certain ways, that that's a form of prejudice?

RZ: Yeah. Everyone has prejudices. . . . If a person got fired because they had a learning disability, that's prejudice. . . .

Q: What about the employer who hires someone who has a learn- ing disability and needs extra time or needs to dictate into a tape recorder rather than to write? Now is that something that an employer should also be required to do? And if they don't do it, is that prejudice?

RZ: No, that's not, that's not, no. Well, I don't know. I don't re- ally like the word prejudice, because when you say prejudice, automatically people think of race. And I don't like that.

Q: I thought I heard you say the word.

RZ: Yeah, well I said it. I said it, but then, now that I'm thinking about it, that's not the right word for it. Discrimination.

Ron initially observes that his experiences—both actual and hypo- thetical—as a person with a learning disability can be compared to the experiences of African Americans. Thus he is able to categorize his girl- friend's rejection as a form of prejudice. He also asserts that being fired because of his learning disability would be a form of prejudice com- parable to racial prejudice, and by analogy would be illegal. However, when asked about a hypothetical refusal to provide what might be con- sidered a "reasonable accommodation" under the ADA, Ron hesitates. No, he says, that would not be an example of prejudice, because prej- udice in his mind suddenly is restricted to race. Ron says he does not like it when people think of race in connection with issues of disabil- ity and accommodation. He distinguishes the concept of "prejudice" in this sense from the more all-encompassing concept of "discrimination," which applies to situations of unfairness that have no racial analogue and are, in his mind, less egregious.

Ron's distinction between prejudice and discrimination raises a num- ber of questions, the answers to which are not at all obvious. Prejudice may suggest to him a visceral dislike for members of a particular social group, whereas discrimination may suggest a more calculated policy that works to their disadvantage. If so, it is understandable why Ron il- lustrates what he views as the many meanings of prejudice with a story about his former girlfriend's dumping him when she discovered he had a learning disability, yet he refuses to apply the term to an employer who is unwilling to provide accommodations in the workplace.

Ron is confident that he would press a legal claim if an employer exhibited a visceral, irrational "prejudice" against him because of his learning disability—and fires him—but not if the employer "discrimi- nates" by refusing to provide reasonable accommodations. In the passage quoted above, Ron claims that he would sue if he were fired because of the mere fact of his learning disability, which he characterizes as an example of prejudice comparable to racial prejudice. But Ron is less confident that he would take legal action against an employer who refused to provide needed on-the-job accommodations: "Personally, I wouldn't bring up my rights. . . . That would be my last resort. . . . Taking someone to court is, everyone's suing everyone now, and it's not right." Ron then repeats that he would not invoke his rights unless he were actually fired because of his disability.

We hesitate to read too much into the philosophical reflections of a high school senior, even one as mature and thoughtful as Ron Zander. But it appears that Ron's somewhat inconsistent thoughts about the invocation of disability rights in the workplace are shaped by the discourse of racial justice. Specifically, Ron readily invokes this discourse to communicate his beliefs about "prejudice"—the irrational rejection of another person based solely on his or her membership in a minority group—but not to communicate his thoughts about entitlement to on-the-job accommodations. Ron appears to view such accommodations as an appropriate and reasonable step but not a matter of right. We think Ron may feel himself precluded from viewing reasonable accommodations in terms of rights because he assumes the equivalent concept in the discourse of racial justice is affirmative action. We think he hesitates to place himself in the position of a claimant in an affirmative action case, perhaps because he disapproves of such claims; but the discourse of racial justice preempts him from thinking or talking about his rights to reasonable accommodations in any other terms. He cannot get outside the discourse of racial justice and view on-the-job accommodations from any perspective except that which requires the employer to take affirmative steps on his behalf—steps that would not be required for other employees. Thus, Ron fumbles for an appropriate expression to describe the employer's hypothetical refusal to provide reasonable accommodations. It is not "prejudice"; perhaps it is "discrimination"—another term Ron borrows from the discourse of racial justice. But discrimination alone, Ron asserts, should not justify bringing a lawsuit. Ron would not bring a lawsuit to obtain reasonable accommodations unless he was about to be fired.

Ron thinks a legal claim for needed accommodations is an example of overlitigious behavior. He is concerned that Americans tend to sue one another too often, and he refuses to consider bringing a lawsuit that might be characterized as frivolous or excessive. Perhaps Ron even views some rights claims by African Americans as overly litigious. The possibility is implied but not expressed. If that is Ron's view, then it further illustrates the ambivalent effects of race on his understanding of disability rights.

Whereas Raymond Militello's narrative illustrates how, in his view, the discourse of racial justice creates strategic opportunities for persons with disabilities, Ron Zander's narrative illustrates how this same discourse is both enabling and limiting for a young man about to enter the workforce. The discourse of racial justice on the one hand enables Ron to construct an identity as a worthy and capable employee in the eyes of any fair-minded employer, but, on the other hand, it limits the claims Ron might make in good conscience against a boss who may be in violation of the law. Even if the ADA guarantees Ron's right to reasonable accommodations, Ron could not assert this right because it has no counterpart in the law of racial justice that is legitimate in Ron's mind. Lacking the legitimizing analogy to racial prejudice, such a rights claim would be frivolous. For this reason, Ron feels foreclosed from taking legal action and would be inclined to forgo the unique rights Congress created to enable him to function effectively in the employment setting.

The Discourse of the Market

We turn now to a second discourse that pervades our society and affects the ways in which individuals with disabilities think and talk about their employment experiences. The discourse of the market characterizes disability employment issues in terms of the economic arguments for and against hiring or accommodating persons with disabilities. This discourse typically emphasizes cost-benefit analysis—that is, it purports to compare the cost to the employer of hiring and accommodating employees with disabilities to the economic benefits of doing so. When this discourse appears in our life story narratives, it is usually the benefits *to the employer* that are compared to the employer's costs rather than benefits to the individual rights holder, to people with disabilities as a group, or to American society as a whole. In short, the use of the discourse of the market tends to emphasize the employer's perspective on the "fairness" of inclusion,[3] and it takes existing work arrangements as a given rather than emphasizing the malleability and relativity of work arrangements suggested by Minow's "social relations" approach (see chapter 2). The ADA itself reflects the cost-benefit conceptualization of market discourse, and its focus on the employer's bottom line,

3. Compare Alan D. Freeman's (1998) distinction between the victim's perspective and the perpetrator's perspective in judicial interpretations of civil rights law.

in its definition of "undue hardship" for determining when an accommodation is reasonable.[4]

Our interviewees tend to use the discourse of the market not as an analytic tool for comparing costs and benefits or measuring economic efficiency but as a way to convey basic assumptions about their identity as employees in a business enterprise. We view their use of this discourse in terms of its expressive qualities, since they rarely engage in an actual economic calculation. Market discourse can construct our interviewees' identities in different ways in relation to disability rights. Some use the discourse to distance themselves from rights while others use it to affirm rights. For example, as we show in this section, Sid Tegler rejects rights under the ADA in order to underscore his belief that he truly belongs in the workplace. His refusal to invoke rights, in his eyes, makes him just like the other employees and reinforces the fact that an individual who uses a wheelchair "belongs" in the workplace as much as any other employee. The attraction of market discourse, to Sid Tegler, lies in the fact that by using it he can legitimate his identity as a potential employee. On the other hand, Sean O'Brian uses market discourse as a starting point for explaining why ADA rights are fair and why their guarantees of inclusion and nondiscrimination are reasonable requirements. For Sean, discourse of the market demonstrates that his insistence on rights is a sober and practical position and that he is not a naive idealist who is unaware of the constraints employers actually face in their daily business.

Among the interviewees who consistently employ the discourse of the market, Sid Tegler's narrative is particularly striking in its skepticism about rights. We earlier presented Sid Tegler's life story and have discussed his experiences in chapter 3. Sid, it will be recalled, has used a wheelchair since a skiing injury in junior high school. Now a self-employed CPA in a small village in western New York, Sid places great value on independence and self-sufficiency. At times he minimizes his

---

4. ADA §12111(10)(B): In determining whether an accommodation would impose an undue hardship on a covered entity, factors to be considered include

(i) The nature and net cost of the accommodation needed under this chapter;

(ii) The overall financial resources of the facility or facilities involved in the provision of the reasonable accommodation; the number of persons employed at such facility; the effect on expenses and resources, or the impact otherwise of such accommodation upon the operation of the facility;

(iii) The overall financial resources of the covered entity; the overall size of the business of a covered entity with respect to the number of its employees; the number, type and location of its facilities; and

(iv) The type of operation or operations of the covered entity. . . .

distinctive identity as a person with a disability by comparing his mobility impairment to the difficulties of his middle-aged high school classmates who have developed trick knees and bad backs. Sid tends to use a quip or sarcastic remark to dismiss rights to accommodations for persons with disabilities, and he observes that he himself has learned to get around without invoking such rights. He believes curb cuts and automatic door openers for wheelchair users are cost effective only because they are also convenient for other members of the community, such as children on bikes or parents with baby carriages. For the most part, however, Sid perceives accommodation rights as incompatible with his sense of full citizenship, and he maintains that he does not want or need them. His assertions support his image of an individual who participates fully in the political and social life of his community and an employee who is self-sufficient and asks for little if anything from an employer.

Sid's use of the discourse of the market tends to focus attention on the ways in which hiring and accommodating workers with disabilities might affect business operations, evaluated in terms of his view of the employer's short-term costs and benefits and the productivity of employees. The influence of market discourse is apparent, for example, when Sid readily takes the side of a potential employer, assessing legal rights to accommodations that might help Sid as an individual but reduce profits for the business as a whole: "I really don't feel that the government or any large organized group, whether it's the employer or the government, owes me something unless I can make a profit, or further their cause in some way. . . . I can see arguments on the other side [i.e., the employer's side] that say there's really no economic justification for it, or relatively little." Sid justifies his rejection of employment rights by linking them to the employer's bottom line. In his view, paraplegia generally merits no special considerations in employment. Neither an employer nor the community should be under a special obligation to offer accommodations to Sid or persons like him.

When Sid Tegler links accessibility rights and reasonable accommodations to the market, he exemplifies a discourse frequently used by our interviewees. Sid is not the only one to voice reservations about asserting rights in the employment setting because of a concern for the employer's bottom line. In using this discourse, some interviewees contrast what they believe to be the ADA's absolute and inflexible requirement of on-the-job accommodations with the employer's need to balance costs and benefits. In drawing this contrast between the rigidity of legal rights and the pragmatic realities of the market, they justify their own refusal to invoke rights if the costs of enabling them to work impose a net burden on the employer. Few of these interviewees acknowledge that the

ADA itself expressly incorporates a flexible requirement of "reasonable accommodations" that requires a balancing of the cost of such accommodations against the resources and capacities of the employer, and none connects the discourse of the market with the comment in the ADA's regulations that the determination of a "reasonable accommodation" may require employers and employees to engage in face-to-face negotiations and reach a reasonable compromise in cases of disagreement (29 C.F.R. 1630.2(o)(3)). Rather, they speak as if an employer's need for profit establishes an absolute limit on the accommodations that employees should expect to receive.

A rather different perspective is seen to be appropriate for educational settings as compared to employment settings. Interviewees who are students, though sometimes conflicted about seeking academic accommodations, could justify their requests on the grounds that they paid for their education. In return for their tuition payments, they could expect the college or university to incur some costs for accommodations. By contrast, in the employment setting, the same interviewees feel it harder to justify requests for accommodations from the individuals who pay *them* their salaries. As employees, they believe that the burden is on them to meet the employer's expectations rather than to demand that the employer incur additional costs for their benefit. For interviewees like Sid Tegler, their reasoning has little to do with an actual weighing of costs and benefits, since they believe it unfair to require an employer to go to *any* additional expense no matter how productive the individual might become with accommodations or how many employees might benefit.

Under present circumstances, Sid rejects employment rights for himself and for persons with disabilities in general. His statement that employers should not have to pay for accommodations that affect the bottom line expresses his belief that he is a capable employee without accommodations, and that belief is consistent with his satisfaction in achieving the status of a self-employed professional. Although Sid does not feel that he needs the ADA's rights to be a successful CPA or to participate in the life of his small community, his frustrating employment experiences on the East Coast suggest to us that rights to accommodations might have made a great difference to him at an earlier point in his career. Sid, however, does not share the sense that rights would have helped him to become a full citizen or a capable employee or that rights would have enabled him to fulfill an employer's expectations. He interprets his experience with East Coast accounting firms to mean that he could have worked with minor adjustments, not legally mandated accommodations, but that the principal barrier to employment was employers' irrational perceptions of him—prejudice. Little will change, he believes, until such perceptions of persons with disabilities are transformed, which can only happen over time. Sid thinks that law can do relatively little to accomplish such a transformation.

Because of his emphasis on the discourse of the market, Sid criticizes the influence of prejudice and stereotyping on the grounds that they distort a rational evaluation of the costs and benefits of employing people with disabilities. Sid believes that he could perform up to market expectations for employees in his profession—with no more than minimal accommodations—but that he was blocked from employment by the intrusion of illegitimate factors that had no role in a proper market-based analysis of his capabilities. Thus, by describing the unfair behavior of employers in his discourse of the market, Sid deemphasizes the importance of rights while emphasizing his capacity to work and to be integrated into the mainstream without accommodations.

For Sid Tegler and a number of other interviewees, market discourse provides a powerful expressive medium for talking about disability concerns in relation to employment. Some interviewees who employ cost-benefit analysis emphasize the low cost of most accommodations relative to the benefits associated with hiring talented new employees with disabilities. Sid does not employ market discourse in this way. His purpose is to argue that the ADA is generally an inappropriate intrusion on managerial prerogatives, but that it is nonetheless ridiculous for an employer to weigh costs and benefits irrationally by using measures that are distorted by prejudice. Although Sid would expect no accommodations for himself as a matter of right, he is disgusted by employers who would deny him a job simply because he uses a wheelchair. The language he uses to express his disgust is the discourse of the market, which provides the terms, concepts, and symbols that highlight the irrationality and self-defeating quality of discriminatory behavior.

Sid Tegler's use of market discourse operates primarily to express an identity. By employing this discourse, he places himself inside the web of relationships that constitute the workplace and associates himself with the norms and structures of the market. Positioning himself in this way, he identifies himself as an employee who belongs, not because of rights asserted against the institutions and values of the workplace, but because his place in the mainstream is legitimated by the market itself. For other interviewees, however, market discourse operates quite differently. These individuals do not share Sid's assumption that rights undercut their identity as capable employees. They use market discourse to affirm rights rather than to reject them. For these individuals, rights can be justified in cost-benefit terms because as employees they will produce a net benefit for their employer, even if the employer must initially incur some costs to provide accommodations. Market discourse, as it is used by these interviewees, underscores the fact that only an employer whose thinking is distorted by prejudice would ignore the economic efficiency of hiring people with disabilities and providing them with reasonable accommodations. Interviewees like Sean O'Brian view the right to accommodations as consistent with and even *expressive of* their identities as capable employees.

Sean, like Sid, suffered a spinal cord injury causing permanent physical disability—in Sean's case, quadriplegia. Sean's injury occurred in a car accident when he was a nineteen-year-old junior college student and required him to abandon his plan to pursue a career as a commercial pilot. Sean credits the strong value system instilled in him by his family for his determination to rehabilitate after his injury and pursue a college degree and a job. Whereas he recalls that others in his rehabilitation unit tended to "whine" and complain, Sean claims that he simply told himself, "Well this is where you're at and make the best of it. . . . I don't think my family or my friends would have stood for anything less either." Eventually, Sean returned to college and obtained a bachelor's and a master's degree in library science.

Sean has seldom asked for or desired accommodations, even when he might have been entitled to them under the ADA. After completing his studies, he obtained a job as a volunteer in one of his university's specialized libraries, which led to a paid temporary position in cataloguing and reference work. Remaining self-sufficient in his job is a high priority, and he has considered how to obtain accommodations that would make him more useful to the library. His first thought is to search for grant money to purchase electronic aids so that he will not "have to interrupt somebody else's time, which is not the way I want to do things." Sean thinks it is important to pay for his own accommodations whenever possible and to avoid confrontation. If Sean needed an accommodation that he could not afford, he would evaluate the reasonableness of his request in terms of whether the accommodation might benefit other employees as well as himself. Thus, Sean's frame of reference is general distributive fairness, not individual legal entitlement. For example, he explains that the CD-ROM technology he finds useful also benefits other librarians. Sean is wary of rights claims, in part because they lead to confrontation and also because they may not reflect his belief that accommodations should be of general, not personal, benefit. Even with respect to accommodations Sean needs for himself, he argues that the benefit to others is an essential element—in this case, future employees with disabilities: "I'm doing it for me, but there's also others that are going to benefit from it, and if I just moused out and gave up then I'm not being fair to somebody else also."

Like Sid Tegler, Sean O'Brian feels a strong commitment to the value of self-reliance. Like Sid, Sean sometimes uses the discourse of the market to express this value and to claim an identity as a legitimate participant in the workplace. He emphasizes that he would not request an accommodation that "makes the position more expensive than what it's worth." This appears to be a form of cost-benefit analysis, sensitive to the financial concerns of the employer. Sean does not want to use his rights under the ADA to confront an employer or to disrupt the employer's usual calculations for determining when software, hardware, or other technology would be affordable and useful. By acknowledging these cost-benefit concerns, Sean can reinforce his identity as a self-sufficient participant in the workplace.

Yet Sean differs from Sid in his readiness to embrace rights despite his occasional use of the discourse of the market. Sean, unlike Sid, finds it possible within this discourse to justify the use of rights to persuade an employer that some accommodations would benefit Sean *and* other employees, thus broadening the terms of a narrow analysis of costs and benefits. Furthermore, Sean believes that some kinds of accommodations that benefit himself alone may be justified, even if their costs exceed their immediate financial benefits to the employer, simply because they enhance Sean's ability to work and to be independent. Such accommodations would be fair, Sean thinks, because they place him on an equal footing with others: "I mean, I didn't ask to be disabled. I didn't do anything where I should have to foot the entire bill or something like that on my own, and I'm not asking them to cope with my mental adjustment. I'm just asking for help in being able to just kind of be on an equal plane with the rest of my profession." Sean expresses a readiness to consult a legal aid attorney if necessary to obtain this sort of accommodation, despite his ambivalence about deploying rights to challenge existing practices in the workplace.

The discourse of the market operates differently in the life story narratives of Sid Tegler and Sean O'Brian. For Sid, the discourse makes legal rights under the ADA irrelevant. If an accommodation is cost effective, a rational employer will provide it regardless of the ADA. If the employer acts irrationally, because of prejudice toward people with disabilities, Sid would simply seek work elsewhere rather than invoking rights. Use of the discourse of the market provides Sid with a vocabulary for expressing his sense of self as a legitimate participant in the marketplace. For Sean, the situation is different. Although Sean also values self-reliance and is wary of the disruptive effects of rights in the workplace, he does not believe that rights under the ADA are completely preempted by the norms and practices of the market. For one thing, he notes that many accommodations are useful not just to the rights holder but to other employees, both present and future. As long as his request for an accommodation is not financially excessive, moreover, he thinks he is entitled to ask the employer to assume part of the cost even when it would benefit Sean alone. Cost-benefit analysis is not the ultimate criterion for every accommodation, particularly if Sean's ability to participate in the workplace is at stake. Sean "didn't ask to be disabled" and shouldn't bear all of the consequences for the accident that made accommodation necessary. Sean, unlike Sid, expects employers to contribute to the reasonable costs of inclusion, and he believes that it is fair to invoke rights to force them to do so. The discourse of the market, for Sean, is consistent with shared responsibility for enabling persons with disabilities to become self-sufficient workers.

The Discourse of Faith

As our interviewees discuss their lives and their employment experiences, a third discourse emerges along with the discourses of racial justice and the market—the discourse of religious faith. Sociolegal scholars have generally ignored religion in America as a factor affecting the role of law and legal rights, although it is clear that religion today, as in the past, remains a pervasive element in American communities and consciousness.[5] A few studies demonstrate how powerful a force religion can be. Greenhouse (1986), for example, shows how the discourse of faith frames the perception of conflict and social change among Baptists in "Hopewell," Georgia, and determines the place law occupies in their moral universe. Similarly, some of our interviewees incorporate religious beliefs and practices into their narrative accounts of interactions with others, experiences of fairness and unfairness, expectations for the future, and attitudes toward rights. For them, the discourse of religion is a resource that enables them to understand and express their concepts of self, disability, employment, and the law. At times our interviewees explicitly mention religious faith, but at other times it is implicit—yet unmistakable—in their life story narratives. In either case, we view the discourse of faith as a factor that can have great significance for understanding how rights become active.

Georgia Steeb, whose life story narrative precedes this chapter, draws expressly on her religious beliefs when interpreting her experiences and

5. The puzzling neglect of religion in sociolegal studies is discussed in French 1998.

her own conduct. Georgia was not raised in a religious family, but she became a born-again Christian at the age of twenty-one after meeting a Baptist minister in a hospital. Georgia refers both to the law and to her religion when discussing the barriers she has faced because of her use of a wheelchair. She often mentions the availability of rights; but, at the same time, she recognizes that her Christian beliefs require tolerance and forgiveness of others' treatment of her, a perspective that she sometimes feels to be in conflict with the discourse of rights. She has protested conduct that she believes illegal—by speaking to store managers, for example, or by writing letters—and she herself worries that these protests may be inconsistent with her belief in Christian forgiveness. Georgia believes that the pursuit of rights cannot be allowed to compromise the more fundamental definitions of justice that she finds in the Bible and in the life of Jesus.

After Georgia suffered a permanent spinal injury at the age of twelve, she found it difficult to return to school as a student in a wheelchair, and she struggled with the problem of inaccessible classrooms and an uncertain future. Although she completed high school, she has made only partial progress toward a bachelor's degree. There have been difficulties obtaining accommodations for her disability, and she has had problems with anxiety and a lack of self-confidence. Recurrent panic attacks required repeated hospitalization and made her married life difficult. She and her husband divorced after four years, and she has raised her daughter as a single parent. Georgia has had little success with employment, although she did work for a time as an uncertified substitute teacher for the public schools.

In narrating her life story, Georgia's references to rights provide a framework for describing what she considers the unfair denial of opportunities. Her rights consciousness is all the more notable because she attended high school and college before the passage of federal laws requiring academic accommodations and accessible school buildings. Rights come into play "when you go from someone saying 'Consider it a privilege that we're allowing you to go to public school' as compared to now [when] the mandates are 'This must be accessible.'" If current laws had been in effect when she attended high school, she believes that school administrators would have made greater efforts to provide accommodations and would have included her in trips and other activities from which she was barred. Georgia claims that today she is ready to invoke rights to address unfair treatment. When she was asked what she would do if she were denied reasonable accommodations for employment as a teacher, she said she would complain to the school board. If she thought they were in violation of the law, "Oh, I'd report 'em. I'd report 'em quicker than. . . ."

Although Georgia frequently employs a discourse of rights to describe situations in which she has been treated unjustly because of her disability, she has never formally invoked the ADA or contested her treatment by employers on account of her disability. Interestingly, however, she has sometimes referred to the law in complaints about matters not related to her disability. She describes one incident in which she attempted to sue a potential employer who had rejected Georgia's application for a position as a clerk, because, he told her, he preferred to hire a man for the job. Although her disability was almost certainly the employer's real reason for rejecting her application, Georgia interpreted—and still perceives—the employer's conduct as sex discrimination. She complained to a civil rights organization, which declined to file a lawsuit because they believed her use of a wheelchair made it unlikely that she was qualified for the job regardless of her gender. The organization's lawyers, according to her own account, concluded that Georgia was denied the job because of her disability, which at that time would have been lawful, but Georgia persists in her belief that the denial of employment was a clear case of gender bias.

Georgia's rhetoric of rights does not necessarily match her actual behavior. From her narrative, we can see that she has in fact avoided many situations in which she would have to seek accommodations, and when accommodations have been an issue she has seldom confronted the people in charge. For example, she made little effort to persuade administrators at the local university to provide accessible classrooms, and instead she transferred to another school. In many other situations, Georgia has tended to "exit" rather than invoke rights, a choice often dictated by her susceptibility to anxiety and panic attacks.

Among the factors that make Georgia reluctant to invoke disability rights, one of the most important is the influence of religion. Her religious conversion, by her own account, was a turning point in her life. "I accepted the Lord as my savior. . . . I was born again and my life was totally different from that point on." She became a devout Baptist, has remained an active participant in the church, and has raised her daughter in the faith.

As frequently as she mentions rights to legitimate her grievances about unjust treatment, Georgia employs the discourse of her religion and the Bible to support her decisions to let her life take its course. She became reconciled to her divorce, noting "it's what the Bible says, let the leaving depart. You don't keep them." Following her conversion and the breakup of her marriage, she had no panic attacks and ended her ten-year dependence on Valium. Her faith gave her a strong sense of order. "You know . . . you trust in God and . . . there are positions for people. God makes positions for people. . . ." When her panic attacks recurred, her sense of order was not shaken. At first, she resisted her doctor's recommendation that she take medication, recalling her earlier addiction to Valium. She says, however, that "the Lord had a long talk with me and told me, you know, 'Listen.' And so I've been on it ever since and have not had any, you know, not had any major problems."

In Georgia's understanding, the discourse of faith is, in many respects, incompatible with the discourse of rights as a framework for interpreting her identity and her disability. Her knowledge of the law is often quite detailed and encompasses a wide range of life situations ranging from school accommodations to handicapped parking to specific architectural requirements for accessibility under the law. But she also believes that a contentious response is in conflict with her Christian beliefs. For example, she describes a local department store's failure to make display areas accessible and observes that their excuses for narrow, crowded aisles were "malarkey"; but she then backtracks to reconcile her response with her religious values: "My Christian knowledge [and] my heart knows that you don't take that attitude. I'm always supposed to display what Christ would display when he was on earth. And he did take a lot of garbage, but it can't be the attitude that, that you have to [do] what I say or I'm going to . . . you know? My demeanor should always reflect that in which I believe. So I'm always babbling this type of thing but I do notice. . . ." Her self-characterization of "babbling" reflects Georgia's struggle to assimilate her understanding of rights under the ADA into the discourse of religious faith.

When asked what she would do if her employer refused to provide accommodations the law entitled her to have, she says that her decision to take action would depend on a number of practical contextual factors. She would consider how important the job was to her, whether the company could afford the accommodation, and whether the denial reflected a reasonable business decision—in other words, factors relevant to the discourse of the market. She is aware that her efforts to enforce the law might help others. If an employer were to treat her unfairly, she would not automatically adopt either a legalistic or a religious perspective. Rather, she tells us, echoing Ron Zander's distinction between "prejudice" and "discrimination," she would consider the character of the employer, and if prejudice were not involved she would "leave it alone." This moral assessment of the employer's motive appears to be consistent with the framework of religion. At the other extreme, however, if the decision reflected an "an arrogant, Nazi-supremacy type thing" she would be sure to file a legal complaint. It would be a "matter of principle" to have a record made of the injustice. Pursuit of principle could, after all, be reconciled with religion. Christianity, Georgia tells us, is consistent with the invocation of employment rights when an individual's survival is at stake: "I don't say let the chips fall where they may. I'd just say 'Lord take care of it.' You know the Bible says you don't work you don't eat . . . and you know I need a job . . . I don't make a crusade, but if it was a job I really wanted. . . ."

In this last statement, Georgia Steeb constructs a justification for invoking rights that comports with her religious faith. Yet the situation she addresses is hypothetical, and it is clear that in her actual life story she has found the discourse of faith to be in tension with disability rights. Religion, for her, emphasizes forgiveness and acceptance of one's lot in life. Rights, for her, emphasize confrontation and dissatisfaction with the status quo. Georgia's detailed discussion of disability law suggests that she draws on legal rights rhetorically to validate her sense of self-worth, yet in practice she avoids invoking them. When the opportunity arises to move beyond rhetoric to legal action, Georgia cites her religious values in order to justify a nonconfrontational response.

The tension between disability rights and the discourse of faith displayed by Georgia Steeb is more muted, but still present, in the life stories of some of our other interviewees, particularly those who were strongly influenced by a discourse of faith as children but who have not been particularly observant as adults. Sean O'Brian, for example, whose life story we compared to Sid Tegler's in the previous section, professes not to be particularly religious. Yet he was raised in a devout Roman Catholic family, was close to his parents and grandparents, and admired their values and the way they conducted their lives. Looking back on the auto accident that resulted in his quadriplegia and a difficult period of rehabilitation during his late teens and early twenties, Sean emphasizes that his family's religious faith was an invaluable resource: "I just admired them for the way they lived their lives. . . . And I think it is something that carried all the way through my disability and in my car accident and after that. They said the family was always there and always had been, and it's a prize."

Sean credits values instilled by his family for his ability to accept his injury and maintain a positive attitude during his rehabilitation and subsequent efforts to complete his college education, obtain a professional degree, and find employment. During rehabilitation, he met many other individuals with similar injuries who had far more difficulty adjusting than he did.

It made me realize that there were a lot of people who are not quite as fortunate as I was. . . . [It] just came natural for me to just accept the situation. . . . I just think sometimes—I'm not real

religious and I don't believe anything [is] ordained, but there must
have been something along the road that helped my personality
makeup where I was just able to cope with what was dealt me and
just say, "Well this is where you're at and make the best of it."

In many respects Sean's acceptance of his spinal injury has been remarkable. His injury completely changed the reference points for his identity.
He was a high school athlete, and he aspired to become a commercial
pilot, having already picked a college and a career path leading to that
goal. Following his accident, Sean was forced to give up athletics and his
plan to become a pilot, yet he does not allow himself to express regret
at the radical transformation of his identity. Instead, Sean has pursued
the discovery of deeper, more important qualities.

For Sean, the discourse of faith has remained an important element
in his life, even after he began to distance himself from the religious
practices of his family. He repeatedly refers to the values of self-reliance,
concern for others, and acceptance of the hand fate deals us. We believe
that this discourse, although it has been stripped of specific religious
references, originates in the religious beliefs of Sean's family, and that
it profoundly affects Sean's perceptions of disability rights.

Sean's view of rights, like Georgia Steeb's, contains some ambivalence, though Sean does not share Georgia's deep sense of conflict between religious belief and the law. Sean, like Georgia, would probably
reject the invocation of rights in most situations. As a recent graduate
of a library science program, Sean recognizes his right to reasonable on-
the-job accommodations. He asserts a willingness to invoke such rights,
particularly if his value to an employer—in market terms—justifies the
cost of the accommodations he needs. Furthermore, Sean expresses reluctance to request accommodations that benefit himself alone and are
not also of use to other employees. The discourses of faith and the market blend together in Sean's account. Yet we think the discourse of faith
is a resource that enables Sean to articulate a sense of rights that ac-
centuates their unselfish qualities—their value to others—and also the
moral demands they properly make on employers to help their employees strive for a truly inclusive society.

Sean's perspective on what constitutes "reasonable accommodations" differs from the legal standards articulated in the ADA. It seems
clear that he has modified the legal definition of his disability rights
by filtering them through the perspective derived from religion. His
approach to rights reflects his family's religious faith and its emphasis
on self-sufficiency, concern and support for others, and acceptance of
things that cannot be changed. For Sean, the influence of religion does

not mandate passivity, but it does modify the self-referential aspects of legal rights. Sean tends to qualify the rights to which he believes himself entitled by removing those elements that strike him as selfish and by retaining only those elements that promote fairness to others as well as respect for his own self-worth. For Sean, the "reasonableness" of reasonable accommodations is determined by personal values rooted in the religious faith of his family.

Conclusion

Our discussion of the three discourses—racial justice, market, and faith—illustrates their relevance to the process by which disability rights become active in the lives of the ADA's intended beneficiaries. Our argument could have been illustrated by the analysis of other discourses, but we frequently encountered these three in the employment narratives of our interviewees and they are linked to important institutions, practices, and beliefs that we discuss elsewhere in this book. At times, our interviewees regarded these discourses as a resource that enabled them to understand and talk about their life stories. They did not view the discourses as mutually exclusive. Sean O'Brian's narrative, for example, weaves together the discourse of faith and the discourse of the market as he describes the value he places on the employer's bottom line and on the need to demonstrate self-sufficiency and generosity toward fellow employees. Raymond Militello's narrative combines the discourses of racial justice and the market as he analyzes what he takes to be the implications of affirmative action for persons with learning disabilities while also denouncing the intrusive effects of rights on employers' prerogatives. Each discourse, or combination of discourses, functions somewhat differently for different interviewees. The effect of these discourses is palpable but not always predictable.

What, then, is the significance of discourse in these life story narratives, particularly in relation to rights? We suggested earlier that rights become active in situations where potential rights holders perceive a disparity between the treatment they expect and the treatment they actually receive. It is important, therefore, to ask whether and how the disparity is perceived, and we think that these three discourses, among many others, bear on that issue. Discourses enable people to talk about who is and who should be an employee. They provide a framework for perceiving whether an employer is acting fairly or unfairly. They facilitate our interviewees' efforts to evaluate the quality of their experiences in the workplace. In short, discourses, alone or in combination, enable the expression of identity—both the identity of the interviewee and the imagined identity of an employee who legitimately "belongs" in the workplace.

We can see in many of these life stories how the discourses of racial justice, the market, and religious faith can help to position our interviewees in relation to rights. When Ron Zander invokes the discourse of racial justice, he constructs his own identity as a capable worker with a learning disability and argues that discrimination against him on the basis of his disability would be a violation of his rights. The discourse of racial justice is a powerful tool that helps Ron to explain how well he matches up against the "typical" employee and how unfair it would be to treat him differently because of his disability. At the same time, however, when Ron uses the discourse of racial justice, he comes up against his own hesitations about affirmative action claims and for this reason finds it hard to make a rights-based argument in favor of reasonable accommodations for people with learning disabilities. The same discourse that helps Ron articulate a connection between rights and the hiring and firing of workers with disabilities also makes it difficult for him to articulate a connection between rights and on-the-job accommodations.

When Sid Tegler uses the discourse of the market, he signals his support for the cost-benefit evaluations that he considers central to the labor market. By speaking the language of the marketplace, he enhances his identity as a player within it rather than as a "disabled" and disaffected outsider. Sid also uses this discourse to emphasize the irrationality of excluding him from employment on the basis of extraneous considerations—such as physical appearance or erroneously exaggerated assumptions about his incapacity—rather than a hard-nosed assessment of Sid's potential contribution to the bottom line. Sid does not, however, conclude that ADA rights should be invoked when prejudice leads to a distorted cost-benefit analysis. For Sid, unlike Sean O'Brian, the analysis of costs and benefits implies a rejection of rights and a total reliance on the mechanisms of the market eventually to root out discrimination and injustice.

For Georgia Steeb, her frequent use of the discourse of religious faith reinforces her highly ambivalent view of rights. The more she adheres to her Christian beliefs, the more she thinks that she should forgive those who treat her unfairly. Yet her knowledge of disability law makes her keenly aware of treatment that could be considered a violation of her rights. Whether to invoke her rights in an adversarial fashion or to forgive those who violate them is a dilemma for Georgia. Significantly, this dilemma is less urgent for Sean O'Brian, who uses the discourse of faith to establish a clear boundary between the situations that call for the invocation of legal rights and the situations that call for self-sufficiency and generosity toward others.

In considering how rights become active and what role they actually play in the lives of their intended beneficiaries, we think it useful to view rights in relation to the discourses individuals use to perceive, evaluate, and discuss their experience of unfairness. ADA rights intersect with familiar discourses in everyday life and cannot be considered in isolation from them. The interplay of rights with such discourses, however, does not produce a predictable outcome in each instance but becomes part of a broader process through which individuals with disabilities use the resources available to them to construct understandings of self and work. These discourses provide a vocabulary and a set of concepts with which one can evaluate experiences with employment and determine whether those experiences fall short of expectations. Each discourse provides a means by which individuals can express their sense of hope and disappointment, satisfaction and frustration, justice and injustice. By examining these discourses in relation to the ADA, we can advance our understanding of how rights become active in the lives of men and women with disabilities in American society.

five

Life Story: Rosemary Sauter

Rosemary Sauter sees herself reflected in her son, Billy. She was in her mid-forties when we first interviewed her, and Billy was a junior in high school. From his earliest years in primary school, he had struggled with writing and math. Rosemary argued for several years with teachers and school administrators, who refused to acknowledge Billy's special needs and labeled her an overprotective mother. When he was finally diagnosed with a learning disability in the fourth grade, he was sent to a segregated school where he spent two years in a special education class "learning nothing, absolutely nothing." Not until middle school did he begin to receive educational accommodations in a mainstream academic setting.

Billy's experience with special education law and procedures taught Rosemary a great deal about herself and led her to reexamine her entire life history and her plans for the future. "That's when I started figuring out, my brain works as bad as his, but I had actually learned to compensate where he was just lost." Although she had learned to compensate for what she now understands to have been her own learning disability, however, she had always thought that her problems arose from a lack of intelligence: "I never realized, I just thought I was slow. I thought I was dumb. That was what I was. I really did think I was dumb." Her own diagnosis resulted directly from her experience as an advocate for Billy.

It is startling to realize that you are not the person you always thought you were. What would Rosemary do with this knowledge, this new sense of self? The choices available to her in mid-life were liberating; Rosemary could now undertake things that she had previously thought impossible. Yet no one can step completely out of one skin and put on another. Rosemary's personality was constructed out of elements from her past, from experiences, perceptions, and relationships stretching over many years, even though some important aspects of that past—as she now realized—were based on a mistake, on an erroneous understanding. Rosemary's life history before reaching this crossroads in her forties was a unique adventure in which a bright and resourceful young woman struggled against misperception and stereotype.

Rosemary's father was the oldest of nine children born to Polish immigrants. He dropped out of school after the fourth grade and worked as a cabinetmaker and a factory foreman. Rosemary's mother went as far as the eleventh grade but then became a machine operator and a seamstress. Both parents left school because of the Depression, yet Rosemary is convinced that her father also had a learning disability and that the condition is hereditary within her family. Rosemary's father was very strict and used a barber strap to punish his children for their supposed inattentiveness in school. Rosemary recalls frequent reproach and punishment for her academic shortcomings, which she blamed on herself: "I had a very low self-esteem. . . . I felt I was stupid. . . . It took a long time to finally figure out I really wasn't stupid, I just learn differently."

The biggest disciplinarian was my mother, not my father. I had that switched [in our first interview], which is not that unusual of me. . . . She would always say, if you don't behave your father's going to [use the barber's strap]. He did it a couple of times, but she would do it mostly.

Rosemary actually worked quite hard in school, but she was perceived—by others and by herself—as lazy and incompetent. Her response was to become "the class clown," a free spirit inclined toward creative and rebellious behavior in the face of unsympathetic teachers and parents. Some of her recollections of those years are both hilarious and poignant. In a Catholic primary school, she "used to drive the sisters nuts" and was frequently thrown out of class.

> I took off on the nuns one time and hid, because I didn't want to be in school that day; and I hid downstairs in the old ash cans that they had under the stairs. And the whole school, they had the police, the fire

department, everybody out looking for me. They found me about five o'clock at night. The janitor found me. I was in the ash can. . . . I got bored, so I fell asleep in the ash can. And of course when you hear the nuns with those, remember those old beads that they used to wear, you know, the big old long habits? When you heard the beads, you just sat there and froze, because if they found you, they'd beat the tar out of you.

Rosemary remembers being sent to the Sister Superior's office so frequently that she actually had her own desk there. Once the Sister Superior called Rosemary's father to the school and locked Rosemary in a small paper closet until he arrived:

It was a small little closet, and she put a couple of reams of paper in and she said, Now you sit here." And she locked me in there, and I climbed to the top shelf. . . . And it was funny, because she told my father, she said, "When you get home, you beat this child to an inch of her life." She opened the door, and there's no kid. The kid's gone, you know, and my father saw me up top. He said the face on the nun was like, "How can she get out of here now?" But he said it was priceless, because this nun just went, well she went crazy.

The story conveys Rosemary's recollection of a defiant and rebellious childhood, but it also shows another side of her father. Although a harsh disciplinarian himself, this anecdote characterizes him as a covert ally of his daughter in her ongoing struggle against the authority of the Sister Superior. Perhaps he understood from his own experience that much of her behavior resulted from hyperactivity that she simply could not control.

Her own peers seemed to understand Rosemary better than did her teachers. In high school, for example, she was still the "class devil." There were only three minutes between classes, and everyone knew that during one changeover Rosemary went from a class on the third floor to the first floor by sliding down the banister. Everyone made allowances for her except the principal, who was determined to catch her in the act and punish her. The result was predictable: "I took out the principal coming off [the banister], and he stood right there and I just, bam, and that was it. There was no stopping after three floors. I mean I was coming down, and everybody knew I slid that banister everyday."

If I had a kid that did half the stuff I did, I would have killed him. I really would. [Laughs.] The child would not have made adulthood. I don't know how my parents coped with me, I really don't. My mother prayed that I would have another one like me, which I did. I have my son. [Laughs.] And my father just took it with a grain of salt. He said I was just hyperactive. I was always on the go.

Rosemary's rebellious behavior reflects her hyperactivity in a sternly regimented environment, but it also reflects her frustration with schoolwork. Like many individuals with learning disabilities, Rosemary found some academic tasks extremely easy and others extremely difficult. Math was her strength, and she had an exceptional memory. Reading was nearly impossible: she reversed letters, could not decode hyphenated words, and had trouble tracking a text line by line. She was held back for a year in primary school, but her underlying disability was never diagnosed. Her teachers thought she was lazy and undisciplined. Only one teacher saw Rosemary's true potential. In sixth grade, Miss Kennedy worked long hours with Rosemary after school and showed her how to develop her own idiosyncratic approach to reading. Unlike the other teachers, Miss Kennedy told Rosemary that she was "a very bright and intelligent child. I just needed to learn how I learned. And she was the only one that would actually stay there and work with me. . . . She thought I had trouble organizing things. She used to tell me I need to work on my organization, which is part of being hyperactive. You're just concentrating on so much, you can't concentrate on anything."

Rosemary found that many doors were shut because of what she and most of her teachers assumed was her lack of ability. Other doors were shut because of her gender. Rosemary obviously did have ability in math, and she developed a related interest in mechanical drawing, but she was discouraged from pursuing these subjects because they were inappropriate for girls:

> It was funny, because when I was in school, anything that I really wanted to do, any kind of course I wanted to take, I was interested in mechanical drawing. Girls weren't even in that, but I was interested because of the math and all that kind of, and girls don't do that. You can't do that. So it seemed that everything I really thought I could do, everyone was telling me you can't do that, you have to do this. So then I thought, why bother? . . . Back then, if it was an all-boy class, there was no way they were going to let a girl in there. They just, forget it, you can't take it. Because their thought was, the only reason you want to take that class is because the boys are in there. That's what they would say to you, "That's only a boys' class, what are you trying to do, pick up a guy?" And you just look at them, and you'd say, "Well, I'm interested in all this stuff." "That's not what a girl's interested in."

Rosemary's father again was her covert ally in defying these gender-based conventions. He taught her his woodworking skills—"And I can swing a hammer really good." But it was Rosemary's mother who helped her find what was then considered a more gender-appropriate outlet for her talents and energy. In her early teens, Rosemary had developed considerable ability in dance and acrobatics. At the age of fourteen, she passed an audition for the New York City Ballet and could have moved to New York City to begin training. Her parents, however, were unwilling to let their "wild child," as she now refers to herself, leave home and live on her own. She then "auditioned for Las Vegas, until they found out I was only fourteen." Next, because of her skills on the trapeze, she almost joined a cousin who was a circus performer; but her cousin was reluctant to assume responsibility for her and did not feel that the circus life would be a good choice.

I had done a flying ladder routine in a small touring circus, so I had already done that. And then when the circus came and my cousin was there, I used the excuse with my mother: Well, my cousin's there, I can go with him. Well my cousin [said], I don't want no fifteen year old, no way. I mean, he was panicking, because he thought, Oh my God, she's only fifteen. That's a responsibility, and he didn't want any more responsibility than the man in the moon.

Rosemary's mother apparently became concerned about the likelihood that her teenage daughter would drop out of school and leave home. She decided to help Rosemary set up her own business as owner and operator of a dance studio at the age of fifteen. Rosemary taught dance everyday after school until nine o'clock at night. With her mother's help, she created a successful business, earning more money than some of her teachers. More important, she created a life and an identity outside of school that provided a counterweight to her daily academic frustrations and failures. Her dance studio convinced her that she was a capable and potentially successful person, and it placed school in perspective. The negative messages communicated by her teachers became less important. When teachers told her, "You'll never get a job," she could discount their views since she already had quite a good job. When she struggled in a high school course on business management, she could dismiss the criticisms of her teacher because, in her informed view, he was too academic and impractical in his understanding of the real world of business. Her academically superior classmates, as she discovered later at a class reunion, "were scared to death of me because I had my own business. They said I intimidated them."

With her mother's support, then, Rosemary created a parallel life that sustained her during her teenage years. The "free spirit" and rebellious student learned self-confidence and responsibility and was persuaded that she could stay in her parents' home while still giving socially appropriate expression to her unique abilities. At times, she wanted to drop out of school and devote all her effort to her dance studio. Indeed, her sister, who also had a learning disability, refused to attend school after the ninth grade and dropped out to become a meat wrapper in a grocery store. In Rosemary's case, her father put his foot down. He told her: " 'Well, you better do your best and pass, because you are *not* going to quit high school. You *will* graduate.' So it was down to the point where either I graduated or I was going to be in school until I was ninety. He said he didn't care if I was the oldest high school student there, I was still going to graduate."

As firmly as her father insisted on Rosemary's completing high school, however, he just as firmly opposed her going to college. Rosemary considered becoming a nurse, but she recalls that his old-world attitudes rejected this option out of hand: "His family was from Poland, and they didn't believe girls went to school. Girls did not get an education. Girls got married and had children. . . . My mother would have loved for us to have gone on, but father ruled the roost." Rosemary also considered going on for a bachelor's degree in theater, perhaps to work on scenery or costume design, but her father said, " 'I can't see spending 10, 15, 20 thousand dollars on education that you're going to go into theater.' He just thought that was stupid." Instead, Rosemary was supposed to continue with her dance studio after graduating from high school, until she got married and had children. From Rosemary's perspective, however, the dance studio had served its purpose and was becoming too much of a burden after nine years.

When Rosemary married, she was relieved of the burden of running the studio, but once again the decision was not her own. It was her husband who "decided I'd stay home" and shut down the studio. Although a man was still making crucial decisions about her life, Rosemary welcomed the change. Her first child was born when Rosemary was twenty-three years old, and she stayed at home to raise her child and run her household.

I separated from my first husband after we were married seven and a half months. It was a short marriage. He didn't want the dancing studio. He was threatened by it because I made more money than he did. That was a threat. With the dance studio, I was self-sufficient. It was something I could do, I did well. But as a teacher at the time, I made twice as much money a week as he did, and it was a self-esteem thing. So being stupid and naive at the time, I sold the studio thinking everything was going to be fine. I was going to have children. I'd stay home and be the mommy. . . .

At that point, after nine years, I had had enough [of the dance studio]. I was getting tired. You work six and seven days a week, because when you own your own business there's no rest. You don't have a day off. . . .

[I was a single mother] for about three and a half years. I worked at a toy factory, and then I went to another little place where I made starters for motor boats. And that was very good money. And then I was in the big layoff, way back in the seventies, when Ford was the president. And I met my [second] husband, and we've been married for twenty-four years now. . . . My second husband said he wished I had still had the school. He would have worked with me hand in hand with it. . . . He says, "I'd have quit work and worked the dancing school with you." The difference is, he didn't care that I was making a lot of money at the time. To my second husband, it didn't make a difference. And I make good money now.

As Billy progressed through school, Rosemary began to understand the reasons for her own academic frustrations and failures and asked herself what might be possible if she had appropriate accommodations of her own. She began to consider college again. Two elderly women for whom she provided homecare urged her to study nursing. Rosemary told them, "I'm too stupid. I'm too old."

Perhaps at this stage she did not fully believe that she lacked intelligence, and one of the women challenged her directly: "You are not stupid. You are far from stupid." Rosemary decided that the woman might be right. She enrolled in a local college, intending to train as a nursing assistant because she felt that she was "too old and not smart enough to become a nurse." Advisers at the college persuaded her otherwise. In her first semester, she got very good grades, in part because she was receiving appropriate support from the college learning center and from a faculty member who understood her special learning needs and provided one-on-one coaching. Her experiences in nursing school were generally positive, but occasionally she still encountered difficulties with unsympathetic authority figures.

In my last year of nursing school, I had a clinical instructor who did not want me in her clinical because I was dyslexic. And I had a very hard clinical. It taught me to endure anything, let me tell you. . . . [She said,] "I just don't want anybody with a learning disability. I can't handle it." . . . I felt kind of like I was a second class citizen. You know, like it was starting all over again. . . . My girlfriends couldn't understand why she would constantly be picking on me. She would go in and look and see how I made a bed. She told me I didn't make the bed right. There was nothing wrong with the bed, but this was her way of getting at you. She didn't like the way I handed out medicine. She didn't like the way I wrote. She didn't like the way I printed. . . . [Other students] would go back to the head of our whole nursing group there and tell her, "I can't understand why she is constantly picking on Rosemary." . . . She could have failed me. In fact, she told me at the second week of our semester that she was going to fail me; there was no way she was ever going to let me pass. Because people with learning disabilities don't belong in nursing. And that was prejudice on her part. . . . She's in a position of authority. Either she's going to pass you or she's not. And you have no choice. . . .

Rosemary completed her nursing degree and has now begun to view herself as capable and intelligent. She intends to work as a nurse, but she is also considering further studies at the local university. Her difficulty with writing no longer seems an insuperable obstacle to her work or her studies. As she points out, nurses often use tape recorders for dictation rather than writing out their reports, so this academic accommodation could be readily adapted to her work environment without disrupting existing routines. Moreover, she has found that she can write quickly and effectively on a personal computer, which is also becoming a normal part of many workplaces.

Since Rosemary "found out what the law's like with Billy," her own self-understanding has been deeply affected. She knows that the law applies to her as well as Billy and that the arguments she makes on his behalf could support her own claims as well. Although she still thinks of herself at times as stupid, she would strenuously resist describing Billy in this way. She sees him as a bright

young man with a distinctive style of learning and expression, and she understands that he is legally entitled to accommodations in order to participate fully
in mainstream social settings. If she makes these arguments for Billy, how could
she deny their applicability to herself now that she, too, in her mid-forties, has a
similar diagnosis of learning disability? Her transformed self emerges cautiously
from the cocoon of her old self. She sees life and career possibilities that are not
unlimited but are far more extensive than those that had been available to her in
her teens and early twenties. As Billy prepares himself for higher education and
a career, so does his mother.

*[During the five years since our first interview with Rosemary, she has held
several nursing jobs and has even taken some postgraduate coursework. She
currently works as an operating room nurse. Her son, Billy, entered college
and enjoyed some academic success before neglecting his studies in favor of
partying. Rosemary and her husband encouraged Billy to leave school and
get a job. He is now "working his way up" the ladder in a large entertain-
ment company. As for Rosemary herself, she has achieved full acceptance
as a member of the nursing profession, even when her learning disability is
known by the doctors and other nurses.]*

*I go and tell [my supervisors], "I'm dyslexic. I will do some things backwards. I
will write some words backwards occasionally." . . . My supervisor said, "Don't
tell anybody. . . . If you slip up spelling, we'll catch it." . . . One of the big things
when I was doing ambulatory surgery is "patient denies pain" or "patient denies
anything." And I was writing "denise." And finally one of the girls said to me,
"Who's Denise?" "What?" And then that's when they realized, and they started
laughing. They thought it was funny, and I did too. I thought it was a joke. I said,
"I'm dyslexic. I just transposed the letters."*

*Certain doctors have a certain pattern. Like if I'm going to hand you this
[instrument], some doctors want you to flip it one way, some want you to flip
it another. . . . This one doctor is really cute, because I always did it backwards,
and he says, "What are you, dyslexic?" And I went, "Yes." And he just cracked
up! It shocked him, because here he was saying it as a joke to somebody, saying
"What are you, dyslexic? Because you are always doing it backwards." And I said
to him, "Yes, I am." He just said, okay. . . . What happened after that, he would
just say, "Make sure you get on the other side." I said okay, because I would
hand it the opposite way. And it would, he would just, it would become a joke
afterwards.*

*I belong to the union. If there's a problem [at work], you go to the union
steward. Unless I'm doing something drastically wrong, there is nothing they
can do. Like my supervisor, she can't fire me because I'm dyslexic. She can't get
rid of me because she doesn't like the way I write. She can't. I have a union. . . .*

[Rosemary observes that her hospital has some employees with physical dis-abilities. Asked how their hiring came about, she responds:] The laws for the handicapped. Because if somebody couldn't walk, you wouldn't have gotten a job twenty years ago. . . . [Q: Does that law cover you, too?] I don't know. [Laughs.] I really don't know. . . . But I do know that education has brought up a lot of the things with people with learning disabilities, a lot different. It's made people aware that you're not dumb. I always say, I'm not dumb. I just march to a different drummer. I just do things a little differently.

The Effect of Social Circumstances on Rights and Identity

In chapter 4, we suggested that familiar discourses—distinctive ways of thinking and talking about everyday experiences—affect how rights become active or remain dormant. The discourses of race, market, and faith are powerful and appealing because they are explicitly normative, and our interviewees use them to explain their preferences for particular qualities or actions. But how is it that different individuals adopt different discursive frameworks when they talk about themselves, their disabilities, their careers, and their legal rights? The evidence from our interviews points to the importance of social circumstances in this regard. The use of one interpretive frame rather than another depends in large measure on the resources people bring to the narrative task. We use the term "resources" in its broadest sense to include upbringing, education, wealth, and social relationships, as well as personal attributes such as imagination, character, congeniality, and perseverance. In this chapter, we argue that access—or lack of access—to these resources affects life stories, and hence the process of identity formation, in ways that make it more or less likely that employment rights under the Americans with Disabilities Act (ADA) will become active.

We suggest that individuals construct their sense of self out of the materials that are available to them at different points in their lives, and we believe that one's social circumstances can help to explain differing assumptions about careers and rights. For example, families that provide more supportive relationships, have greater knowledge of a disability and its effects, or have instilled useful philosophical or religious values, or families with greater wealth, may offer individuals more alternatives in constructing an identity and career (see generally Gerber and Reiff 1991). Some of these qualities vary predictably along familiar patterns of social difference, such as differences of social class. Other social characteristics might have less predictable implications such as race, gender, and religious beliefs.[1] In this chapter we focus primarily on resources related to family, social class, and race, and we ask how these resources contribute to the telling of life stories and the perception of rights. In chapter 6, we conclude our analysis with a consideration of gender.

We focus here, as we have throughout the book, on the process of identity formation and its relationship to rights. Our discussion in this chapter relates closely to the analysis we began in chapter 4 with our consideration of discourses. We earlier made the point that identity is best seen in light of its *narrative* and its *interactive* qualities. Social and cultural resources become available to individuals at different moments in their lives as they attempt to *narrate* their sense of self, to draw on particular discursive frameworks to talk about their past and future and determine the trajectory of a career. These discursive acts, in turn, combine with other factors to shape *social interactions* and lead to the distribution of identity among family, friends, coworkers, and others. Throughout the process of identity formation, individuals continually reevaluate their self-concept and their sense that they are being treated fairly or unfairly, that they are positioned appropriately or inappropriately in relation to mainstream social experiences such as employment.

We see the significance of some of these social factors in the life story of Rosemary Sauter, which precedes this chapter. Rosemary's identity formation was influenced by the values and work ethic of her parents, who discouraged her, when she was still a teenager, from attending the New York City Ballet School, going to Las Vegas, or joining the circus, but instead taught her to channel her energies and entrepreneurial talents into her small dance studio. Her parents' working-class background and limited education led them to instill certain values in their children, including the priority of practical academic studies over "impractical" subjects such as theater. Rosemary's identity and career evolved as she availed herself of the resources at hand, although her choices were limited by gendered assumptions about appropriate roles for young women, mothers with young children, and middle-aged women reentering the job market (see our discussion of gender in chapter 6).

Rosemary consistently perceived and evaluated her experiences in terms of the frameworks that were available to her at different turning points in her life. Today, she is more inclined than in the past to label a hypothetical act of employment discrimination as unfair, although she

1. "Personal background variables alone should not predict employment integration or economic opportunity for qualified persons with disabilities. Recent studies, however, point to the emerging relationship of gender, race, and disability to possible workforce participation and advancement" (Blanck 1994:875–76).

says little about the law that might be invoked on her own behalf. A sense of her own entitlement has begun to stir as a result of advocacy for her son Billy, whose learning disability resembles her own, and Rosemary's disability support services in college paralleled those she had obtained for Billy in junior and senior high school. But her thoughts about employment rights under the ADA are not well formed, and by the time of our reinterview Rosemary had begun a successful career without any consciousness of her rights. Her orientation toward rights at each stage of her life was to some degree influenced by new social and cultural resources then available to her, but also reflected the lasting influence of the resources that shaped her identity and career during childhood.

In the discussion that follows, we begin by examining the life stories of Louise Dobbs, William Thomas, and Evelyn Gardner, as we consider how resources associated with family, social class, race, and other social factors influence the impact of the ADA on careers and career planning, making legal rights more or less relevant to the experiences of individuals in different circumstances. We then consider the element of timing, illustrated by the life stories of Sara Lane and Bill Meier, who found that different resources were available to them depending on whether a disability began early or later in life. We argue that resource differences in relation to disability and career stage have important implications for the role the ADA plays in the lives of our interviewees. We conclude with a summary of the process through which social factors influence identity formation and career trajectory and help to determine how and when ADA rights become active. Because none of our interviewees invoked the ADA in a formal rights claim, our question is what effect these social factors have on the other ways in which rights become active—including the capacity of rights to change self-perceptions, cause cultural and discursive shifts, and transform social and institutional contexts.

The Influence of Family, Social Class, and Race

In this section, we present the life stories of Louise Dobbs, William Thomas, and Evelyn Gardner as we explore the influence of family, social class, and race on discourse, career, and the role of rights. In Louise Dobbs's story, which is notable for a nearly complete absence of rights in any form, we emphasize the importance of family and social class. In William Thomas's story, which illustrates the context-creating effects of rights, we consider family and social class in conjunction with race. In Evelyn Gardner's story, in which rights affect self-perception as well as play a context-creating role, we discuss family, social class, and race and the significance of her status as an African immigrant in the United States.

Louise Dobbs

Louise Dobbs's life story dramatically illustrates how the absence of social and economic resources can prevent employment rights under the ADA from becoming active, even in the most subtle or indirect ways. From the beginning, Louise's relatively meager resources profoundly limited her perceptions of self and career. She was raised in a working-class family plagued by alcoholism, poverty, and psychological distress. Her stepfather, a truck driver, had a serious drinking problem. He and Louise did not get along, and Louise, the oldest of seven children, depended primarily on her mother for advice and guidance. Her mother's life was also troubled, and the suicide of Louise's younger brother dealt the family a blow from which it never recovered. Louise was not a good student. Because of her family's poverty, she had to pick fruit and vegetables while still in middle school in order to help the family make ends meet. By the end of the eighth grade, when Louise was sixteen, her parents advised her to quit school. Her studies were not going well, and they needed her to contribute more money toward the family's survival. Louise did as her parents wanted. She never had other friends or relatives to whom she could turn for advice. As she now recalls, "I was always by myself." Her mother was an important influence; there was no one else.

At the age of sixteen, Louise began a series of low-wage, manual labor jobs that were to continue until she suffered a serious stroke in mid-life. She cleaned houses, made pizzas, worked on an assembly line at a wax factory making novelty items, and waited on tables. At the age of twenty, she married Mike Dobbs who, like her stepfather, was a truck driver, and they had five children together. They moved to the south and southwest several times to attempt to improve their circumstances, but these efforts never succeeded. They were dogged by bad luck, and their friends and business partners took advantage of them. On one occasion, their apartment burned down, and they lost all of their possessions. On another occasion, while they were attempting to start a new trucking company, Mike's business partner tricked him and left Mike and Louise destitute. On yet another occasion, Mike got involved with some illegal business practices in Alabama and was convicted and sentenced to prison. After each incident, Louise returned to Buffalo to live with her mother until she could resume her own low-wage employment.

Louise's last job was cutting chicken wings at a poultry farm. She worked seventy hours a week and her wages were a penny for each pound of wings she cut. On a good day, "if you hustled," she could cut 1,300 to 1,500 pounds of wings. Shortly after Louise started work as a chicken cutter, her husband was released from prison, and they divorced. Louise continued at this job for twelve years, until one day she collapsed at work. The cause of her condition was unclear, but she had lost substantial control over her muscles and was unable to return to employment. Over time, she became completely paralyzed on one side. Her doctors began to suspect that she had suffered a stroke. She entered rehabilitation and began to improve somewhat, and Mike returned to help her.

Then Louise experienced another series of catastrophes. Mike died unexpectedly. Shortly thereafter, her mother died, as did a nephew with whom she had a close relationship. Perhaps as a result of these multiple losses, Louise says, "I started going down," and she returned to therapy. Walking was very difficult. There was some improvement, but within a few years her condition worsened. By the time of our interview, Louise had to use a wheelchair when she left her house. She was isolated, without prospects, and deeply discouraged about her future.

Louise expresses a hope that she might work again, but she is unable to imagine a job she might perform. She had done manual labor all her life and had always worked with both hands. Louise could not imagine working with just one hand, nor could she think of a process by which she might seek work as a person with a disability. She was alone, and there was no one from whom she could seek advice or encouragement. She was aware of Vocational and Educational Services for Individuals with Disabilities (VESID), the rehabilitation agency in the state of New York that serves as a resource for persons with disabilities, but during her single contact with VESID she was told that she should return when she was ready to go to school or work. Because of her persistent medical problems, Louise felt unable to do either of these things. When we asked what she saw for herself in the near future, rather than offering even a tentative plan she replied, "I really don't know."

Louise's disability and career trajectory superficially resemble those of Barry Swygert, whose life story we discussed in chapter 2. Because of the increasingly incapacitating effects of a spinal tumor, Barry's professional identity was also transformed in mid-career. Yet it is difficult to imagine two life stories more different than Barry and Louise's. Barry was able to reshape his identity as a successful professional and launch a new career in public relations and disability advocacy. By contrast,

Louise had no contact with her employer at the poultry plant after the day she collapsed on the job, nor did she ever speak to another employer about returning to work. Whereas Barry Swygert successfully redefined himself as an employee, Louise Dobbs appeared unable to project herself beyond her current situation, and she passively accepted a condition of isolation, inactivity, and unemployment. She did not know about the ADA; she never viewed herself as a person with rights whom the law might help to work again. Nor did her employer or her work environment reflect the indirect, context-creating influence of the ADA in any way that proved helpful to Louise.

One of the most striking differences between Louise and Barry is that of social class. Louise's inability to move toward employment after the onset of her disability—by returning to school, for example—was not merely a failure of imagination, nor was it a simple limitation in her self-perception that prevented her from seeing viable opportunities that were actually available to her. Barry Swygert's education and middle-class upbringing gave him numerous career advantages, and many of them remained after he became physically incapacitated. By contrast, Louise Dobbs's education was poor, and her family never encouraged her in this regard. They had pushed Louise into taking low-skill and low-wage labor as quickly as possible, even at the expense of her education, so that she could help the family out of its poverty. Her employment history prior to her disability was spotty and unrewarding. Nothing in her history before the onset of her disability gave her the confidence to attempt either to return to school or to carve out a job appropriate to her skills. Moreover, manual labor (literally, "hand" labor) is exceedingly difficult with only one hand, and in this sense her disability was more disabling in terms of employment than was Barry Swygert's quadriplegia for the middle-class professional work he did. Louise's perceptions of career possibilities after her disability were informed by her limited education and her lifelong working-class experience prior to her injury. In order to continue working, Louise would have had to transform the nature of her employment relatively late in life. Nothing in her social origins or in her self-perceived identity had prepared her to attempt such a radical transformation, nor did she view herself as legally entitled to do so.

By considering class, family, social isolation, and conceptions of self, we can begin to understand why Louise's response to her disability differed so strikingly from Barry's, although physically he was more incapacitated than she. Furthermore, given the low wages for which Louise had worked most of her life, it is quite possible that her disability benefits left her just as well off financially as she could expect to be if she succeeded in regaining employment. This was not the case for Barry, whose income level was substantially higher than Louise's.

For Louise, then, there was no significant difference between her current situation and the career trajectory she could envision for herself. The lack of a difference between aspiration and existing circumstances left her with no way of thinking and talking about herself, no discourse, in which concepts of rights might seem relevant, even if she had known about the ADA. At one point, we asked Louise if laws existed to assist a prospective employee with a disability who sought accommodations from a reluctant employer. She replied, "I have no idea." She was then asked to imagine herself in a dialogue with an employer in which she described the accommodations that might permit her to do the work. If the employer refused to provide those accommodations, she stated, "Well then I wouldn't take the job." Perhaps, she added, a counselor from VESID might offer some advice. If the employer changed his mind, she said, "I would take the job." But if the VESID counselor offered his or her suggestions and the employer rejected them, she said, "Then I wouldn't take it." If there were a law, for example, requiring an employer to install a ramp for a wheelchair, would that help? "Probably. I'd be able to get in and out," she replied. But if the employer acknowledged the existence of such a law and still refused to install the ramp, where would that leave her? She answered, "It leaves me without a job."

What is striking in this terse exchange is the absence of a flexible or expansive vision of self, work, and law. Lacking many other resources—relational, financial, educational, and intellectual—Louise is equally unable to conceive of law as a resource she might use. Because she cannot imagine a career that connects her present and past to some future employment, she cannot imagine a space within which employment rights for persons with disabilities might operate. Because her current situation seems to her a "natural" outgrowth of her prior work and life experiences, she does not perceive an illegality on which the law might act to ensure her a place in the world of employment. Her perceptions in this regard are apparently shared by her former employer and by her few remaining friends and relatives. For Louise Dobbs, the ADA's employment rights—if there are such things—are entirely irrelevant to her.

William Thomas

William Thomas and Evelyn Gardner are young African American adults with learning disabilities. In some ways, race affects William and Evelyn similarly as they plan their careers. Both of them experienced the stereotyped perceptions and prejudices of others. Such stereotypes, it has been observed,[2] may alter the experience of an African American child with a learning disability, because teachers and school administrators conflate the symptoms of a learning disability with negative preconceptions about the adolescent behavior of minorities. To some extent, both William and Evelyn were affected by this interaction of disability and the social disadvantages connected with racial difference. While the experience of an African American with a disability may be distinctive, it is also complex. William's and Evelyn's race played a part in their experiences, yet their experiences were quite different. By exploring these similarities and differences in detail, we can understand some of the various ways in which race-related social factors can influence the impact of the ADA on discourses and the shaping of careers.

William Thomas grew up in a poor, urban, African American neighborhood. William's family environment, his early alienation from school, and what he describes as a dangerous neighborhood resemble the circumstances and experiences of many African Americans coming of age in America's inner cities. Evelyn Gardner, on the other hand, was born in a small country in Africa. At the age of twelve, Evelyn's working-class but upwardly mobile parents sent her from Africa to a small upstate New York town to complete her high school and college education. As an adolescent she became an immigrant living in a white American community. Race and class played a role in forming both William's and Evelyn's perceptions of disability, career, and rights, but their experiences were also shaped by their very different family and community origins.

William's teachers diagnosed his learning disability at an early age, and he received special education services throughout his school career. The resources mandated by special education law (a context-creating effect of rights under the Individuals with Disabilities Education Act [IDEA]) have been helpful to William and kept him in school even when many of his friends and classmates dropped out. But William faced other challenges growing up in a poor family in a tough neighborhood. As he prepares to graduate from high school, William considers the main factors shaping his career aspirations to be his placement in a foster home, his mentoring by a neighborhood locksmith who has employed him, and, above all, his ability to play basketball. William's legal rights and his educational entitlements, although important in some ways, have been secondary to these life-altering social and personal factors.

2. See generally Glennon 1995:1333 concerning "the ways in which unconscious and structural racism combine to track African-American students into special education."

William is a star basketball player, and his grades throughout high school have remained high enough to allow him to stay on the team. He was elected student council president in his junior year, and was recruited by colleges interested in his talent as an athlete. By the time of our interview, William had committed himself to attend a nearby junior college. This important career step was not always a likelihood for William Thomas. Earlier in his life, William experienced difficulties that might have prevented him from going to college and embarking on a successful career. In elementary school, William had difficulty reading and writing because of his learning disability. Resource room[3] was available to him as an accommodation for his disability, but he lacked the motivation to do well in school. He often got in trouble and was disciplined. Because his teachers knew he was smart, they promoted him even though he did failing work in several grades. As he entered junior high school, things changed for the worse. School became harder, and teachers were less tolerant.

As a young boy, William received little guidance or encouragement at home. His greatest challenge was not in school or in preparing himself for the future, but rather the challenge he faced on the street. In the neighborhood in which he grew up, according to his current recollections, William had to fight every day. Once, in order to keep from being picked on, he fought the neighborhood gang leader on the sidewalk in front of his home as forty or fifty other boys watched. Although he has since moved to a foster home in another part of the city, William still has friends in his former neighborhood who hang out on the streets or sell drugs.

Overcoming the hazards of the street life in his community has been a key to William's career. During his critical junior high school years, William, unlike many of his friends, was able to establish goals for himself, stay out of trouble, and become a better student. William associates two factors with his transition from street kid and poor student to star athlete and college-bound high school graduate: basketball and the lessons he learned from the neighborhood locksmith for whom he works. In junior high school, just when classes became extremely difficult for William, he grew taller, developed physically, and discovered he had unusual athletic potential. By ninth grade he was a starting varsity basketball player. In high school, he recalls, he possessed "clout"

---

3. A "resource room program" is defined as "a special education program for a student with a disability registered in either a special class or a regular class who needs specialized supplementary instruction in an individual or small group setting for a portion of the day" (N.Y. Comp. Codes R. & Regs. tit. 8, §200.1(rr) (1985)).

because he was big and good at basketball. Teachers would give him a break if he was late for school and had a good excuse.

William also matured in other ways. While he knew he had special standing as a basketball star, William was careful not to abuse the privileges that accompanied his status. He attributes his sensible behavior in part to "good guidance" from teachers who liked him, but he particularly mentions the mentoring by the locksmith who has employed him since junior high school and has taught him the "virtues"—which include "how to be a man, how to carry yourself, how to carry adversity." William practiced these virtues in dealing with customers as an apprentice locksmith. He learned, among other things, how to apply himself, working late on some occasions without expectation of special praise, simply because the job required it.

One might expect that many of the virtues of adult identity that William learned from his employer-mentor would have been conveyed by a parent's instruction or example, but William seldom mentions his parents. Nevertheless, "family" provided a third important ingredient in William's escape from the risks of the street. When he reached junior high school, William was removed from his parents' home and placed with a foster family in a racially mixed, but less troubled, neighborhood. William does not say much about this important move, but he does observe that when his old friends get involved with selling drugs, he now goes home to the family he calls his "grandparents." Referring to his foster parents, he says "my family is strong." This family has provided a steadying influence. His "grandparents" have represented him in negotiations with his high school for the accommodations he receives for his disability.

Unless asked, William does not mention his learning disability, but it seems to have had a negative effect on his self-esteem, as it did for many of our interviewees who were frustrated by their inability to read or write with facility.[4] Through hard work, and with the assistance of

---

4. Similarly, West et al. (1993:462) note that a "barrier identified by a large number of students with disabilities centered on the social isolation, ostracism, or scorn they felt from their instructors and fellow students, either because of their disabilities or because they requested accommodations to which other students were not entitled." In her research, Glennon (1995:1240–41) has encountered this sentiment as well:

> While many students benefit from placement in special education, students placed in special education may suffer the negative consequences of being labeled disabled by their teachers, peers, and themselves. . . . Moreover, placement in special education may diminish students' self-esteem and lead to feelings of humiliation, alienation and failure. As one former student recounted, "[t]he system is telling you that you have a disability and you can't learn at the same rate as other students." The special education label so embarrassed him that he ordered his mother not to tell anyone.

a resource room tutor provided by the school, however, William has remained academically eligible for the basketball team. As a result of the legally mandated services he has received throughout his academic career, William understands that the challenges posed by his learning disability can be overcome, and he takes for granted that he will receive accommodations as a college student. Yet his improved academic performance has not influenced his career aspirations, which remain almost unchanged from his earliest thoughts about work. As a very young boy William wanted to be a truck driver like his father, but now he aspires to become a locksmith, which he compares to working on motors, or he expects to do similar manual work. Although he has been accepted at a local junior college because of his ability to play basketball, he plans to learn practical mechanical skills. If college is too expensive, William will enter the military. His career goals are sensible and practical, but they are far more modest than those of most of our other interviewees with learning disabilities, who plan to use their college degrees to embark on white-collar professional careers. William does not perceive how legally mandated accommodations might make such a career possible for him. His thoughts about a career are undoubtedly affected by the social circumstances of his youth.

When asked directly about the role of legal rights, William makes it clear that they have only a limited relevance to his career planning. The success of William's legally mandated educational accommodations could have led him to perceive the importance of similar ADA-mandated accommodations in employment, but this does not appear to be the case. William thinks it fair for an employer to refuse to hire a prospective employee with a reading disability if the job requires reading, and he does not believe the employer should be obligated to provide accommodations in such circumstances. "If you don't get hired, you don't get hired," William concludes. An employee whose reading skills are inadequate should be treated fairly, but fair treatment does not mean offering reasonable accommodations to enable the employee to work: "You shouldn't discriminate nobody. But if it requires reading and you don't know how to do it, you just can't take the job. It's as simple as that. You just can't take the job. Or shouldn't even apply for the job if you know it's reading." William believes that accommodations should be required only to facilitate a task that the employee can already perform well, rather than a task the employee has difficulty performing. William does not focus on the legal obligations of the employer. Instead, he asserts that it is up to the employee to prove he is qualified without accommodations. William uses his basketball experience to explain how an employee with a learning disability should respond:

[Y]ou would have to keep on just showing him, just keep on showing him. Just like you playing basketball. You can do everything
else but you just can't shoot the three pointer . . . you have to keep
on shooting it. 'Cause you miss one, take the next shot. Show
him that you can shoot. It's the same thing freshman year, I had
to show . . . them I could play. . . . And all employers don't look
at what you can do. They look at how you listen, how you carry
yourself, how you act, how you treat others and stuff like that.

William's own experience with deprivation and prejudice contributes
to his emphasis on self-reliance rather than legal entitlement. He has
learned how to conduct himself responsibly as an employee, but he has
also drawn the conclusion that unfair treatment of persons with disabilities by employers may be something he will have to live with. William
believes that his career objectives must be established without reference
to the enhanced opportunities that reasonable accommodations might
make possible:

Just live with it because there's ignorant people everywhere so you
just have to learn how to live with it. And that's one of the down-
falls of having a disability. You always going to get put down. Every single day somebody always going to tell you, "Oh, you can't
read." Or somebody always going to be trying to put you down
and that's why you got to just say to yourself, "Man that's why
you just work hard. . . ." Make the ignorant people look like fools,
that's what I think. Make them look like fools.

In contrast to the spirit and purpose of the ADA, William believes that
in the employment setting his learning disability is something he must
overcome on his own. At most, an employer can be expected to "accommodate" him by employing him and assigning him a job that he
can perform without special arrangements, rather than a job that his
learning disability would make it difficult for him to perform.

At no point in the interview does William refer to his race to characterize his upbringing or treatment by others. Yet, we believe that race
played a role in shaping William's career trajectory and the role he perceives for rights. His practical but limited career aspirations are, in part,
a product of the systemic racism that affects our society. The resulting
deprivation of economic resources in his family and in his neighborhood have shaped his identity and his concept of a career. William has
had success in overcoming many of the risks posed by family difficulties,
a dangerous neighborhood, and early failure in school. William eventually found counselors, teachers, and foster parents who encouraged
him to complete high school and to consider obtaining a college educa-

tion. Indeed, race may have indirectly played a role in guiding William out of danger, since his attraction to basketball may have been partly inspired by the success local and national African American role models have enjoyed in this sport. During the interview, however, William does not invoke the discourse of racial justice to argue for the deployment of ADA rights. Although he does observe that "you shouldn't discriminate nobody," William does not think or speak about his learning disability in terms broadly analogous to the struggle of African Americans for civil rights.

Thus, while it is likely that many of William's experiences and perceptions have been shaped by his race, the role that race has played is complex. Further, many of William's experiences may be associated with the social circumstances of a working-class family or with William's individual qualities and perceptions. For these reasons, we cannot attribute his particular self-image, its relationship to his disability, or his career aspirations solely to race-related factors. Yet, in spite of his unique success relative to many of his peers, William's perception of the role of rights does reflect the fact that he grew up in a society where racism often produces inequality of wealth and opportunity. William's limited views of his own legal entitlements are closely connected to his limited career aspirations—in comparison, for example, to those of Evelyn Gardner. He cannot imagine a set of reasonable work accommodations for his learning disability. We think this is in part because he may not fully perceive his own abilities and career potential or the likelihood that accommodations could help him develop and utilize those abilities. Self-reliance, but not rights consciousness, has been the hallmark of the earliest stages of William's career. Perhaps college will transform his career path and will open a new space in which the ADA could play a role. For the time being, however, as William stands on the threshold of adulthood, the ADA has exerted little influence on the trajectory of his career.

Evelyn Gardner

Evelyn Gardner, an African American college student with a learning disability, grew up far from the impoverished inner-city neighborhood that shaped William Thomas's experience, and race had a very different influence on her perceptions of career and disability rights. Evelyn's life has bridged two different family experiences, one characterized by close relationships among members of her biological family in Africa, in the small, predominantly black country of her birth, and a second experience living among strangers in a predominately white community in the United States. An older brother brought Evelyn to America and left her "like baggage" with a white family in a small town in upstate New

York without relatives or friends. Evelyn spent a number of lonely and frustrating years in her new surroundings. Her learning disability was not diagnosed until she reached college, seven years after her arrival in the United States.

Evelyn describes herself as a "hands on" person born into an African family that valued formal education and had white-collar aspirations for their children. Her father worked at the post office, and he placed great emphasis on his children's upward mobility. Her parents sent her oldest brother to the United States to attend college, and they likewise expected Evelyn to do well as a student. Her father forced her to leave home after fifth grade to complete her education in the United States, despite her mother's and her own objections. Although virtually abandoned in the United States by her family, Evelyn's adaptation to American culture and American schools was guided by the sense of educational purpose imparted to her by her father.

Prior to leaving Africa, Evelyn attended a Baptist school, where she found reading and math extremely difficult. She was held back in the fourth grade. Her poor performance in grade school may be explained by her undetected learning disability, but in Africa, she recalls, she was simply a student who performed poorly. Evelyn observes that in her home country one was considered either smart or stupid. There was no such thing as special education for students with learning disabilities, and "stupid" students were held back. From her earliest years, Evelyn sensed her unexplained difference, a difference that she initially attributed to a lack of intelligence. Even after diagnosis of her learning disability she expresses doubt that being a good "hands on" person is the same as being smart, and she still thinks she is not as smart as her brothers.

Like William Thomas, Evelyn Gardner was influenced by her family and cultural background, in particular by the value her family placed on education. Unlike William, Evelyn's skin color was not a highly significant factor in her life until she became an immigrant in a small, predominantly white American town. As an immigrant, she became conscious of her cultural as well as her racial differences from other members of the community. She had to get used to "just everything, the way people talked, the way people looked at you." Further, in striking contrast to the support she received from her family and community at home, as an immigrant she was considered an outsider: "I was made fun of when I came here. Because you know if you're different from any American, you're just weird; you're inferior and all this other stuff. So I went through it all day in school and at the home I was living in."

Evelyn's status as an outsider affected her life in many ways. In school she was the subject of jokes and insults by other students, and she regularly got into fights. If she had been living with her own family, her parents might have intervened to make sure that the school protected Evelyn from the cruelty of other students. But Evelyn was living with strangers. Instead of providing support, the family in whose care Evelyn had been left by her brother treated her poorly.

Although schools in the United States are required to offer diagnosis and appropriate accommodations for children with learning disabilities, Evelyn's learning disability was not diagnosed until she reached college. Before then, her disability was masked by her identity as an immigrant. Evelyn was placed in English classes for speakers of other languages and was not given accommodations because neither the school nor Evelyn herself realized that she had a disability. Her slow start and difficulty in reading and math was expected of immigrant children. Even a supportive English language teacher to whom Evelyn frequently turned for help did not suspect that Evelyn had a learning disability. Although she had been sent to America because the schools seemed to offer better educational opportunities, she had the same difficulties with school work that she had had in Africa. As she points out, however, in America she had no brothers to help her with her homework.

Even though Evelyn struggled in school and did not know that her difficulties were due in part to a learning disability, she displayed remarkable tenacity in completing high school and pursuing admission to college. She had little contact with her family in Africa, but her father wrote a brief letter every month to remind her to pursue her studies. Evelyn jokes that her father simply photocopied these letters and mailed one each month, but she was faithful to his goal of finishing school. Evelyn overcame barriers by seeking out adults at her school who could provide the support she needed. Her English language teacher became her mentor. When her assigned guidance counselor told Evelyn she was "not college material," Evelyn found another counselor who was more helpful to her in applying to college. Evelyn's relationship with her host family remained strained and difficult, but she felt very close to the family of a good friend on the track team. Her friend's mother was positive and enthusiastic about Evelyn's ability, and she even helped Evelyn obtain permission to reenter the United States after an emergency visit to see her mother in Africa. Her friend's mother became Evelyn's "angel" and "mom." She told Evelyn she was smart and capable, a very different characterization from the "stupid" self-image she had carried from her childhood, and this enthusiasm rubbed off on Evelyn. With her "mom's" support she was able to overcome setbacks and self-doubts in high school. She moved in with her friend's family after high school.

Evelyn was motivated to complete high school and enter college, but she did not have a clear idea about the kind of work she might do. Her self-concept as a hands-on person suggested a skilled trade, possibly cosmetology, and she also considered becoming an interior designer. Her options for college were limited because she was not a top student. Her ability as a track star won an invitation to apply for admission to a small private college, but she soon realized that neither she nor her family, who were now in the midst of a war in their African country, could afford the tuition. Instead, she worked for a year flipping hamburgers and enrolled in a local community college, initially in a tourism and travel program. A professor immediately identified Evelyn's difficulty in reading and interpreting text or speech and referred her to the special education staff, who quickly diagnosed Evelyn's learning disability. At this point in her life, rights became active through their context-creating role in the college where she studied. Evelyn's diagnosis had a profound effect on her self-perception and her concept of a career. She discovered that, with legally mandated accommodations for her disability, she could be a good student and could choose among a number of fields that were appropriate for her abilities. Her undergraduate counselor suggested that human services might be well suited to Evelyn's "people person" skills. With the advice and support of her "mom" and her special education counselor at college, she decided to pursue a degree in human services. Eventually, she made plans to begin work toward a bachelor's degree in social work after completing her two-year program at the community college.

The diagnosis of Evelyn's learning disability significantly affected her expectations for employment. Although many people had earlier told her that she had great potential, the diagnosis reduced her own uncertainty and self-doubt. She began to see herself as a person with unique skills, as someone who could earn a professional degree. Gradually, her work experience began to support this identity and career expectation. She was invited to become a summer intern at a halfway house for teenage boys during her two-year program at the community college. She found that she related well to the boys and could understand their problems. She received high praise from the program's director, who invited her to apply for a job when she finished her community college program.

Despite diagnosis and the assurances of her mentors and American "family," and despite her positive work experience, Evelyn still harbors doubts about her career and how future employers might respond to her disability. Like William Thomas, she feels reluctant to share this knowledge with a prospective employer. She fears that an employer, like society in general, would not understand that she is indeed an able employee despite her disability: "I don't know if your label will follow you. I'm sure it does somehow . . . the label that you have a learning disability or you don't read well or you don't do this well. So it's, if there's somebody else in mind who's got all A's in school and reads 500 words a minute, whatever . . . he or she's going to be more fit for the job that I'm going for. . . . I don't personally think so, but that's how society thinks."

She understands such confusion well, partly because she herself was confused about her ability until she was diagnosed. Disclosure of her disability could produce stigma and bias that might jeopardize her career prospects. On the other hand, Evelyn thinks it may be more fair to a prospective employer to tell him or her about her learning disability so that the employer can choose an employee who is right for the job: "[It] depends on if it's going to interfere with my job. . . . I would want them to know why . . . because if they knew, they'd try to find somebody who they think wouldn't have a problem. . . . If I'm not going to be fully qualified to perform the way that I know I'm capable of, then that would, you know, it would kind of be holding me back and holding the employer, the place of employment, back." In this statement, Evelyn echoes William Thomas's assumption that the burden is on a prospective employee to establish her or his qualifications for a job without reference to the reasonable accommodations the ADA might require the employer to provide.

Evelyn, like William, thinks first in terms of self-reliance in the workplace rather than of legally mandated reasonable accommodations. The discourse of racial justice appears to have little to do with the way she thinks and talks about her options. If she already had the job, she might not tell an employer about her learning disability as long as she could find ways to prevent it from interfering with her work. On the other hand, if her disability interfered with her work, then she might tell her employer "so that if they can help you, they will help you." Here, Evelyn, unlike William, does perceive a space where rights might become active. She imagines what it would have been like if her high school teachers had known she had a learning disability and had offered her the accommodations that have made college a better experience. Evelyn struggles in drawing the line between what is fair and not fair to ask from an employer. Yet she states emphatically that if her employer were extremely rigid and refused to make any allowance for her disability, whether or not she could do the work unaccommodated, she would invoke her rights under the law: "We, whatever we are, disabled, we have a right to full equal employment just as anybody else." She would litigate this issue to open the way for future employees, although she probably would not work for such an employer even if her claim were successful.

Nevertheless, we can see in Evelyn's interview an element that was missing in both William Thomas's and Louise Dobbs's—a sense that the ADA is available to make employment possible for a person with a disability who requires reasonable on-the-job accommodations. Evelyn's consciousness of rights is associated with a more expansive view of the career opportunities she might pursue. We can even detect an oblique reference to the discourse of racial justice in phrases like "a right to full equal employment" for persons with disabilities. Evelyn's career aspirations and her awareness of ADA rights exceed those of William and Louise by a considerable margin.

As for race, it is a crucial part of Evelyn's life story, but not in the same sense as it is for William Thomas. For Evelyn, race is primarily associated with cultural differences and with her experience as an immigrant rather than with social class or economic deprivation. When she arrived in America, she was perceived as "weird" (to use Evelyn's word) because of differences in language and culture, but her middle-class outlook and career aspirations were similar to those of her white classmates. As her schooling progressed, the most painful and stigmatizing difference was being perceived as "stupid," both by her peers and herself. Although she has not yet overcome this demeaning self-perception, Evelyn has been told—and to an extent believes—that she is in fact intelligent and capable. Evelyn's outlook at this stage of her life differs significantly from William's. As a middle-class, African American woman with upwardly mobile and highly ambitious parents, Evelyn now thinks and talks about her career in a way that opens a space in which rights might become active. Whether she would actually invoke her ADA rights remains uncertain, yet rights have already had an impact on her career simply by affecting the future she imagines for herself and by validating her expectations of fair treatment by prospective employers. The influence of rights occurred because of their context-creating role in college and their transformation of Evelyn's self-perception. For Evelyn Gardner, unlike Louise Dobbs and William Thomas, rights guaranteed by the ADA have already helped to determine the trajectory of the career for which she has begun to prepare.

Social Factors and Timing: The Intersection of Disability and Career

In the preceding section, we saw that access, or lack of access, to social and cultural resources can affect how individuals think and talk about their employment-related experiences and can thus determine whether a space exists in which rights might seem relevant. Resources are not fixed and unchanging, however, in relation to the developing sense of self. Access to resources can change during one's lifetime. At certain moments in their lives, Louise, William, and Evelyn had closer or more distant family relationships, greater or smaller incomes, more or less supportive academic or work environments. Even factors such as race, which appear constant, had greater or lesser salience at different points in their lives. Thus, we suggest in this section that the issue of resources must be linked to timing. At each life stage, the resources *then* available to an individual affect the way he or she perceives options and choices, including the relevance or irrelevance of legal rights.

In our interviewees' life stories, access to social and cultural resources appears particularly important at the point when disability and career first intersect. Almost invariably, each narrative takes us back to the time when the disability occurred or became known, and describes how the effects of the disability disrupted or were integrated into the sense of who the narrator was and where he or she belonged. In the case of physical disabilities, it matters *when* an injury or illness causes mobility impairment, and whether it develops gradually or suddenly, in childhood or adulthood. For learning disabilities, as with physical disabilities, timing is a crucial factor. Although learning disabilities are generally present from early childhood, it matters *when* in life they are recognized, understood, and accommodated. Identity and career develop differently for an individual whose learning disability is not recognized until middle age, like Rosemary Sauter, or early adulthood, like Evelyn Gardner, as compared to a person who is diagnosed and provided special education services in elementary school, like William Thomas. Each of these variations suggests a different pattern of interaction over time among disability, social circumstances, and career.

Perhaps time matters most obviously in establishing the point when new rights become available as a matter of law. An individual whose disability occurred or became known after passage of the ADA might think about career and employment rights quite differently from someone whose disability occurred or became known decades earlier. The enactment of disability rights at a particular point in time makes it possible from that point forward, of course, to invoke such rights discursively or in a formal legal proceeding. In addition, the more diffuse or symbolic effects of rights may shape careers in different ways for individuals whose disabilities occurred or became known before and after passage of the ADA. In our discussion below of the life stories of Sara Lane and Bill Meier, we consider the difference that the timing of a disability makes in relation to the date of passage of the ADA.

While we focus in this section on the life cycle of the individual rights holder, we also consider other, less obvious connections between timing and the impact of the ADA. A child, an adolescent, a young adult, and a middle-aged adult might draw on different kinds or combinations of resources at the moment they first experience their disability. Reliance on one set of resources at a particular life stage may establish a behavioral pattern or an attitude that affects an individual's identity and career for many years. Orientation toward or away from rights may be determined by these circumstances related to life stage, as well as by the actual date of passage of the ADA. Such considerations suggest a complex and subtle interrelationship among timing of disability, career, socioeconomic resources, and rights consciousness. This interrelationship and its implications for the ADA is illustrated by comparing the life stories of Sara Lane and Bill Meier. Sara and Bill are both middle-class professionals who use wheelchairs. They are similar in many respects, except that Sara's disability originated in a childhood illness whereas Bill Meier's spinal cord injury occurred during adulthood just when his professional career had begun to take off.

We discussed the experiences of Sara Lane, a successful newspaper reporter, in an earlier life story narrative. Sara contracted polio as a young child nearly four decades before the enactment of the ADA. Although legal rights were not available to her while growing up, she had an invaluable resource on which to rely during her childhood: a highly active and supportive family, who taught Sara to aim high in her professional goals and who were wealthy enough to provide her with an excellent education. Sara's parents pushed her hard and offered substantial support. By the time Sara entered journalism school, she was an academically accomplished student and had developed adaptive skills that served her throughout her adult life. Working at several different newspapers, she learned to devise makeshift accommodations and persuade her employers to provide them even in the pre-ADA era. As Sara's career progressed, she became a successful young woman who could deal effectively, in most instances, with her employers. In addition to her professional skills, she also learned the importance of a positive self-presentation and attitude.

We think that the intertwining of timing, social class, and disability has played a crucial role in the construction of Sara's identity and career. Her outlook was influenced by the time period in which she grew up as well as by the early onset of her disability. Sara speaks of being raised as a "type A polio victim." She possesses the perspective of a generation that was taught to respond to childhood polio with resilience and to pursue lofty career goals with high expectations. Since disability rights did not exist during her childhood, she and her parents faced a set of stark alternatives: the brand of sturdy self-reliance that they embraced for Sara or the isolated and dependent existence assigned to the majority of individuals with paraplegia and quadriplegia in the 1950s and 1960s. Drawing on the resources available to her from early childhood, Sara shaped her career trajectory with the help of her middle-class background, her excellent education, her high intelligence, her outstanding social skills, and her indomitable spirit. She is aware that others in her generation were less fortunate and that her career success is the exception rather than the rule. Many individuals with physical disabilities similar to Sara's lacked the resources she used, and they were unable either to imagine or to achieve the career she has enjoyed.

Sara's utilization of these personal and material resources since early childhood explains why, even after passage of the ADA, she views rights with ambivalence. Despite numerous frustrations over work assignments and the reluctance of her employer to provide an accessible bathroom, Sara has always relied on her powers of persuasion and on the intervention of others. She has never invoked her legal rights. She is concerned about being perceived as a "whiner," and she does not want to jeopardize the chances of future employees who have disabilities. The resources on which she depends today are the same ones she learned to use as a young child.

Sara Lane's life story therefore illustrates the importance of timing—both the time period in which she grew up and the point in her life at which the onset of her disability occurred. In both of these senses, timing determined the array of resources available to Sara in pursuing her career and contributes to her current reluctance to invoke the ADA in situations of conflict with her employer. This is not to say that the passage of the ADA had no effect on Sara's career. She is aware of the ADA, and speaks readily about her rights. Enactment of the ADA affected her sense of fair treatment in the workplace and determined the issues she is willing to advocate. Rights became active in Sara's life by affecting her self-perception and her feelings of entitlement. Rights produced cultural and discursive shifts that advanced Sara's career. For example, when coworkers and, in particular, female supervisors at the newspaper intervened on her behalf at crucial times, it seems likely that they acted not only out of compassion but also because the ADA affected their own perception of Sara as a well-qualified worker with a disability.

Rights also played a context-creating role that benefited Sara. The battle over the accessible bathroom was resolved in Sara's favor when her employer unilaterally recognized that the ADA applied to him and his newspaper. Because the onset of Sara's disability occurred in early childhood at a time when the resources available to her instilled a last-ing philosophy of self-reliance and high professional expectations, she is less likely to bring rights into play on her own behalf. Yet the phi-losophy she learned in childhood led to a professional career and to supportive friendships that may have made it somewhat more likely that the ADA, enacted many years later, would have indirect and sym-bolic constitutive effects that have been helpful to her notwithstanding her reluctance to assert her rights.

Bill Meier, whose life story we have not yet presented, is another high-achieving professional who uses a wheelchair. Unlike Sara Lane, Bill first experienced paraplegia as an adult and had to adjust the trajec-tory of his career in mid-course in response to the new factor of phys-ical disability. He found this readjustment to be a difficult challenge. Unlike Sara, Bill did not have years of preparation and planning while still living with his family before entering employment as a worker in a wheelchair. He did, however, have two advantages that she lacked: he had already begun to establish a positive professional reputation before his disability occurred, and the ADA had just come into effect when he resumed employment after his injury.

Before his accident, Bill was a talented young executive, whose ear-lier years involved what he now calls "taking it whatever way the wind blows." It was clear, however, that Bill's education and his parents' ex-pectations had prepared him to pursue a career in business. With ma-turity and marriage, he realized that it was important "to set a goal and then strive for it," and not simply to drift from one opportunity to another. Accordingly, shortly before his injury, he accepted a high-paying new position in his organization, which required him to travel extensively throughout a large geographical region.

Less than a year after accepting the position as a regional manager, Bill suffered a spinal cord injury at a party and spent the next year and a half in a rehabilitation facility. His return to work in a wheelchair produced uncertainty and bad feelings. On the one hand, he now sees that the regional assignment was inherently flawed: structural changes in the organization had made the position untenable, and another re-gional manager had simply stopped working the month before Bill's return. On the other hand, Bill feels betrayed by his boss, who had mouthed platitudes—"He said he thought I could do it. I had the mo-tivation to be able to get out there and do it."—but was actually setting Bill up for failure. Bill now sees his boss as a heartless person concerned only with the bottom line and not with people or personal relation-ships. He is angry that his boss seemed unconcerned with Bill's struggles in his difficult assignment and that his boss never communicated with him personally about the problems Bill faced.

When Bill describes his struggles as regional manager, he reveals his ambivalence about the effects of his disability and about his own capabilities. On the one hand, he views his disability as irrelevant to his difficulties because he believes that the position to which he was assigned was unworkable, even had he not had his injury: "No one in my position could do that job." On the other hand, he implies that his boss could have cooperated with him to restructure the job in a way that would have allowed Bill to succeed. Even if this had happened, however, Bill doubts his capacity to handle the job after his injury: "Well, I couldn't do the job. With all that travel, it's just impossible. . . . I couldn't get everything that was expected of me done, although I wouldn't admit that to my boss at that time, because that would have been an easy way to let me go."

Bill's account alternates between a condemnation of his insensitive and uncaring boss and his realization that both his disability and the job itself made it impossible for him to continue as a regional manager. At one point, asked what his boss should have done, Bill responds: "What he should have done is have this whole job somehow customized for me without any major—you know—it could have been done." At other times, however, Bill speaks more in terms of the enormous change that occurred in his life and his unreadiness to deal with its consequences: "I was not psychologically ready to 'get out there.' I went from being 6' 3" and an athlete to 4' 1" in a chair that people would cross the street so they don't have to interact with you. It's an unbelievable transition. The physical barrier's not a problem, but the ability to look people in the eye, the ability to act confidently. I just went from sitting in a house and doing rehab to going out there again. That was impossible." Even when Bill's dissatisfaction with his boss became most intense, however, he did not perceive his boss's behavior as a denial of Bill's rights under the ADA. Bill never stated to his boss or to us that he had been denied his legal entitlement to on-the-job accommodations.

Bill's difficulty in resuming his position as regional manager marked a watershed in his career. Just as he began a lucrative but extremely challenging new assignment, his injury intervened and transformed his identity as a worker. Whereas Sara Lane knew of her disability from childhood and could therefore plan and prepare for a career for many years, Bill was required to rethink his identity just as his career was about to take off. The timing of his disability marks a crucial difference between his career path and Sara's, because Bill had already invested a significant part of his life in an identity and a career before his injury. Bill's transformed career might have developed differently if he had worked with a more sympathetic and supportive boss or if the job itself had been structured more realistically, but the timing of his disability would inevitably have required him to recreate himself as a worker and redirect the path of his career.

Although his injury created an enormous challenge to his identity as a capable employee, Bill managed to devise a satisfactory career path by drawing on the resources he had acquired up to that point. The resources available to Bill included a philosophy that it is essential "to set a goal and then strive for it, not . . . take it whatever way the wind blows," a set of professional credentials that established him as a well-educated and capable young businessman, a current position from which he could not easily be fired or demoted, and a recently enacted civil rights statute whose effects were only gradually being felt in the American workplace. Relying on all of these resources, Bill Meier reimagined his future. The president of his company's Buffalo office offered him a position that did not require Bill to travel from city to city. The office needed someone to work in sales and public relations. The president described the tasks that needed to be performed and invited Bill to "write your own job description." Bill became one of the three directors in the Buffalo office. His new boss, unlike his former boss, talked extensively with Bill about accommodations that would enable him to do his work effectively, and he even hired a consultant to make sure that the workplace was physically accessible. It appears that many factors, including the ADA, played a part in the positive redirection of Bill's career. Bill thrives in his new position and can now state with some confidence, "I'm the best membership sales representative that's ever been here."

The onset of Bill Meier's disability later in his life undoubtedly created substantial problems, requiring him to "take a step back" and think carefully about how to move forward again to succeed. Yet he identifies a very important advantage associated with the later onset of disability. At one point in the interview, he speculates on how difficult it would be if he had not already achieved some success and held a position of importance before his injury occurred. If he had first entered the job market as a person in a wheelchair, even after enactment of the ADA, would he ever have attained the position he now holds? Bill thinks not:

> If I were to just quit here one day and send my resumes out, I don't
> think I would get a lot of calls if my resume said "disabled" on it
> or whatever. I think if I went out on interviews, there would be

very few people that would put me in the final cut, so to speak, solely based on the fact that the guy's in a wheelchair, there's no way he can do his job. Or he's going to want this and that and the other thing as an accommodation, and we simply can't afford to address those needs. So I don't think, in this kind of perspective—other people have disagreed—I don't think I'm that employable at the level of employment that I'm at now in other places. . . . It's difficult, and most employers don't realize it's difficult, and I don't think they're going to want to take the time or money or whatever it takes to have a "special needs" employee, which is why I lead my life as a "non-special needs" kind of person.

Paraplegia certainly transformed Bill's identity in many important ways, but his persona as a highly capable employee was familiar before his circumstances changed. If he were to present himself in a wheelchair to strangers as a job applicant with no employment history, he doubts whether his future would be as bright, regardless of the ADA.

It is striking that Bill never mentioned to his former boss, or to us during the interview, the employment rights he has under the ADA. Yet, we believe that rights played a role in shaping his career and enabling him ultimately to succeed in a different assignment in the same organization. It is clear that Bill is aware of the ADA—he distributes a brochure on this very topic as part of his job. We think that rights contribute to his sense of employability, his image of himself as a working professional, and his sense of entitlement. Because of the personal and material resources available to Bill at the time of his injury, anything short of a successful professional career would have violated his expectations. For this reason, when Bill experienced difficulty on returning to his regional manager job, he perceived a clear disparity between the treatment he expected from his former boss and that which he in fact received. At times his narrative suggests the influence of the ADA. After reassignment to the Buffalo office, as the implications of the ADA became increasingly apparent, both Bill and his new boss thought it obvious that they should sit down together and work out the necessary accommodations for a valuable employee who had suffered an injury. Neither Bill nor his second boss appears to have mentioned the ADA explicitly during these discussions, yet their negotiation of reasonable accommodations conforms precisely to the bilateral procedures outlined in the ADA's regulations. Bill never invoked his rights, but it is reasonable to conclude that rights gradually became active in his career. At the same time, however, it must be recognized that Bill's sense of entitlement and his high expectations for himself also drew on his previous professional employment and middle-class background. Had he lacked the resources associated with education, professional success, and social class, rights alone would have been much less likely to have played a part in his career.

Conclusion

In this chapter, we have examined the influence of family, social class, and race on the perceptions and role of rights in the lives of men and women with disabilities. It is quite probable that these factors affect the frequency—and, in the case of our study, the infrequency—with which formal rights claims are brought by individuals who believe they are the victims of ADA violations. Because none of our interviewees lodged formal claims or even consulted lawyers, however, our discussion in this chapter has examined how family, social class, and race affect the other ways in which ADA rights become active. Referring back to our discussion of the constitutive effects of rights in chapter 2, we have pointed out numerous instances in which ADA rights have transformed self-perceptions, produced cultural and discursive shifts, and played a context-creating role in the lives of the interviewees whose stories we have presented in this chapter. By facilitating or impeding these constitutive effects, the social factors we have considered significantly affect the role of rights under the ADA. Moreover, we have suggested that the effects of these social factors are not fixed and unchanging for a given individual. Their significance varies over time, and we stress the influence these factors exert at the moment in one's life that a disability occurs or becomes known. The point at which disability intersects the trajectory of a career proves to be crucially important for an individual's orientation toward rights.

The effect of social factors such as family, class, and race is to make available (or unavailable) a combination of resources with which to construct an identity and a career. Sometimes these factors combine in surprising fashion to enable an individual with a disability to think and talk about herself in new ways and to move ahead, as was the case with Evelyn Gardner, a middle-class West African immigrant who overcame problems associated with an undiagnosed learning disability and virtual abandonment by her family in a predominantly white community to prepare herself for a career in social work. Sometimes these same factors can prevent an individual from envisioning a viable career, as was true for Louise Dobbs, whose working-class background, limited education, low-wage jobs, and broken marriage provided few resources for coping with the debilitating effects of a stroke in middle age. The effects of each of the cultural, social, and material resources of the kind we have discussed may be multifaceted. Families, for example, can impart resilience, determination, knowledge, and faith in oneself. All of these qualities are extremely valuable resources for some of our interviewees. But families may also instill other qualities whose value is more uncertain, such as a religious faith that counsels acceptance of adverse experiences or a philosophy of dependence on family members that limits development of self-sufficiency.

The influence of social class is similarly complex. Although the effects of social class are often apparent, our interviewees were not necessarily disadvantaged by their working-class origins as compared to those raised in middle-class families. Rosemary Sauter, for example, gained advantages from the manual skills, practicality, good judgment, and determination of her working-class parents that proved more valuable to her than the resources many other interviewees found in their more affluent, middle-class homes. Of course, it is usually an advantage to have more money rather than less, but the effects of social class on identity and career—while often highly significant—do not lend themselves readily to a simple scale.

The social effects of race, too, have a very significant yet complex influence on identity and career. For William Thomas, the socially imposed career disadvantages of young African American men growing up in impoverished urban neighborhoods certainly limited his career aspirations. His mature attitude toward work and potential employment obstacles reflect an invaluable and, in his case, a race-related resource he has already acquired: a keen understanding of how to succeed in the face of adversity. His youthful experiences with the effects of race and racial discrimination may in the long run make him better able to envision how rights under the ADA could contribute positively to a successful career. Nevertheless, when we compare William's life story with that of Evelyn Gardner, who is also a young African American with a learning disability, we can see how her middle-class background served as a resource that enabled her, in her early twenties, to envision a more ambitious and challenging professional career than could William as he prepared to enter college.

We think it important, then, to consider the resources available to individuals with disabilities as they construct their identities and careers, but not to assume that each social factor has the same significance for every individual. We have attempted in this chapter, as we have throughout the book, to emphasize a new understanding of the *process* through which rights become active. In this process, social factors such as family, social class, and race can contribute significantly to identity formation. In turn, identity is closely connected to the capacity of individuals to perceive themselves as appropriately or inappropriately located in relation to social boundaries, and as receiving or being denied the kind of treatment they expect. When the sense of self leads an individual to perceive a disparity between expectation and reality, a space is created within which ADA rights may seem relevant. Such was the case for Evelyn Gardner and, potentially, for William Thomas, but not for Louise Dobbs.

We have also emphasized that the significance of resources should be thought of as dynamic, rather than static, over time. Our comparison of Sara Lane and Bill Meier underscores the significance of timing in relation to resources, identity, and rights. Coming from relatively affluent, middle-class backgrounds, Sara and Bill are both high-achieving professionals who use wheelchairs, and their identities and career trajectories are similar in many ways. Yet Sara's disability dates from early childhood while Bill's occurred after his career was already underway. Timing probably contributes to Sara's reluctance to avail herself of her rights, even in informal discussions or negotiations, because she had learned from an early age how to make her way by relying almost exclusively on her own accommodations and adjustments. Bill, who also avoids any direct invocation of his rights, differs from Sara in that he engaged in explicit negotiations concerning accommodations with his new boss, precisely as the ADA and its regulations require. Although neither Bill nor his boss mentioned the statute or its guidelines, their negotiations represented an application of an ADA-mandated procedure that Sara never experienced. Rights have played a constitutive role for both Sara and Bill, but in rather different ways. We think these differences arise, at least in part, from the different times in their lives when disability intersected career trajectory.

Besides family, social class, and race, other social factors also influence identity and the role of rights. Our discussion is meant to be illustrative rather than exhaustive. In our analysis thus far, we have omitted one obvious factor of great significance: gender. Our omission was intentional. We think gender is so important, and contributes in such complex ways to the role of the ADA, that it merits consideration in a chapter all its own. We undertake that consideration in chapter 6.

six

Life Story: Beth Devon

[We were unable to incorporate any comments Beth Devon might have had about our version of her life story; sadly, she died before a reinterview could be arranged. Although we recognize that the following account may contain flaws that stand uncorrected, we dedicate this version of Beth's story to her memory.]

Beth Devon sometimes muses that a shift in the wind caused her to contract polio at the age of nine. Shortly after she participated in a political rally at a sports stadium one evening, she and four other children in attendance came down with polio: "We all said some wind went through that stadium." Although her comment is undoubtedly facetious, the imagery is significant. Beth views her disability as the result of happenstance, of a change in wind direction—fortuitous events in people's lives that lead some, like her, to use wheelchairs while others do not. The distinction between persons with and without disability is not, in her mind, dramatically marked. Her social identity is shaped in terms of shifting contingencies that require sensible, strategic responses.

Beth had just celebrated her sixtieth birthday when we interviewed her in the living room of her comfortable home. She had been a "disability activist" long before that term came into use. The mother of two children and the grandmother of five, Beth had pursued a professional career as an executive assistant in a successful small business and, later, as a solo professional. She had joined, and in some cases had led, numerous voluntary organizations that benefited persons with disabilities. At the time of our interview, Beth lived alone; her husband had died of cancer five years earlier: "He was able-bodied. He didn't have any handicaps at all. I never figured that he would go. I'd be the one. But fate plays funny tricks on you sometimes." Beth still led a very active life, and through her example she demonstrated to other wheelchair users how they might pursue careers in the social mainstream. Yet, for Beth Devon the law has little significance or relevance in her everyday dealings with others. The law is like the weather: at some times more favorable than others, but not particularly relevant to her own life. The absolute categories of the law are intrusive, clumsy, and inconsistent with her understanding of social and professional relationships.

Beth's personal philosophy might easily have been different. She spent most of her childhood in socially segregated institutions. After two years in the hospital following the onset of her illness, she moved to a rehabilitation center where she received therapy and schooling for four more years. It was only in the middle of her senior year of high school that she rejoined her classmates in the local public school system she had attended before her illness. She had maintained friendships with her classmates over the years, however, and continued to view the graduating high school class as her peer group. Indeed, the polio epidemics of the 1940s affected so many that it became a shared experience for a sizeable minority of the children in her community. She did not feel that she alone had been marked as "different" during a time when the hospital wards overflowed with polio patients and donated buildings served as temporary annexes to house the many children who were receiving treatment. Hers was a generational experience, and, despite the years of separation from her classmates, it may have been easier for her to maintain an identity as part of her high school class than for teenagers whose physical disabilities resulted from accidents or other exceptional circumstances that were more difficult for their classmates to understand and accept.

Although neither of her parents had attended college or even completed high school, there was no question in Beth Devon's mind about her plans after graduation. Her test scores had determined that she was college material, so she applied and was accepted into a program where she could receive professional training. She studied for two years in a college that was an obstacle course for people in wheelchairs: the campus was hilly and the buildings were inaccessible.

She had to pay students to carry her up and down the stairs; but this otherwise inconvenient and even humiliating experience was not all bad, for it was how she met her husband, who was among the students who carried her to and from classes. Teachers and administrators were not always understanding, however, and on one occasion she was forced to accept an unsatisfactory grade in a course because she could not get to the classroom. On another occasion, a professor called her to his office to accuse her of cheating: two different handwritings appeared in her homework. To his consternation, Beth laughed at his accusation. As a result of her polio, she had taught herself to write left-handed as well as right-handed. When writing in large, heavy ledger books that were difficult for her to lift, she wrote on the left side with her left hand and the right side with her right hand, and thus it appeared that two different people had collaborated on her assignments. She recalled that the professor was surprised and apologetic when he heard her explanation: "Now that's something I'll have to think of the rest of the school term, that one person can put out two different handwritings. . . . I'll never forget that."

Despite her frequent encounters with adversity, Beth interpreted her experiences in terms of gains and losses, of setbacks and steps forward. Her narrative rejects absolutes, and nowhere does she convey or acknowledge a sense of rigid categorization on her part or on the part of those she encounters. From the potentially degrading experience of being lifted up and down the stairs came a close and loving relationship with the young man who carried her and eventually married her. From the unfounded accusation of cheating came a humorous story of a professor who learned to be less judgmental and more understanding. Her life story, as she tells it, is free from recrimination against those who may have treated her unfairly or committed acts of discrimination on the basis of her disability.

Although her father believed that women should not drive cars, Beth Devon became the first woman in her family to circumvent his wishes. Her friend secretly taught her how to use the hand controls he had installed, and they switched seats before returning to her home so that her father would not suspect that she had defied him. After college, she took and passed her driver's test. Later, her ability to drive would serve as an inspiration for injured or paralyzed war veterans who felt helpless until they were driven around the city by a young woman volunteer whose disability was as extensive as their own. Returning home from the driving test, the same friend took her to meet a businessman who was starting a new auto dealership and needed an accountant. The job interview was a success, and she became an employee not long after graduating from college. She held this job for twelve years and played a key administrative role as the business succeeded and expanded rapidly.

It was in this position that Beth refined her philosophy of dealing with people and with situations and became skilled in developing strategies to ensure accessibility. Knowing how and when to suggest the need for workplace accommodations, she persuaded her boss to make the office accessible to an employee in a wheelchair. Eventually, he agreed to rearrange and widen the doors, and fellow employees assisted with parking so she had direct access to the rear door without having to go through the snow or rain. She read the moods of her boss carefully and gauged exactly the right moment to ask for an accommodation that he was likely to approve. She would start small and evaluate his response before asking for larger and more expensive changes: "Before you ask for the world, ask for just a small island. That was my attitude, was to feel it out and just see how far you could [go]." When he resisted, she would threaten to resign; but her threats were always carefully calculated. She knew exactly how far she could push him on a given issue and never went beyond what she thought realistically she could get: "You have to pick and choose your days, too. When they have a real bad day at home, you're not going to ask until the situation [improves], so you've got to look it over pretty good."

Beth recalled that many of her customers did not even know that she had a disability. When she worked, she sat in a regular desk chair. Occasionally a customer would see the wheelchair nearby and exclaim, "What in the world happened to you?" That was, she recalled, "a fun time." It was only at such moments that she talked to them about her disability. They would then acknowledge, "You know, I never did see you get up and run around." This recollection underscores Beth's view of her own disability as circumstantial and superficial rather than one that places her in a separate social category. Once the office was remodeled to be generally accessible, her identity as a person with a disability nearly vanished. The "fun" was to play with people's perception, to show how easily one identity can be exchanged for another, to demonstrate how inconsequential her use of the wheelchair was, and to remind the customers that her disability had little to do with her professional identity as a skilled and valuable employee. This kind of play was available to one who was thoroughly professional and had the strategic skills to persuade an employer to provide the accommodations necessary to allow her to do her job.

Yet even a person as skilled in interpersonal dealings as Beth Devon can sometimes encounter resistance, and she discovered over time that she could not persuade her employer to provide an accessible bathroom. For reasons that appear irrational, or perhaps were related to a man's refusal to acknowledge that women have to use the bathroom just as men do, or perhaps to some distorted notion that bathrooms are not proper subjects for men and women to discuss with one another, Beth's employer refused to modify the office's bathroom despite his willingness to introduce other extensive modifications throughout the building. She had to work the whole day without going to the bathroom, and, as a consequence, she eventually developed a disabling kidney disease.

Why did her otherwise successful strategy fail on the issue of an accessible bathroom? According to her own account, Beth Devon recognized over time that her employer would never concede this issue to her. When she raised it with him, he told her to use the bathroom in a restaurant at lunchtime. Although he spent far more money on other accommodations, "[h]e was just touchy and funny about this bathroom thing." Interestingly, she never threatened to resign over his failure to provide an accessible bathroom; she believed that he would never give in, that he would call her bluff and she would be out of a job. Beth felt that she had to accept the situation as one that could not be changed, however painful and harmful it was to her, and she lived with it until she retired to raise a family.

Beth Devon's philosophy was tested to its limits by the problem of the inaccessible bathroom. Her incremental, strategic approach foundered in a situation where the employer simply would not budge. No matter how skillfully she read his mood and gauged the appropriate moment to push, threaten, or cajole, his response was unyielding. At this point, her basic approach provided no workable solution. She felt that she had no choice but to accept the situation so long as she wanted to continue working for him. As far as she knew, the law then provided no remedy, except that it entitled her to disability payments for her kidney disease caused by workplace conditions. Yet even if the law had at that time required her employer to provide an accessible bathroom, it is not at all clear that Beth would have invoked her rights and tried to force her employer to change his position. Her comments on disability rights activism suggest that the law may have no place in her strategy for dealing with recalcitrant employers.

After retiring from the auto dealership, Beth worked for individual clients but never sought full-time employment with another business. Her time was taken up with family, with accounting jobs she handled from her home, and with numerous volunteer organizations. Although she never had to negotiate accommodations with an employer during that time, she is aware of the legal and social changes that have occurred in recent years, and she offers advice to others on how to pursue their career objectives.

As a general proposition, Beth opposes preferential hiring and is uneasy with new disability laws that, as she understands them, might give an advantage to a prospective employee on the basis of disability: "Because you're handicapped you get extra points; and because you're Oriental you get other points; because you're Spanish you get other points; because you're a Negro race you get other points, you know what I mean? And I don't think that works too good, because you just cause dissension among those that have no points to grab in there, because the jobs are taken up by all those who can grab up the points—maybe not because of their ability." Her impression that the Americans with Disabilities Act (ADA) confers "points" on job applicants with disabilities resembles that of Raymond Militello, whose life story we presented earlier. Unlike Raymond, however, Beth feels that no one should claim an entitlement because of a disability. Instead, she urges prospective employees to make themselves attractive to employers by developing their qualifications to such a high level that they outbalance the disability as hiring considerations: "You've got to overly meet the other criteria like, say, your appearance, and your clothes, and your personality, or whatever. You've got to overly do it, so that your disability or handicap is maybe overshadowed by these, and overcome by these other good points that you can bring out. And maybe your handicap, per se, is overlooked a little bit more, not right up in the light maybe, if you can present yourself a little better."

Her observations about needing to "overly meet the other criteria" should be understood in the context of her negative comments about people in wheelchairs who complain of hiring discrimination without ever considering whether (as Beth suspects) their own sloppy and dirty appearance, not their disability, might have been the determining factor. She confronted one such individual and asked him whether he ever thought about wearing clean, neat clothes and making himself look more presentable and not like someone who had just gotten out of bed. He responded by saying that it was the employer's bias rather than his own appearance that caused his job application to be rejected. But Beth observes that it was not only the man's physical appearance that was unattractive: the wheelchair itself was filthy. She comments that "a lot of men don't clean their chairs," but she spends hours at a time cleaning hers until "all the lines [are] sleek." Significantly, she considers the wheelchair to be just like any other article of clothing, requiring the same care and cleaning: "Your chair is part of you, just like your shoes."

This view of the wheelchair sheds light on Beth Devon's general attitude toward her disability. The wheelchair, in this account, is not a highly charged symbol of difference, but an ordinary part of one's wardrobe—like shoes and clothing. She rejects the assumption expressed by some people with disabilities that the wheelchair is a lightning rod for discrimination. Rather than regarding it primarily as a symbol, she insists that it is a mundane, unexceptional part of one's overall self-presentation. If it is kept clean, the wheelchair will not detract from one's qualifications in any determinative sense, but could function as a "weakness" that can be overcome by emphasizing one's overqualification with respect to other hiring criteria. The unsuccessful job applicant should not assume that the wheelchair is the problem; he or she should begin, Beth urges, by looking in the mirror rather than crying discrimination. She rejects the proposition that society creates rigid categories that mark persons with disabilities as "different," and she emphasizes instead that persons with disabilities who cultivate their social skills and know-how can participate fully in most social arenas.

Beth Devon's "legal consciousness," then, predictably leads her to minimize the role of law in the employment process. Even under the ADA, which she acknowledges has expanded the rights available to persons with disabilities, the job applicant who encounters a blatantly biased employer should not assume that the law will prove useful: "Even if the law is behind you, makes it easier for you, once you get there [it's] not going to help you that much. You've still got to get your abilities straightened out, you've got to have all your schooling right. And I don't think anybody should get hired just because of their handicap; they should be able to do the job and do it well." At most, she suggests, those who encounter blatant discrimination should notify the Better Business Bureau.

At one point, we asked Beth if she thinks the ADA will cause more people to request accommodations from employers. She agrees that this is likely to occur, but then tells an anecdote that appears at first to be unrelated to the issue of increased rights claims. The story concerns a locally prominent man who uses a wheelchair and is fond of racing it recklessly wherever he goes, even in places where he might run into frail or elderly people. His wheelchair has no brakes: he simply throws it into reverse when he wants to stop. "He burns out a motor once a month, by throwing it in reverse all the time—and this he's proud of."

At first we did not understand the relevance of this anecdote, but after some reflection we saw how it connected to the question we had raised. We had asked Beth to consider whether the new law would lead to an increase in rights claims by individuals with disabilities. Acknowledging that it might, she then thinks of a person who, in her view, flaunts his disability and makes himself conspicuous by dramatizing the symbol of his disability, the wheelchair. His attitude toward his wheelchair contrasts with the attitude Beth expressed earlier in the interview: the wheelchair is merely a part of her wardrobe, like a pair of shoes. Her strategy is to downplay the importance of the wheelchair in her dealings with other people, but the man she describes in her anecdote behaves in precisely the opposite way. Unlike Beth, he exhibits the wheelchair flamboyantly, even exuberantly, as he conducts his public business.

The contrasting attitudes toward the wheelchair, and toward disability in general, are consistent with differing attitudes toward legal rights under the ADA. Beth Devon had earlier stated that the disability should be downplayed in employment negotiations, that it should be regarded as perhaps a slight disadvantage in some circumstances but one that could be outbalanced by overqualification on other criteria. She does *not* believe that the disability should be at the center of hiring considerations, nor of on-the-job accommodation discussions. The idea that individuals would increasingly make claims of rights under the ADA seems closely linked in her mind with the inappropriate social behavior of an individual who makes his wheelchair a conspicuous part of his social identity, who flaunts his disability to the extent of jeopardizing the safety of others through his reckless driving. In the case of asserting rights under the ADA and in the case of the reckless wheelchair user, disability is no longer treated as an ordinary part of the everyday world—one aspect of an individual's identity among many other aspects—and instead the disability comes to dominate the perception of that person. For Beth Devon, a longtime disability advocate and counselor, rights granted by the ADA represent a potential threat to her view of how individuals with disabilities should achieve inclusion and success in the mainstream of society.

Gender and Disability Rights

Perhaps no factor influences the discourses of work and rights more profoundly than gender. In this chapter, we consider how gender affects the way men and women with disabilities think and talk about their sense of self, their career path, and their perceptions of the American with Disabilities Act (ADA).[1]

Gender influences both aspects of identity formation that we have emphasized in this book: how one interacts with others and the narrative of self that evolves over a lifetime. Life stories like those of Beth Devon and the other interviewees we discuss in this chapter illustrate the profound and often complex effects of gender and disability on expectations for a career. Gendered expectations are communicated directly and indirectly by parents, teachers, and peers, and these expectations shaped our interviewees' emergent self-concepts. Much of the significance attributed to gender results from images and social practices that people associate with biological difference. In different social circumstances, the influence of gender on identity may vary significantly, and individuals learn to experience, talk about, and perceive gender in different ways. Through life stories like that of Beth Devon, we can see how gender combines with family influences, social class, race, and other factors considered in the previous chapters to shape the way persons with disabilities think and talk about themselves, their expectations for employment, and their perceptions of rights. At the same time, our interviewees demonstrate an extraordinary capacity for creative behavior that defies the seemingly inflexible societal constraints imposed by gendered roles and stereotypes.

1. We gratefully acknowledge the helpful comments and suggestions of our colleague, Dianne Avery, who read an early draft of this chapter and contributed significantly to our thoughts about these materials.

213

Our discussion of gender and disability rights brings together many of the central themes from earlier chapters. Of particular importance is that fact that gender, like disability, has had a pervasive influence on the organization of work and the expectations that employers have for potential employees—and, indirectly, the expectations that potential employees have for themselves. The gendering of particular jobs and relationships within the workplace has historical roots similar to the origins of the social and legal construction of disability and work discussed in chapter 3. The social construction of work often dichotomizes both "able" versus "disabled" *and* "male" versus "female" employment, and these dichotomies tend to channel individuals toward or away from particular jobs. The social dichotomies of able/disabled and male/female create a doubly complex dilemma for persons with disabilities, who must confront two different yet interrelated sets of presumptions about their identities, abilities, and employability.

As we have seen in the preceding chapters, the development of identity depends on the social circumstances and experiences that provide an individual with disabilities access to opportunities, resources, interpretations, and discourses. Our research demonstrates how gender, too, contributes to the process of identity formation among our interviewees. In this chapter, by contrasting men's and women's life stories and their employment experiences and differing orientations to the law, we return to our fundamental question of how rights become active. The ADA addresses the effects of stereotypes and misperceptions of disability, but it says nothing explicitly about gender. We think it essential to consider how rights under the ADA become active in relation to the gender-related considerations about which the ADA itself is silent.

This chapter, then, examines in detail how gender, in combination with other social factors, affects the formation of identity for men and women with disabilities and how the gendered identities thus constituted may predispose individuals to embrace or reject rights as they pursue their careers. The first section of the chapter considers how gender becomes an important element in the process of identity formation for men and women with disabilities. The second section, drawing on the life story of Mary Williams, provides a more detailed illustration of the role of gender in shaping a career. The third section focuses on the relationship between gender and the role of rights. There we present the life stories of four men and women with disabilities. The first pair, Beth Devon and Sid Tegler, have constructed a career and a gendered identity that rejects the role of rights, while the second pair, Jill Golding and Al Vincenzo, have turned toward rights in their quest for inclusion in the workplace.

Gender and Identity

In this section, we begin our discussion of gender by considering how it contributes to the process of identity formation that determines careers as well as orientations toward disability rights. As we have observed previously, rights do not appear relevant until the potential rights bearer perceives a disparity between actual experiences and those that he or she anticipates. Gender has a powerful effect on the experiences people anticipate in the workplace. In chapter 3, we described work as a social construct in which jobs are presumed to exist only for "able" workers, and we observed that individuals with disabilities who seek employment must contend with this categorical presumption. In focusing now on gender, we encounter the source of another pervasive system for classifying identities. As in every culture and society, the manifest physical differences between men and women are associated in American society with assumptions about gender-appropriate physical and intellectual practices. Gender is tied to rigorous social and cultural codes concerning appropriate bodies, behaviors, and jobs. These codes severely constrain both men and women in our society and shape perceptions and assumptions about careers from early childhood until the age of retirement.[2] Both gender and disability trigger assumptions about work that is deemed appropriate or even possible for men and women in our society.

Gender, like disability, is a social construct deeply rooted in the organization of work and in the ways employers have historically perceived their employees.[3] Women—and men—have often been perceived as preferring and best suited for particular jobs and working conditions (see Amott and Matthaei 1996; Kessler-Harris 1982; Brown and Pechman 1987). These perceptions have, of course, historically operated to the disadvantage of women who seek equal job opportunities and

2. Reskin and Hartmann (1986:51–55) note that in 1980, more than 80 percent of the workers in 275 out of the 508 occupations listed in the most detailed U.S. census enumeration were the same gender. Of course, the gendered character of particular types of work may change over time, and gendered assumptions about jobs may be disrupted by overt challenges to long-established customs and perceptions of men and women in the workplace.

3. Kanter (1993:263), a scholar of corporate employment, observes about the gendering of jobs that "[t]o a very large degree, organizations make their workers into who they are. . . . What really happens is that predictions are made on the basis of stereotypes and current notions of who fits where in the present system; people are then 'set up' in positions which make the predictions come true." See also Reskin and Padavic 1994:126 ff, describing processes that lead to gendered construction of the workplace. The authors note that the gendered construction of the contemporary workplace is a product of intentional and unintentional actions of many role players, including employers, coworkers, customers, and workers themselves.

pay. Men and women with disabilities must grapple not only with the dilemma that most jobs are designed for and expected to be filled by "able" workers, but also with the fact that either men or women workers are expected to fill particular jobs. The effects of these two systems of expectations rooted in the culture of work are not a simple double barrier, for there are circumstances under which the effects of a disability may alter gender identity (or vice versa), making the effects of gender and disability on identity complex and interactive.

These complex interconnections among gender, identity, disability, and work have already been explored by scholars whose work was not, like ours, concerned specifically with the effects of the ADA. Some of these scholars have noted that disabilities, particularly "visible" physical disabilities, affect the lives of men and women differently (see, e.g., Wendell 1996; Silvers 1998). An influential essay by Asch and Fine, for example, observes that disability for men can "contradict" conventional gender images, whereas for women it can "replicate" them: "Having a disability was seen as synonymous with being dependent, childlike, and helpless—an image fundamentally challenging all that is embodied in the ideal male: virility, autonomy, and independence. Yet this image replicated, if in caricature, all that is embodied in the ideal female: emotionality, passivity, and dependence" (1988:3).

In this sense, disabilities can "handicap" both men and women, but for women, some have argued, the results can be a "double disability" (see Deegan and Brooks 1985), or even "two handicaps plus" (Hanna and Rogovsky 1991). These researchers suggest that the doubling effect may have particular relevance for employment, since women in the workplace, even if they have no disability, generally tend to occupy unequal positions and earn inferior wages (see generally Brown and Pechman 1987; Reskin and Hartmann 1986). Women with disabilities, it is suggested, may find it particularly difficult to identify jobs for which society views them as well suited. They may experience heightened levels of exclusion or discrimination for which rights might seem an appropriate remedy.

OuYang (1990:19) argues that women with disabilities are—like all women—disproportionately excluded from jobs perceived as essentially masculine in character. In addition, OuYang argues that to the extent women are viewed as "asexual," particularly women with physical disabilities, they may also be excluded from jobs perceived as "feminine." As Hahn (1994:118) observes, the social disadvantages of sexual objectification for most women are compounded by the social disadvantages of "asexual objectification" for women with disabilities. Hahn's point is obviously relevant for women with *physical* disabilities, but, in more subtle ways, the processes of asexual objectification may shape the identities and careers of women with *learning* disabilities as well (see the story of Mary Williams in the next section of this chapter).

The identity- and career-distorting effects of disability on the identities of women are readily apparent in the life stories of our interviewees. It does not necessarily follow, however, that men with disabilities in the workplace are better off than women with disabilities or encounter less frequent infringements of their employment rights.[4] Men's identities, like women's, may be radically changed by disability, but in rather different ways.[5] Referring specifically to men with *physical* disabilities, Hahn (1994:136) suggests that the "double disability" of women finds its counterpart in disadvantages associated with the "conflicted identities" of men with physical disabilities: "Disabled men are conflicted; they have one attribute—disability—that is generally devalued and another feature—masculinity—that is usually interpreted as a sign of strength or even physical prowess. But the latter characteristic does not necessarily give them an advantage in most situations. In fact, disabled men who rely exclusively on their masculinity often find their efforts subverted both by the connotations of disability and by the inherent fallacy of traditional male privilege."

Our study confirms such effects in the lives of some men who use wheelchairs. Bill Meier, as we saw in chapter 5, experienced a profound

4. Rough comparative data on employment of men and women with and without disabilities appear to suggest that gender does not necessarily enhance the disadvantage of workers with disabilities. For example, data provided by Jans and Stoddard (1999:22 [citing U.S. Bureau of Census website]) provide the following mixed insights into the "double disability" hypothesis: (1) The *labor force participation rate* for women without disabilities is 85 percent of the rate for men without disabilities, while the ratio for women with disabilities is slightly higher—88 percent. (2) Similarly, in terms of *median monthly income*, women without disabilities earned 67.1 percent of men's monthly earnings, while women with "nonsevere disabilities" earned only a slightly lower fraction (64.6 percent) of the monthly earnings of men with nonsevere disabilities; and women with "severe disabilities" actually earned a higher fraction (79.2 percent) of the median earnings of men with severe disabilities (ibid.:23 [citing McNeil 1993]). (3) The same pattern is apparent in relative rates of poverty. While more women than men are poor, disability does not force proportionately more women than men into poverty. Jans and Stoddard (1999:24 [citing U.S. Bureau of the Census]) offer statistics showing that for those with no "work disability," men's poverty rate is 67 percent of women's poverty rate. For those with a "work disability," the ratio increases to 72 percent—that is, proportionately more men than women are forced into poverty by a disability. And for those with a "severe work disability," the ratio is 77 percent. Thus, these rough data suggest that gender disparities in the workplace are not exacerbated by disability. But Anita Silvers (1998:89) cites 1984 census data to argue that women with disabilities have a "much lower socio-cultural participation rate" and are more likely to be unemployed than nondisabled women and disabled men.

5. As Murphy (1987:94–95) notes, the identities of men with physical disabilities are significantly compromised in the eyes of society: "Paralytic disability constitutes emasculation. . . . For the male, the weakening and atrophy of the body threaten all the cultural values of masculinity: strength, activeness, speed, virility, stamina, and fortitude."

identity change as the result of a spinal chord injury he suffered as a young adult. Bill is keenly aware of the social implications of his disability, commenting that "I went from being 6' 3" and an athlete to 4' 1" in a chair that people would cross the street so they don't have to interact with you." He also suggests that it was unlikely that he could have been hired for an attractive, well-paying job like the one he currently holds if he had sent out resumes and begun interviewing *after* his injury. Bill believes that he was able to make the transition to his current position of responsibility only because he had already begun a successful managerial career before his injury.

Bill Meier's story also suggests that the life stage at the onset of a physical disability may influence gender identity and employment. The timing of disability may be particularly important in determining the magnitude of the effects of a disability on men who use wheelchairs. Men like Rick Evans (discussed in chapter 1), who experience physical disability before adolescence, may find it especially difficult to combat gender-related stereotypes and establish a conventional "masculine" identity as an adult who uses a wheelchair. By contrast, men who first experience physical disability during adulthood, such as Bill Meier, may reap more of the social and economic advantages associated with their gender despite the disadvantages related to their newly acquired disability.

It is not clear whether the timing of disability has the same effect on the gendered identities of women who use wheelchairs. Some of the women in our study, such as Beth Devon and Sara Lane, have enjoyed success in their careers despite using wheelchairs from early childhood. It is possible that early onset of a physical disability tends to reduce the career advantages men in wheelchairs would otherwise enjoy over similarly situated women. This possibility, which suggests a slightly different perspective on the "double disability" hypothesis, is consistent with the views of some writers who observe that wheelchair users of both genders are seen, stereotypically, as asexual, as persons for whom the cultural categories of male and female, like many other cultural categories, are less significant.[6]

For individuals with *learning disabilities,* no less than those with physical disabilities, the interrelated effects of gender and disability can

6. As Murphy (1987:135) observes: "Just as the bodies of the disabled are permanently impaired, so also is their standing as members of society. The lasting indeterminacy of their state of being produces a similar lack of definition of their social roles, which are in any event superseded and obscured by submersion of their identities." Some have suggested that a physical disability may yield unexpected benefits by removing gender roles as a source of concern, as well as by increasing one's sense of self-reliance and accomplishment in overcoming barriers in daily life. See Deegan 1985; Hahn 1994.

shape the development of identity from childhood through adulthood. Consider, for example, the divergent paths followed by Rosemary Sauter (whose life story we presented earlier) and Dick Seaton, a woman and a man with much in common except for gender. Like Rosemary, Dick had a learning disability that was never acknowledged or understood during childhood. Both Rosemary and Dick were perceived as unintelligent students with little promise for college or a professional career, a perception arising from the effects of their learning disabilities and from stereotypes associated with their working-class backgrounds.

In large part because of their gender differences, however, Rosemary and Dick traveled down very different paths toward adulthood and adult careers. Dick, whose parents were poor farmers, was expected to use his muscles and his "shop skills" to earn a living. When Dick struggled with certain courses in school, his teachers and parents simply assumed that he lacked academic ability and pushed him toward a career in manual labor. Dick, who discovered as an adult that he has an IQ of 140, was told as a teenager that he was not college material. He enrolled without permission in a few college preparatory math courses and enjoyed the intellectual challenge they offered, but on the whole his record was poor. After graduation, he became a house painter. By contrast, Rosemary, whose father was a woodworker, was never expected to use her muscles or her shop skills, although she possessed both in abundance. Career paths open to Dick were closed to Rosemary because of her gender, while career paths that required higher education were closed to both because of their disability and social class.

Gender, in combination with social class and disability, provides an explanation for similarities and differences in the development of Rosemary and Dick's identities. Rosemary's decision to open a dance studio while she was still a high school student, although an unconventional choice, proved an effective way to deal with societal expectations of femininity for a teenage girl who was physically hyperactive and academically unsuccessful. Later, Rosemary gave up her career as a dance instructor for gendered reasons: her first husband did not want her to work, and she was expected to stay home with her two children (one of whom has a learning disability like her own). This career restriction was never imposed on Dick Seaton when he started his family or on any other male we interviewed. Over time, Dick achieved success in his career as a painting contractor while Rosemary remained outside the workplace. Eventually Rosemary decided to attend nursing school at the urging of two elderly women for whom she had provided home care. Many of our interviewees with learning disabilities—all of them women—chose careers as nurses or hairdressers. Although these careers may also be chosen by men, they were never considered by any of our male interviewees, including Dick Seaton.

By contrast, when Dick discovered as an adult that he had a learning disability, he considered pursuing a career as a doctor or psychiatrist, but in the end decided it was too late to begin a medical career and chose instead to return to college and study counseling. The thought that he might become a nurse never entered his mind, although nursing might have been more similar to the medical career he wanted the most. Had he been a woman, nursing might have suggested itself to Dick as it did to Rosemary.

Work and identity developed quite differently for Dick Seaton and Rosemary Sauter despite the similarity in their backgrounds and abilities. Gender affected their career choices at every turn, and it also influenced the perception of their learning disability and its role in their identity formation. Moreover, their stories suggest that the effects of gender on the identity formation of men and women with disabilities are contingent on other factors such as family, social class, and race.

While reaffirming the importance of gender in tracing the careers of individuals with disabilities and the role of disability rights, we prefer to avoid categorical conclusions about the impact of gender. We reject the notion that the intersection of gender and disability invariably affects the careers of women one way and of men another, regardless of other social factors or the type of disability and the time of onset or diagnosis. Rather, we urge the importance of viewing gender as a key component in the *process* of identity formation over time. Furthermore, because of the feedback effects of work on education and identity formation, the nature of work itself, with its pervasive gender coding, affects men and women with disabilities from early childhood through job training, job applications, hiring, and promotion. Consider, for example, the interplay between gender, work, and the evolving sense of self in the life story of Mary Williams in the section that follows.

Gender and Career

We view a career not merely as a phenomenon of adulthood but as a *process* that has its origins in early childhood, in the development of a sense of self within one's family, in school, and in taken-for-granted assumptions about what the world will offer a child or adolescent when he or she becomes old enough to work. Gender has a profound effect on this process. The life stories of individuals with disabilities reveal the continual effects of gender. In this section, we offer a portrait of one interviewee, Mary Williams, whose career emerged over a long period of time from the often painful experiences of her earlier life.

When we interviewed Mary Williams, she was in mid-career, working as a self-employed hairdresser and attending college in order to obtain teaching credentials so she could become a cosmetology instructor. Mary, then in her late thirties, had been married for nearly fifteen years and had two children with learning disabilities, yet Mary herself did not realize she had a disability until she decided to return for adult education classes in the local community college. As a hyperactive child who could not read but was never diagnosed, Mary's early academic and social experiences were painful: "I used to think, What's the matter? What's wrong? How come? . . . I couldn't read. I couldn't do anything. Everything relating to school I failed." During her early years, her disability made it impossible for her to fit in. Because she lacked what she and others perceived as a "normal" female identity, she found it hard to envision how she could enter the social mainstream as a child or an adult.

In school, Mary was constantly humiliated by her inability to do the work and by failing every test: "Any time they passed you a paper, I would sit there and cry, because I couldn't do it. And everybody would be done, and I was, it was a bad scene. It was bad, real bad." Mary recalls that she had no friends in elementary school. She fell several years behind her peers, her classmates called her "dummy," and she was "pretty ugly" and had "bad zits." Mary's memories of this period in her life combine the elements of perceived physical unattractiveness, lack of intelligence, and social rejection. Making matters worse, she recalls, her alcoholic father beat her each time she failed. His violent, abusive behavior punctuated each academic failure and left her feeling incompetent, lost, and alone.

As a schoolgirl, Mary's identity became compromised in large part because she lacked what were considered gender-appropriate traits such as attractiveness, poise, good manners, charm, and intelligence. Her fantasies of the future drew on culturally defined, conventional social roles for women. She was unable to envision herself in any professional career and instead wanted to be a housewife and have "a lot of kids." Since she found herself outside the conventional boundaries for girls who were "feminine," popular, and successful, however, her dreams of becoming a housewife and mother seemed unattainable.

In the sixth grade, Mary reached a dramatic turning point in her life when she decided to turn her apparent gender-related shortcomings to her own advantage:

I was always very strong. So one day, I came home crying, and I said . . . tomorrow, I go in and the next one that abuses me . . . I'm just going to beat the shit out of them! So I went in school, and it didn't take long. I was only in there for ten minutes, and we were all out on the lawn, and this Sally Green, and everybody thought she was the toughest jock queen. . . . I forget what she said, she didn't even finish it, and I went nuts on her. . . . I beat this girl. I beat her so bad, she had two big black eyes, a big fat lip. She was a mess. And then she was down on the ground, then don't I pick her up and brush her off! I says, "You know, you shouldn't have said that to me." [Laughing.] I mean, that's how bad I am. All right, you shouldn't have said that to me, all right, and I'm helping her up after I *killed* her.

Mary's reading of the sixth grade social scene was astute. After she beat up Sally Green, the jock queen, her classmates viewed her differently. Although they still kept their distance, they no longer ridiculed her as a failure and a misfit:

It just took once, one time. . . . I was smart enough to know, if I give myself this reputation, they won't do it to me no more. . . . That day was the end of the abuse for me. It was the last day, because then I'd be walking down the hall and everybody would move right over. Ohhhh, cool! That was better than having this right in my face. You know, maybe ten feet down the hall there, but that's fine. Before they were doing it right to me. So that was the end of it.

Mary had discovered that her strength and athleticism could compensate for her compromised identity as a preadolescent girl, at least to the extent that she was no longer made a victim by her insensitive classmates. It took a fistfight with another girl to stop her classmates from picking on her. If resort to physical violence complicated her gender identity, it helped to mitigate some of the stigma associated with her disability. She did not yet fit comfortably into any conventional, gender-defined category, but she had created a space in which she could explore her options and seek a path toward successful adulthood and, eventually, a career.

As Mary moved through middle and high school, she continued to struggle academically, and her father continued to beat her. Prospects for a conventional adult identity and career remained uncertain. She used her physical toughness to her advantage, but her difference from other girls made her lonely and depressed: "You'd go and you would work your butt off and you'd still get F's. And then I'd get my ass kicked [by my father]. And I was like, man-oh-man-oh-man." At the age of fourteen she made the first of several attempts to commit suicide, an indication of the seriousness of the despair she felt at the time, despite the humor with which she now narrates her life story.

Mary's life changed somewhat for the better when she began to spend three hours each day away from her high school at a special vocational school. Here, she suddenly discovered that she could excel academically and that the pursuit of a career might actually be possible. She explored a number of practical vocational fields, and she learned enough about auto mechanics to repair her own car, but the subject that most appealed to her was hairdressing. Gradually, Mary began to envision a future that combined academic success with professional employment in a field she enjoyed. She noted that being a hairdresser, unlike an automobile mechanic, was consistent with society's expectations for women. For the first time in her life, Mary perceived herself as conforming to a conventional gender role in her studies and in her thoughts about the future.

Mary had reached a second turning point in the process of identity formation and career development. Drawing on an aggressive and sometimes reckless determination, she achieved success in a field that society considered "feminine" and acceptable. As graduation drew near, however, Mary's plans for the future were placed in jeopardy by her continued struggle with academic subjects at her private high school. On the verge of failing a required social studies course and flunking out, Mary requested a meeting with the principal and several other administrators. As she describes the meeting, she rescued her career prospects by adopting a feisty and aggressive persona that must have seemed completely at odds with their expectations for the behavior of a teenage girl:

> I went down there and I called a meeting with the principal. I said, "Come on, boys, we have to have this meeting." And they all laughed and said okay. I said, "Now you know I really tried hard this year, and I came every day. . . . I really want this diploma. . . . I really would hate for youse to lose the money. Because I'm going to drop out, then, and you're going to lose a lot of money. . . ." I always knew what I was doing, when I said I was going to quit. I just wanted my way. I always got it.

The principal agreed with Mary, and he persuaded the social studies teacher to give her a score of sixty-five so that she could receive her diploma. She was now on her way to a career in cosmetology. To escape her abusive father, Mary moved to her grandmother's house and began to work. From a child who did not fit any of the "normal" images associated with young females in American society, she emerged as an adult who drew on her strengths to forge a career consistent with conventional gender expectations.

Mary Williams married at the age of twenty-three and had two children. She achieved considerable success as a hairdresser. The owner of the salon where Mary worked wanted her to serve as manager, not knowing that she could not read. Mary said she would take the position, but only on the condition that someone else would handle the books. Because she was such a capable and trusted employee, they agreed. No one at work knew about her disability. Mary found other ways to improvise accommodations that allowed her to "pass" and succeed in society. For example, when she went to the Department of Motor Vehicles and had trouble reading the forms, she simply removed her glasses, pretended she left them at home, and requested the assistance of another customer.

Perhaps Mary's most impressive self-devised accommodation involves a woman, Barbara, whose hair Mary cuts and whom Mary regards as a confidant. When Mary told Barbara that she had been unable to fill out her own Rolodex, Barbara offered to help. Gradually, Barbara took over more and more of Mary's paperwork in exchange for free haircuts. Barbara now manages all of Mary's finances, writes her bills, and handles her correspondence. The arrangement is strictly private, based on a barter exchange. Mary has found a way to function effectively as a professional with a severe learning disability without legal intervention and without the assistance of any government program or private organization.

At the time of our interview, Mary had returned to college in order to obtain a degree that would allow her to teach cosmetology. For the first time, Mary was tested and diagnosed with dyslexia and attention deficit disorder. As a result, she receives some of the indirect, context-creating benefits of rights: her college provides Mary with tutors and oral testing conditions and allows her to tape her classes. To her own surprise, she gets excellent grades in college—all A's and B's. She feels smart for the first time in her life, and enjoys using some of the fancy words she encounters in her college courses. Nevertheless, despite the rewards of these legally mandated accommodations, Mary is reluctant to identify herself openly as a person with a learning disability rather than "passing" with the benefits of improvised accommodations. She describes, for example, a tutor at her college who assumed that she would give him an incompetent haircut because of her learning disability. People who have invisible disabilities, Mary concludes, are usually better off concealing them in order to avoid stigma and prejudice. Moreover, Mary is unaware of the existence of the ADA and has no knowledge of the obligations it imposes on an employer: "Are they required to do this? I don't know. I'd have to find out."

The effects of disability and gender stereotypes combined throughout her life to make it difficult for Mary to imagine a career and a place in the social mainstream. Her identity as an adult now fits readily into familiar gendered images of mother, wife, and working professional in a field stereotypically considered appropriate for women. The effects of her disability no longer disrupt conventional gender categories, as they did during childhood. To friends and colleagues, to employers and teachers, Mary must seem a strong, vivacious, and forthright woman, a talented and respected hairdresser, an outstanding student and a prospective teacher. Mary has attained what was only a fantasy during childhood: she has conformed to societal expectations for women both in her family life and in her career. But throughout much of her adolescence and early adulthood, Mary shared the limited expectations others had for her. Because expectations were low and Mary's self-perception remained entangled with the effects of her disability, there was little disparity between expectations and reality and rights had little space in which to become active.

Improvising her own accommodations at work and at home, Mary Williams has now created a career in the social mainstream and has achieved an identity as an employee, wife, and mother that exceeded her childhood imaginings—but without invoking rights. Ironically, her unique methods of adapting to expected gender roles have rendered rights even less relevant because her career has far outpaced her expectations. Mary's silence on the subject of rights may be contrasted with the explicit discussion of rights in the life stories we next consider.

Gender and Rights

We turn now to narratives in which the role of legal rights receives express consideration. In this section, we discuss the accounts of men and women who are more aware of the ADA than is Mary Williams. Even for them, however, the role of rights is problematic and is complicated by societal assumptions about gender and employment. Consequently, some of our interviewees reject rights while others embrace them. For most, rights become active through their indirect, context-creating effects. In this section, we ask how gender affects and is affected by the various direct and indirect manifestations of rights.

As we have noted, the ADA itself is silent on gender, but gender is central to identity and the ADA was intended to transform the identities of individuals who were formerly the victims of exclusion and stigmatization. We may assume, therefore, that the ADA's drafters intended the transformation of identity to include the fair and rational treatment of gender difference, since the prior history of American civil rights legislation suggests that Congress intended its benefits to be available equally to men and women,[7] and that closely related—and, in some cases, overlapping—rights-based protections could address exclusion on the basis of *both* disability and gender. As we turn once again to our life story interviews, we ask whether this goal has been realized in the role rights actually play in the experiences of our interviewees.

We explore this question in the context of two pairs of life stories. The first pair—Beth Devon and Sid Tegler—turn away from rights as they construct careers that match their expectations for male and female employees in the social mainstream. The second pair—Jill Golding and Al Vincenzo—view rights as an important part of the process through which they attempt to create identities and careers that are consistent with prevailing images of men and women in American society.

Turning away from Rights: Beth Devon and Sid Tegler

We begin with the life stories of two accountants—Beth Devon and Sid Tegler—whose careers and identities diverged markedly yet whose negative attitudes toward rights were in the end quite similar. A comparison of their life stories provides insight into the profound importance of gender and gendered identities in relation to the provisions of the ADA; yet the ultimate similarity in their cautious view of rights serves as a reminder that no single social factor, including gender, translates simplistically into a predictor of rights consciousness.

Beth Devon and Sid Tegler, subjects of life stories presented earlier in this book, are both middle-aged and live in small towns in western New York. Both trained as accountants and have worked for many years in that field. Both have used wheelchairs since childhood. Yet, these similarities notwithstanding, the lives and employment histories of Beth and Sid are strikingly different. As we compare Beth's and Sid's life stories, we see that their disabilities and perceived gender roles led them to different career options and choices at every stage in their lives, although both eventually achieved professional and personal success.

---

7. In prior civil rights statutes, such as the Civil Rights Act of 1964 and Title IX of the Education Amendments of 1972, Congress made it clear that gender equity is necessary to achieve full participation by women and men in employment and in society generally. Both of these statutes prohibit unfair treatment based on stereotypes and irrational assumptions about men and women as citizens and as workers.

Even more significant is the fact that these two very different individuals embrace a similar philosophy that emphasizes self-reliance and individual responsibility rather than legal rights.

Beth Devon has defined her identity at each life stage in terms of her relationships with others. A strong and determined professional woman, she attained success and fulfillment in life within culturally familiar roles: as the high-achieving daughter of a strong-willed father, as the lifelong companion of the husband she met in college, and as the indispensable office manager for a male boss. Even when she became a part-time self-employed accountant, her motive for leaving her job as office manager was related to her commitment to familial relationships. And even as a solo practitioner, she devotes a significant part of her life to her relationships—as an adviser and counselor—with other persons who have disabilities and who need her help. Thus, while advocating independence and autonomy for persons with disabilities, Beth Devon has also affirmed the importance of conventional gender roles and the nurturing and support stereotypically associated with women in our society.

Beth, who contracted polio at the age of nine, had always assumed that she would attend college and become a professional. The inaccessibility of her college campus proved to be a problem, but it also introduced her to the man who would become her husband. Beth relied on male students to carry her up and down stairs. This experience of vulnerability and dependency was, in Beth's retelling, embarrassing; but being carried by a strong male student was also, at least in part, romantic. The initial relationship of dependency proved entirely consistent with the formation of a self who could enter the social mainstream and devise accommodations that allowed her to participate on her own terms.

Sid Tegler had similar experiences as a college student, but gender roles led him to interpret them quite differently. Sid, too, encountered inaccessible university buildings and grounds. He, too, was carried up the stairs by male students, but his most vivid description is being hoisted up the outside of a dormitory in order to attend a party on an upper floor. Sid, like Beth, was forced to depend on the extra efforts and the muscle power of others in order to join the social mainstream. He does not, however, describe this experience in terms of vulnerability and dependency, and certainly not romance, but rather in terms of male bonding and equality. Sid tells the story of being hoisted up the side of the building in order to describe the process through which he became one of the guys. He, like his friends, was young and reckless, a student more interested in drinking and partying than studying. Beth and Sid interpreted parallel experiences in college differently for reasons of gender, yet in both cases these experiences are described as laying the foundations for a life of self-sufficiency in the social mainstream.

As Beth and Sid began their careers, gendered roles and relationships continued to exert an influence. Beth took a job with a domineering and sometimes bullheaded male boss, and she used her patient, flexible, competent personality to establish herself as a "girl Friday" in the office.[8] Beth's boss understood and accepted this familiar gender role and came to view her as indispensable. Beth, in turn, worked within the culturally recognized employment relationship to carve out a remarkable career, albeit one founded on archetypal gender inequality.[9] She learned how to deal with her boss's moods and stubborn responses, and gradually developed a feasible work environment and office routine in which her disability became essentially irrelevant to her career. Although a male employee with a physical disability like Beth's might have developed a similar relationship and a comparable career, we think it would have been far more difficult. Our culture does not usually offer the same relational options to men in employment situations as it does to women.[10] Beth used the elements that were available to her, including societal assumptions about workplace gender roles and relationships that she herself may have endorsed, and, with great skill and resourcefulness, constructed a career that lasted many years.

Again, the contrast with Sid Tegler's life story is instructive. For Sid, there was never an option to work as anyone's "girl Friday." As in college, he assumed that participation in the workplace required him to be

8. Our colleague Dianne Avery, through her comments and suggested readings, has helped us understand the history of jobs that people in the 1950s, and perhaps nowadays as well, refer to when talking about someone's being a "girl Friday." This history further demonstrates how gender becomes a part of the social construction of particular types of work. Thus, Reskin and Padavic (1994:49–51) observe that in an earlier era, subordinate office roles were occupied by males rather than females. The growth of bureaucratization in the twentieth century created a massive market for clerks and office assistants. Women were hired for these positions because they were available and their wages were low. The current prevalence of women in such roles is in part a result of women's increasing availability in the low-wage labor market in combination with the tendency of relationships within employment settings to replicate relationships—and reinforce stereotypes—in the society at large. Men were retained for positions of greater authority in the office.

9. Although being a "girl Friday" may exemplify gender inequality in the workplace, Beth Devon's success in this role must be recognized as an achievement. Asch and Fine (1988:30) suggest that a woman with a disability may consider it a victory to attain a status that some women without disabilities might view as unequal or even oppressive.

10. Although camaraderie among males may be typical in some work settings, Asch and Fine (1988:30) observe that a man's physical disability conflicts with the gender identity required for male camaraderie or a "masculinized" job, while a woman's physical disability may reinforce the gender identity required in a "feminized" job such as Beth's and may interfere less with interpersonal relationships with coworkers.

like—or functionally equivalent to—the other men. When an accounting firm perceived him as unqualified because he could not climb to the top of an oil tank to measure its contents, it evaluated his job skills by exactly the same standards it applied to other male applicants. Sid believed that the evaluation was flawed but not the assumptions underlying it. He expected employers to be flexible, to assign him to functionally equivalent jobs, but his career aspirations developed within a framework in which he was one among equals, not someone's indispensable subordinate. He developed a hard-boiled persona to deal with unreasonable, inflexible employers. At one point, he describes conversations with African American friends who, like himself, encountered prejudice in the workplace: "They said, 'Well, now we know what it's like to run around on tire rubber.' And I said, 'Well, now I know what it's like not to have to worry about sunburn.' They said, 'Yeah, okay, yeah.' But it was that kind of thing, and it was, you go and do your thing, I'll do mine, and see you in a week, and maybe we'll get a cold one together, whatever. And that was it." It is difficult to imagine Beth Devon participating in this sort of offhand, Hemingwayesque dialogue as the result of encountering painful and humiliating discriminatory behavior.

Beth Devon and Sid Tegler both achieved professional success while adhering to a philosophy that emphasizes self-sufficiency and is inconsistent in their minds with the assertion of rights. For Beth, gendered images of incapacity or of subordination transformed themselves into social roles and relationships that she describes as fulfilling, including her role as a valued and highly competent employee. Determined to construct a career out of the cultural elements that were available to her, Beth skillfully positioned herself in the social mainstream. Sid has achieved success as a self-employed professional with deep roots in his community, but he has done so on his own and not from a subordinated status within a hierarchical organization. Like Beth, Sid achieved success by working with the cultural elements available to him, particularly those emphasizing autonomy and self-reliance. But as a man in a wheelchair, he found the cultural images associated with physical disability—incapacity, fragility, immobility—difficult to translate into a social role as a "normal" employee in a high-powered business establishment. In her fifties and sixties, Beth also turned to self-employment. This choice may also have resulted from a range of options narrowed by her disability, and to this extent her career resembles Sid's. Yet we sense that his range of options was more drastically narrowed from an earlier point in life than hers, and this narrowing stemmed in important ways from special problems associated with men in wheelchairs who attempt to participate as equals in the workplace.

Notwithstanding the different ways that gender has influenced their careers, the narratives of Beth and Sid have marked similarities, particularly in their characterization of disability rights. Both emphasize self-reliance and maintain that their success or failure in pursuing a career usually lay within their own power. Consequently, Beth and Sid reject rights as an answer to the barriers faced by persons with disabilities. Beth has made herself a living example of self-help, and her faith in the importance of self-presentation and a positive attitude makes her reluctant to assert rights that could disrupt the all-important impressions a good employee should make on an employer. Moreover, Beth has little faith that rights can help an individual on the job. Most important, an employee "should be able to do the job and do it well." She believes that a person with a disability should possess social skills that enable employers to see her or his competence and minimize awareness of the wheelchair. Individuals themselves are responsible for acquiring such skills, which are far more effective than disability rights.

Sid also dismisses disability rights, often with a quip reflecting his sardonic, offhand sense of humor. Although he believes that he has encountered deeply ingrained discrimination because of his disability, he does not perceive a role for rights in addressing such problems. The interplay of gender and disability have impeded Sid's career, and he has responded by emphasizing his belief in rugged individualism and the rewards of the market. His individualistic views leave little room for rights, and he expresses opposition to laws that single out persons like him for special treatment. Just as he prided himself on rugged individualism in adapting to his college environment, Sid emphasizes camaraderie within the business world—acknowledging the prejudices he encounters in that world but choosing to play by its rules because they reinforce his belief in his own independence. He thinks that his ability to assume this male role would be undermined if he gained admission to the business world by asserting disability rights. Although Sid believes that the prejudice he encountered while on the job market was irrational, because he was denied work for which he was well-qualified, he does not think that the ADA will improve such attitudes for many years. In the meantime, persons with disabilities should get on with their lives.

Although the process of identity formation was very different for Beth and Sid, they ultimately came to hold similar views of disability rights. Their reluctance to embrace rights can be explained in part by the similar niche they occupy in the business communities of their respective small towns, where the assertion of rights is likely to be viewed by friends, neighbors, and colleagues as disruptive and inappropriate. Yet Beth and Sid came to occupy their niche through very different paths, determined in large measure by gender-related factors. Their current occupation, and the images and beliefs about rights associated with it, represents a late stage in a long process of identity formation, and that process can be understood only in terms of the interaction between gender and disability within a particular cultural and social framework. In the case of Beth Devon and Sid Tegler, this process led them to turn away from rights guaranteed by the ADA.

Turning toward Rights: Jill Golding and Al Vincenzo

For Jill Golding and Al Vincenzo, the influence of gender on identity formation has produced a more positive attitude toward rights. Unlike Sid Tegler and Beth Devon, Jill and Al embrace rights, although in very different ways. Jill believes that rights can reinforce, and even create, caring relationships. Al's assertiveness about rights reflects his struggle to narrate an active, even aggressive, male identity. In different ways, each uses rights to help reconstruct gendered elements of a self that has been rendered ambiguous by disability.

Jill Golding, whose life story is one of the first recounted in this book, now believes that she is both competent and cared for as an adult woman. Earlier in her life, her self-concept was quite different. The effects of Jill's undiagnosed learning disability explain her poor performance in primary and secondary school and, later, in college. Her mother and teachers, who did not suspect the existence of her learning disability, thought Jill was lazy and were highly critical of her. Their perceptions had a devastating impact on her identity, and even later in life, after diagnosis of her disability and successful completion of her training as a nurse, these perceptions have a lingering influence on her self-concept.

Following graduation from high school, Jill pursued her dream of becoming a health care professional. Her still undiagnosed disability, compounded by low self-esteem and an abusive marriage, led to failure in her first attempt to complete college. Entering therapy marked a turning point for Jill, and her identity underwent a radical transformation. As she gained self-confidence, she reentered college, and her disability was diagnosed soon afterward. Her transformed identity enabled her to complete her professional training and to begin a successful career as a nurse.

As her identity changed and her life altered course, Jill Golding embraced rights. Jill's career in health care builds on values and skills she first learned from her nurse-mother and a school nurse who was her protector during her difficult school years. Jill, now a nurse herself and happily remarried, makes a strong connection between rights and the ethic of care that has guided her to her chosen profession. In her view, her right to accommodations for her disability requires her employer to care for her and to meet her individual needs in the same way she cares for each of her patients. She believes that if she had been offered the accommodations to which she was legally entitled as a girl in school, her childhood would have been transformed.

Jill's understanding of rights, unique among our interviewees, is that they reinforce, and even create, caring relationships. Although Jill does not discuss the relationship between rights and gender, it is apparent that she considers rights to be closely related to a *gendered* concept of caring. For Jill, her own caring for patients as a nurse is associated with the caring she should have received from her mother during childhood and the caring she now exchanges with a loving and supportive husband. Far from feeling restricted by her participation in an occupation that is often stereotypically associated with women workers, Jill embraces nursing because it is associated with values that have shaped her identity as a successful adult and as a woman. She experiences no conflict between either the gendered or professional attributes of her employment and asserting her rights as an employee. Quite the contrary, for Jill, asserting her rights positively reinforces her perception of herself as a nurse and a woman.

Unlike Jill Golding, whose identity as a girl and a young woman was problematic and unresolved, Al Vincenzo (whose life story we have not yet discussed) experienced no uncertainties about his male identity prior to a serious injury to his spinal chord at age twenty-one. Before his injury, Al devoted himself to playing hockey, partying, and fishing. Suddenly his life was transformed. Al's childhood and early adulthood had involved behavior that he understood to place him squarely within conventional gender categories, but the sudden onset of a physical disability at age twenty-one undermined his participation in those categories and required him to begin the work of redefining his identity as a young man with quadriplegia. His narrative illustrates how rights can contribute to the process of reconstructing gendered identities after a major disability has disrupted them.

Al describes himself as an underachiever during his middle school and high school years, graduating with a C average despite his high academic aptitude. He had an interest in writing and in art, but two other passions consumed him during those years: hockey and drugs. Al's substance abuse began at an early age:

Between thirteen and eighteen or nineteen, I'm in school during the day, smoking pot with my buddies between classes, and then at the bar the rest of the night. . . . I think I always had the inner niceties that I think I have now, but with drug and alcohol problems, they tend to cover up good parts of your personality. . . . I worked in a pharmacy, and for an addict to work in a pharmacy is like a rooster in a hen house. So I got in a lot of trouble there, as far as stealing things and all these associated problems that go along with abuse.

His addiction became so serious by the time he finished high school that he "was just thinking about where the next fix was going to come from." He missed his high school graduation ceremony because he was in a drunken stupor at a friend's house. Shortly afterward, unable to control Al's behavior, his parents asked him to leave the house. He rented several different apartments and was evicted from each of them for excessive partying. After six months on his own, Al awoke one December night under a dumpster and realized "I was about as low as you could go." At that point, he began rehabilitation.

Surprisingly, despite his problems with substance abuse, Al achieved considerable success as a young hockey player. He never conditioned himself properly, but he had a great deal of raw talent and assumed he would eventually become a professional. He recalls that he could shoot a puck eighty-seven miles per hour, "which is as hard as they can shoot it in the NHL." Ironically, Al's drug abuse and lack of conditioning had nothing to do with his injury, which occurred when he tripped over a fallen player and hit the boards head first. Al lost all sensation in his limbs and knew immediately that his neck might have been broken.

I heard a big snap and a big boooom, and as that sound got more quiet, everything went numb. It seemed like it took ten minutes to happen, but it only took the snap of the fingers. . . . It took them an hour to get to the rink and an hour to get me off the ice. There was a three inch hole in the ice melted the shape of my body where I was laying for two hours, with the police saying, "Turn him over." And I'm like, "Don't touch me." I knew what I did right away. I was just hoping that it was a bad pinched nerve.

In that instant, Al's identity was transformed. Prior to his injury, Al's personal qualities, both positive and negative, were readily associated with young American males. His athletic ability, his swashbuckling attitude toward life, even his excessive partying and his substance abuse are culturally acknowledged as "male" qualities and problems. This is not to say that young women cannot also devote their lives to sports or become addicted to drugs and alcohol. Indeed, Al's sister is, by his own description, an avid athlete. Nothing in Al's life prior to his injury was exclusively or intrinsically "male," yet from the perspective of the society and culture in which he lived, Al's interests, his behavior, and the very body he inhabited were all gender coded. He was easily recognizable as one iconic male type: a jock, an outdoorsman, a "bad boy." After his accident, he no longer fit the gendered stereotype.

Al's disability disrupted many aspects of his life, but our interest here is the way in which his quadriplegia undermined gender-coded features of his physical presence and behavior. Since some aspects of his personality had been dysfunctional, disruption was in certain ways desirable. Indeed, Al himself had begun to address his self-destructive behavior before his injury and was undergoing rehabilitative counseling for his substance abuse. He was ready to shed his "bad boy" behavior, but he was not prepared to give up hockey for life in a wheelchair. Some researchers, such as Hahn (1994) and Murphy (1987), have described this latter transition as one that can render males asexual by depriving them of symbols of masculinity considered significant in our culture—such as stature, physique, and athletic pursuits. Such descriptions suggest the gendered quality of the life change Al now faced. Al himself, however, does not tell his story in these terms, nor does he dwell only on losses.

Al spent months pondering the transformation he had undergone, and then he decided for the first time to attend college. In his own words, "After about a year and half of sort of laying around on my ass all day long and listening to my father tell me that I better do something with myself, I went back to school." By the time of our interview, Al had nearly completed his college education as an English major. Unable to be an athlete, Al has emphasized qualities and interests that had always been present but never as conspicuous as his more explicitly "virile" pursuits. He had always enjoyed writing. He had played the guitar and harmonica before his accident and had written songs for performance by local bands. Now these interests and abilities appear to be strengths on which he can build a college education and perhaps a career. Al also likes to draw and paint, and he views computer art or even cartoons as potential career options as well. Al talks about freelance work after graduation. He would like to submit poetry and short stories to newspapers and magazines.

The transformation of Al's identity and his career plans has involved the loss of some qualities that were overtly gendered, and in their place he now emphasizes qualities that are less overtly coded as "male" but are generally considered culturally appropriate for young men. The physical transformation was not inevitably emasculating, but did involve a refocusing from athletics to creative and artistic activities. Al does not see these two areas of interest as incompatible. "I'm a very artistic person," he observes. "So I think that part of art came out in me in sports and in hockey as a skater and a goal scorer."

The transformation we have described has not been easy for Al; he suffers from physical symptoms of stress and is often in great pain. He describes himself as a positive and "easygoing" person, but the competitive side of his personality that was so obvious in his athletic pursuits is still apparent. When Al speaks of discriminatory behavior by potential employers or of hypothetical situations in which employers might refuse to provide reasonable accommodations, he displays a strong awareness of his rights under the ADA and a professed willingness to act aggressively to protect them:

> I'm not one to scream lawsuit, lawsuit all over the place, but if it came down to that, I think I would use every means necessary to get what I thought was right for myself. I don't want to screw anybody out of money or whatever, but . . . if any law out there can, or any organization can help me get what I want, I'll use it. . . . I get pretty aggressive when it comes to trying to get what I want, so I would use whatever means necessary, I would say, to get and to keep a job.

For Al Vincenzo, as for Jill Golding, reference to his rights under the ADA helps to establish who he is and what he intends to do with his life. Jill makes a connection between rights and caring relationships that sustain her self-perceived identity as a woman. Rights enable Al to connect his self-perceived identity as a man in a wheelchair to his identity as a former star athlete. The urge to compete athletically still manifests itself in Al's speech and conduct, but it is now redirected toward fighting when necessary for the right to participate in the workplace. If some in our society would characterize this form of behavior as "macho," then it could be interpreted as a vestige of Al's activities before his injury. Al uses rights discursively to mitigate the gender-compromising effects of disability and to "normalize" his identity as a prospective employee within conventional concepts of male-female differences.

Although Al has not yet found occasion to invoke his ADA rights explicitly or formally, he claims that he is quite willing to do so. We take his claim at face value. Rights play a profound role for Al, clarifying the "conflicted identity" (Hahn 1994) of a young man in a wheelchair and helping him to reclaim, in altered circumstances, some essential aspects of the person he was before his injury.

Conclusion

Gender, like family, social class, and race, influences the formation of identity and the role of rights in the lives and careers of men and women with disabilities. Gender does not always operate in a clear or predictable fashion in relation to rights under the ADA, yet its significance is nearly always apparent in the way our interviewees think and talk about their life stories. These narratives suggest four different ways in which gender affects how rights become active.

First, gender operates over a long period of time to shape the identities of people with disabilities in the workplace. Rosemary Sauter's and Dick Seaton's experiences and opportunities throughout their lives have been influenced by the fact that she is a woman and he is a man. Gender has contributed to the formation of their personality, their social relationships and interactions, their perspective on life, their likes and dislikes, their political views, their career aspirations, and the ways in which others perceive them. All of these factors affect their perceptions of themselves as employees.

Second, gender combines with other resources to influence an individual's willingness to embrace rights. We have seen that gender interacts with such elements as family and educational background, social class, race, religion, ethnicity, and other social and personal factors in a *process* that operates over time to make rights more or less active in people's lives. Gender alone cannot explain differences in consciousness and perceptions of rights. We can contrast Jill Golding's and Al Vincenzo's openness toward the protections of the ADA with the rejection of rights in the narratives of Beth Devon and Sid Tegler, who also drew on—and were influenced by—conventional images and expectations for men and women as they fashioned their careers over time. For Beth and Sid, the relatively successful paths of their careers, influenced by gender from beginning to end, make the enactment of ADA rights seem unimportant or even undesirable. But for Jill and Al, rights offer a welcome guarantee of access to work that might otherwise be denied them on account of their disabilities. Rights for them are consistent with their self-perceptions and their ideals.

Third, entanglement of gender and disability helps explain the singular absence of references to rights in some narratives, such as Mary Williams's. Like many of our interviewees, Mary's struggle to separate the effects of her disability from her sense of self left little space in which rights could become active. Gender affected this struggle, in part by redirecting it. Because she had little knowledge of her learning disability until she reached adulthood, Mary's perceptions of her problems—

and her creative adaptations—focused on her "unfeminine" behavior rather than on the learning disability that remained undiagnosed and unknown to her. Even if she had been exposed to information about the ADA or the possibility of disability rights, the information in all probability would have seemed irrelevant. Formerly, Mary did not think of herself as a person with a disability but as someone with little academic aptitude and an unconventional, and sometimes unruly, personality. She would not have imagined that disability rights applied to her. Now that she has experienced success beyond her expectations in the conventional gender roles that she values—through marriage, motherhood, and pursuit of what she considers a gender-appropriate occupation—the likelihood of rights becoming active in her life is diminished even further. Rights appear to offer little beyond what she has already attained in her pursuit of gender-related goals.

Fourth, ADA rights can clarify the gender identities of men and women with disabilities in the workplace and facilitate entry into jobs that tend to exclude those whose gender identities are sometimes perceived as ambiguous. Disability may compromise or blur conventional gender identities, thus making it difficult for men and women to fit into the workplace and its often stringent gender constraints. While many of our interviewees had to contend with these blurring effects, some used or referred to ADA rights explicitly to clarify their gender identities. Jill Golding, for example, deployed rights to strengthen her self-concept as a person who was both caring and cared for as a woman. Her use of rights to reinforce relationships with others contrasts sharply with Beth Devon's concerns about rights as a disrupter of gendered relationships in the workplace. The iconic masculine characteristics of Al Vincenzo's personality before his injury were threatened by his physical disability and by the "conflicted identity" (Hahn 1994) associated with men who use wheelchairs. Al speaks readily about rights and states that he is willing to file a formal rights claim if necessary. One of the effects of rights in Al's narrative is to help him reconstitute his self-image as a feisty, competitive, even combative male—much like the semiprofessional athlete he had been before his injury. By contrast, Sid Tegler reinforces his gendered identity by rejecting rights and insisting instead on rugged self-reliance.

Finally, in all of these cases, we view the quest for so-called normal gender identities as a problematic issue in itself. Allusions to "masculine" or "feminine" identities in these life stories refer to cultural norms that are often based on irrational gender stereotypes and unequal or oppressive practices. For example, Beth Devon's success as a woman in the workplace owed a great deal to her ability to fit herself into a role of

gendered subordination as a "girl Friday" in an office. It was a remarkable achievement, but at the same time it became part of a broader pattern of gender inequality in employment. Sid Tegler's difficulty in finding employment arose in part from his rejection of any subordinated
role, because he was determined to participate in the workplace as one
among equals or not at all. Both Beth and Sid achieved success within
the constraints imposed by conventional gender roles in the workplace,
but these constraints drastically limited the career options available to
them. Achieving the elusive goal of normality, as defined by prevailing
social norms and practices, does not necessarily bring equality, since
"normal" gender roles may be inherently unequal.

Conclusion

Sara Lane, a newspaper reporter who contracted polio as a young child, benefited from the disability rights movement and from accommodations provided by employers, but she fears that asserting her rights might undermine her professional identity and jeopardize the opportunities of future reporters with disabilities. Jill Golding is an aspiring nurse whose recent awareness of her rights has led her to reinterpret her career prospects as well as her childhood experiences with a learning disability that went undiagnosed and unaccommodated. A young business school graduate with dyslexia who plans a career in his father's company, Raymond Militello views the Americans with Disabilities Act (ADA) as a mistake but argues that he would be a fool not to take advantage of the opportunities it affords him. Sid Tegler, a wheelchair user who opposes the ADA's guarantee of rights, reflects on his career as a self-employed CPA in a small town and his earlier struggles with employers in big-city accounting firms. Georgia Steeb, paraplegic since an accident in high school, endorses rights under the ADA but has never asserted them and at times expresses concern that the invocation of rights could violate her religious faith. A nurse from a working-class immigrant family that questioned the value of higher education for their daughter, Rosemary Sauter eventually obtained professional training with accommodations for her learning disability but has little awareness of or interest in the rights the ADA confers on her as an employee. Beth Devon, also the child of working-class parents, has followed a philosophy of self-sufficiency since becoming ill with polio in childhood, and believes that her success as an office manager and a CPA owes more to her skills and personal strengths than to the dubious benefits of legal rights.

The life stories of these individuals, and many others like them, form the basis of our book. As we write this conclusion, we look back twelve years to the date President George Bush signed the ADA into law, and we ask whether these life stories are different as a consequence. All of the men and women with disabilities whom we interviewed feel that they have experienced injustice in some form, many in connection with employment, yet none has filed a rights claim and none has asserted rights explicitly to confront what he or she perceives as unfair actions by an employer. Does this mean that rights have been inactive in their lives and that they would have told their life stories in much the same way if the ADA had never been enacted? We think not. We have argued that our interviewees' stories actually illustrate a broad spectrum of effects, and that rights have played a vital role for some of them while having little significance for others.

As we reflect on the role of rights in the lives of their intended beneficiaries, we are struck by the fact that these variable and highly significant effects would scarcely be noticed in most discussions of rights among policymakers, scholars, media commentators, and the public at large, because their discussions focus almost exclusively on formal claims and litigation. Analyses confined to the formal assertion of rights could not account for, or even see, the effects we have identified and might very well conclude that ADA rights have been inactive for all the individuals whose stories we have presented in this book. We reject this conclusion and we question any view of rights that ignores all but their most formal manifestations. We have presented an alternative view, a different theory of the sometimes subtle and pervasive role of rights in the lives of rights holders. Our theory draws illustratively on the effects of the ADA, but we think it applicable to civil rights in general.

Our finding that rights can play a significant role even in the absence of formal claims has led us to ask—and attempt to answer—further questions: Why are rights embraced by some of our interviewees, rejected by some, and unfamiliar to others? When rights become active, even when they are not explicitly asserted, why are the consequences dramatically positive in some but not all cases? Under what circumstances are rights most likely to promote the goals of inclusion, accommodation, and nondiscrimination that the drafters of the ADA envisioned?

From our earliest focus group discussions to our final individual interviews, the men and women who participated in this study have guided us toward answers that emerge from their autobiographical narratives. They have convinced us that identity provides the key to understanding how and when rights become active. The sense of self that emerges over a long span of time, from early childhood to adulthood, may be affected in different ways by a disability, and the intersection of disability and identity can make rights appear more or less relevant, useful, or attainable. We have proposed a view of rights that begins with a consideration of identity and then asks about the circumstances in which rights and identity constitute one another over time.

A Recursive Theory of Rights and Identity

The fundamental connection between rights and identity became clear to us soon after we decided to focus on the employment provisions of the ADA. Throughout history, the term "disabled" meant unable to work. The aim of Title I of the ADA was to enact rights that would ensure that greater numbers of men and women with disabilities *could* work. The drafters of the ADA contemplated a basic transformation of the identities of millions of Americans, extending far beyond the workplace. Our educational system to a large extent reflects the needs and expectations of the workplace. If people with disabilities are seen as capable of employment, then teachers and parents may change their perceptions of students with disabilities and may help them to construct an identity that anticipates inclusion rather than exclusion. In the same sense, because of the value our society places on self-sufficiency and employment as indicators of citizenship, enabling persons with disabilities to work should also transform their status in the community and should contribute to a new social identity founded on equality and autonomy.

In short, the aspirations of the ADA enabled us to see quite clearly the fundamental connections between rights and identity. Indeed, we have suggested that other theories of rights also contain important, but unstated, assumptions about identity. Classical rights theory assumes that rights contribute to the identity of the idealized democratic citizen who is entitled to full political participation. The rights and relationship model assumes that rights can undermine identity by damaging community networks and relational ties that are essential to social life. Critical rights theory, at least in its original form, contends that rights have damaging effects on identity by creating false hopes for their efficacy and then dashing those hopes when power is actually contested. Feminist legal theorists and critical race theorists have defended the role of rights, because they assume that under certain conditions rights can contribute positively to the social identities of those who have been disempowered and excluded. Thus, our interest in the connection between identity and rights has roots in earlier theoretical models, but we think the connection is far richer and more complex than has been recognized.

We have argued that the relationship between identity and rights runs in both directions. It is *recursive* in the sense that not only does identity determine how and when rights become active, but rights can also shape identity. Our recursive theory of rights derives from a body of sociolegal scholarship emphasizing the mutually constitutive relationship between law and society. What can this perspective tell us about the role of rights? We think it tells us this: identity involves basic understandings of who one is and where in society one belongs. The process of identity formation makes individuals more or less ready to see rights as relevant to their experiences. The experience of exclusion—from a building, a job, an education, a social network—may seem natural and appropriate unless it is inconsistent with one's identity, in which case it can appear unnatural and unjust. Perception of a disparity between actual and expected treatment creates a space in which rights might appear relevant as a yardstick to measure unfairness. But what is the source of our assumptions about who one is and where one belongs? Surely rights can—recursively—contribute to these assumptions, and thus to one's identity, by shaping the development of a sense of self in many ways, direct and indirect, symbolic and practical, from early childhood to middle age or later. Rights may influence identity by altering how individuals perceive themselves or by changing how they are perceived or treated by others, bringing about a new perspective on who one is and what one expects. The self, so constituted, acquires an identity that can, under certain circumstances, lend itself to the perception that he or she is being treated unfairly—that rights are being violated.

An important aspect of the recursive relationship between rights and identity is that it extends over many years. In developing our theory, we found it essential to listen to the life stories of our interviewees, since we sought to understand a long-term process in which the self develops and in which rights may or may not play a role at different moments. Even those who subscribe to a mutually constitutive theory of law and society do not necessarily study the interactive process over such a long span of time. Our interviewees continually reminded us of the importance of doing so, by returning in their narratives again and again to the significance of family, early education, childhood friendships and struggles, and high school and college training. Thus, we have concluded that it is important to explore the recursive effects of identity and rights in research that has considerable temporal depth.

It is also important to acknowledge the many important, though informal, ways through which rights may become active. Unlike traditional theorists of rights, we do not confine our attention to litigation, formal claims, or even explicit articulations of rights. Instead, we suggest that individuals use resources and form relationships in their social environment in different ways as identity emerges, shaping ideas about who they are and how they expect to be treated. Knowledge of rights may have direct effects, but rights may also become active without the rights holder's participation or awareness. Our interviewees sometimes described situations in which friends and colleagues in their social networks perceived the relevance of rights and the importance of accommodations. In these situations, rights became active because of the efforts of others rather than those of the rights holders themselves. The recursive relationship between rights and identity must also be understood in terms of the effects of rights on social institutions, such as the workplace, the family, and schools. In fact, we have identified at least three ways, other than explicit claims or formal litigation, in which rights become active and shape identities and careers.

First, rights can change the self-perceptions of individuals with disabilities, enabling them to envision more ambitious career paths by incorporating in their plans the reasonable accommodations and the nondiscriminatory treatment guaranteed by the ADA. Some of our interviewees, such as Jill Golding and Barry Swygert (pp. 100–104), viewed themselves as qualified for professional careers because they assumed that rights would help to make such careers possible. The availability of rights can create more positive and confident self-perceptions, encouraging individuals with disabilities to formulate career aspirations and to perceive many obstacles as the product of unfair treatment rather than personal shortcomings. Further, as individuals with disabilities incorporate rights into their self-image and their career planning, their everyday interactions with friends, co-workers, and supervisors may begin to reflect rights-based assumptions.

Second, ADA rights become active through cultural and discursive shifts even when rights do not directly transform an individual's self-perceptions. By becoming part of everyday speech, thought, and action, ADA rights affect the way others perceive individuals with disabilities as employees. Sara Lane, for example, never invoked rights, but it is apparent that the ADA contributed to a shift in the behavior and perceptions of many people in her workplace, partly because of her own interactions with them, and partly because of the broad and diffuse cultural transformations that the ADA helped to promote. These broader cultural shifts derive from many sources, including media reporting of the ADA and the relatively rare acts of enforcement it has spawned. As a result, Bill Meier's second boss (see pp. 200–201) voluntarily initiated precisely the sort of employer-employee dialogue about accessibility that the ADA was intended to promote, although neither he nor Bill apparently mentioned the ADA explicitly.

Third, ADA rights may become active through institutional transformations that are not directed at any particular individual. As a result of cultural and discursive shifts, as well as the fear of legal enforcement, rights are sometimes implemented unilaterally by third parties, including employers, rather than through advocacy by the rights-bearers themselves. Rosemary Sauter, Sean O'Brien (pp.163–65), Mary Williams (pp. 220–25), Evelyn Gardner (pp. 189–94), and other interviewees found that their colleges provided reasonable accommodations and educational services to all qualified students. Sara Lane's workplace became more accessible when the editor of the newspaper engaged in a general assessment of his organization's responsibilities under the ADA.

Closely related to our last point, we have learned that the impact of special education laws and practices on schools, apart from the enactment of the ADA, has had a dramatic effect on the rights consciousness of children and adults. Young adults who benefited to some extent from the IDEA may be more inclined to incorporate rights into their thoughts about future employment. Because they viewed themselves at an earlier age as rights-bearing individuals, they and others may perceive higher employment aspirations as appropriate. At the same time, they may be uncertain about the consequences of attempting to implement disability rights in the workplace. Individuals who had no experience with the IDEA are more likely to be unaware of their rights under the ADA and may not be able to envision how legally mandated accommodations could make an ambitious career possible for a self they may still view as "disabled."

These sometimes subtle and indirect effects of rights hold great significance for the workplace. As we have suggested, the identity of workers with disabilities is especially problematic because of the historical dichotomization of "disability" and "work." Employees or would-be employees rarely assert rights explicitly against their employers, in part because of the identity issues we have already discussed and in part because, as in the case of our interviewees, many consider it self-defeating to seek inclusion and acceptance through confrontation and claims of law violation. Furthermore, it is anomalous for the ADA to require its beneficiaries to prove their entitlement to employment rights by demonstrating first that they are unable to work. It is also problematic to define the reasonableness of accommodations exclusively from the vantage point of the employer who creates a barrier to access and then claims that change is too costly. For all of these reasons, individuals are reluctant to assert adversarial rights claims in the workplace, and our interviewees depended almost exclusively on rights becoming active in some other way—through the support of coworkers, through the unilateral actions of their supervisors, through corporate decisions to alter workplace environments or practices, or through more diffuse attitudinal changes or cultural and discursive shifts. In some life stories we can discern these transformations actually taking place, but in others the workplace appears impervious to all but the most direct and aggressive attacks, which our interviewees were not willing to undertake.

Making Space for Rights

A recursive theory of rights and identity might suggest a continual evolution toward greater rights consciousness and an ever-increasing role for rights, but our study does not lead us to such a conclusion. Although rights and identity can and do act reciprocally upon one another, many of the life stories we collected point to factors that can change the indirect or symbolic effects of rights or even prevent them from becoming active. We think that one of the values of the theory of rights that we present in this book is to explain in broader terms why rights become active in different ways for different individuals and, for some people, not at all. Our interviewees report that the ADA's employment rights have been neither uniformly beneficial nor uniformly harmful. Instead, the effects have varied dramatically and are dependent far less on the formal qualities of the law than on the evolving identities of its beneficiaries and the social circumstances of their lives.

Explaining the variable effects of the ADA's employment rights has been a central goal of this study. We can summarize our conclusions by pointing to the elements of identity that have provided a focus throughout this book: identity's interactional and intersubjective qualities and its narrative dimension. We have examined a number of factors that affect an individual's capacity to engage in social interactions or to narrate their life stories in ways that are likely to enhance or diminish the various roles of rights. Some of these factors might be characterized as personal attributes while others are social circumstances that make different kinds of resources more or less available.

Personal Attributes

Personal attributes of a potential rights holder can make a great deal of difference. Certain individuals, for reasons that cannot always be explained, have greater resiliency, ambition, perseverance, creativity, congeniality, and courage. These attributes endow them more than others with a capacity to engage in constructive social interactions and to narrate stories of the past and future that are consistent with successful careers. We consider these attributes a key to the construction of identity, but of course they are also components of identity and are recognized as such by persons with whom an individual interacts. The effect of these attributes can be the creation of a shared perception that for some people but not others employment is possible and that a space exists in which rights may become active.

Very often, as we have observed, this perception of a space for rights is facilitated by the ability to construct a sense of self that is separate and distinct from the disability. An individual who cannot make this distinction has a blurred identity that tends to inhibit the perception that rights might be relevant, but individuals who more clearly separate the "able" self from the disability are likely to appear worthy of accommodation, inclusion, and employment. And yet, paradoxically, for a few individuals who possess an abundance of the personal attributes we have listed above, rights remain inactive because of success and not because of incapacity. That is, for people like Beth Devon and Sid Tegler, the extent of their professional and personal accomplishments leads them to perceive no gap between where they are and where they want to be. Their perseverance, determination, and creativity enables them to achieve many of their ambitions without rights and to conclude that the drawbacks of rights are not worth the additional benefits they might confer.

Among the personal attributes that explain variations in identity and the role of rights, one of the most important is the nature of the disability itself. Individuals with learning and with physical disabilities encounter very different problems, not only because the workplace may present different barriers to their participation but because their disabilities affect identity in quite different ways. The two disability types that we have included in our study have dissimilar effects on the interactional or intersubjective dimension of identity. A learning disability is invisible and the option to conceal it is attractive to those who fear stigmatization or misunderstanding. By contrast, those who use wheelchairs may feel their disability is *too* visible and that it tends to overpower all other attributes in its effect on social interactions. Our interviews revealed differences between individuals with these two types of disability regarding expectations of others, cultural environments, degrees of understanding, and discourses about their disability. As a consequence, the process of identity formation for an individual with a learning disability can be quite unlike that of an individual who uses a wheelchair, and perceptions of the relevance of rights may vary accordingly.

Social Circumstances

In addition to personal attributes, we have attempted to explain variations in the role of rights by pointing to the social circumstances of our interviewees. We suggest that, because of differences in their social circumstances, individuals have different resources available to them with which to construct an identity and a career. The personal attributes discussed above constitute one such resource, but we have also discovered that our interviewees have variable access to other types of resources in their social environment and that these differences affect how and when rights become active. Differences in social circumstances include family, class, race, and gender, but they do not always lend themselves to simple predictions about the resources an individual may find available. For example, both Sean O'Brian (pages 163–65) and Rick Evans (pages 54–57) come from close-knit and supportive families. Sean learned from his family how to construct a tough and resilient identity and an ambitious career path, while Rick did not. In understanding how social circumstances translate into personal resources, it is important to avoid overly deterministic or reductionist conclusions. Nevertheless, our interviewees consistently pointed to their families as one of the most important resources available to them, and we conclude that family circumstances provide a crucial interpretive key to understanding the formation of identities and careers as well as the potential role of rights.

Similarly, social class and race explain differences in our interviewees' access to resources that enable them to construct an identity that is more or less consistent with a role for rights. Our comparison of Louise Dobbs and Barry Swygert (pages 100–104) illustrates how two individuals who experienced very similar physical disabilities in midcareer have responded in dramatically different ways. Differences in social class help to explain why Louise could not gain access to resources that might enable her to construct an identity and a career after suffering a stroke on the floor of a chicken processing plant. Her limited education and her history of low-wage manual labor employment left her unable to construct a sense of self that was consistent either with continued employment or with any conception of the role rights might play in facilitating her return to work. By comparison, Barry Swygert's middle-class upbringing, education, and employment history provided him with ample resources for reconstructing his identity and his career as a wheelchair user with quadriplegia, and ADA rights reinforced his new sense of self as well as his understanding of the contribution he might make to future employers.

Once again, we do not mean to suggest that differences in social class invariably confer advantage or make it more likely that rights will play a role, but we do think that education, income, and social status provide important resources that many of our interviewees have been able to deploy as they construct an identity for which ADA employment rights appear appropriate. We also think that the effects of systemic racism on a community can explain why William Thomas (pages 183–89), a young African American man, has had access to fewer resources and has consequently constructed a less ambitious career objective—with a more limited role for rights—than have his white counterparts. Racial difference does not always equate with a diminished role for rights, as the example of Evelyn Gardner reminds us (pages 189–94), but it is a social circumstance often associated with limitations on the resources available to construct a career that could incorporate disability rights into one's conception of what is possible.

Gender is a social circumstance as well as a personal attribute. It is a social circumstance in the sense that entry into particular kinds of social activities, including employment, has historically been influenced by cultural assumptions about appropriate activities for men as compared to women. Our comparison of the lives and careers of Rosemary Sauter and Dick Seaton (pages 219–20), for example, reveals how gendered assumptions about employment and family for working-class men and women led them down very different paths despite similarities in their disabilities. Gender-based assumptions affected our interviewees throughout their lives, shaping the sense of their own career potential as their identity developed from childhood. Thus, gender as a social circumstance made different kinds of resources available to the men and women we interviewed, and permitted them to engage in different ways in the social interactions and narrative practices that form an identity. For many of our interviewees, gender and its role in identity formation became closely connected to the perception that they were appropriately or inappropriately situated in relation to work and, as a consequence, that rights did or did not have a role to play in defining the fairness of their experiences.

All of these social circumstances—family, class, race, and gender—help us to understand variations in the ways individuals think and speak about themselves, which we have referred to as the "discourses" they employ. We have suggested that certain widely used discourses can in themselves serve as a resource to facilitate identity formation or to characterize one's situation as appropriate or inappropriate. Among the most significant of these discourses in our interviewees' life stories are the discourses of racial justice, the market, and religious faith. We contend that because of differences in their social circumstances individuals may have variable access to these discourses and that the use of one rather than another can shape understandings of fairness and unfairness, justice and injustice, and the relevance of legal rights.

Timing

In examining how personal attributes and social circumstances contribute to variations in identity formation and the role of rights, we have emphasized an additional consideration: the timing of a disability's onset or diagnosis. Identities are shaped not only by the slow processes of socialization and child-rearing but also by more rapid and traumatic changes, such as an automobile or sports accident or the diagnosis of a learning disability. When an identity is suddenly reshaped in this way, different resources may come into play. For Sara Lane, early onset of her physical disability meant that she benefited from a long period of preparation for self-sufficiency in a middle-class family that strongly encouraged her to develop an identity consistent with a professional career; but for Rick Evans (pages 54–57), early onset led to his isolation from social networks and opportunities to develop a "normal" identity as a potential employee. For Bill Meier (pages 198–202), the later onset of his physical disability meant that he could draw on existing professional credentials and connections—and on the shift in cultural practices resulting from the recently enacted ADA; but for Louise Dobbs (pages 180–83) the later onset occurred at a time when she had lost her network of supportive friends and relatives and had acquired few credentials or connections that might enable her to imagine future employment. Thus, we argue that it is essential to consider the nature of the resources available to an individual at the moment when disability intersects the lifespan and in the time that follows.

What Difference Do Rights Make?

We have chosen to examine the influence of a civil rights statute in part because we think such laws embody the highest and most expansive expectations for rights. Civil rights are rights of inclusion and are intended to bring about fundamental changes in the lives of rights holders and in society as a whole. Earlier civil rights laws reflected similar lofty expectations for groups that historically had been excluded and oppressed, in particular persons of color and women. Our analysis of the ADA is intended as a case study that may have implications for the analysis of other kinds of civil rights. We hope that our suggestions for new kinds of research and new conceptualizations of the effects of rights will contribute to improved understandings of civil rights in general and not just those associated with the ADA.

We contend that legal consciousness, which other writers have shown to be mutually constitutive of a wide variety of rights, is always related to the evolution of an identity. We argue that identity must be viewed across a broad span of time, and we suggest that one way to obtain such a view is to elicit life stories. When identity is presented in this way, its complex interconnections to rights are more clearly revealed. Furthermore, it is possible to perceive the many different ways in which rights become active and to transcend the narrow constraints of a litigation-based perspective. The result is a richer and more nuanced understanding of the difference rights make and the variable social circumstances that cause rights to make a greater difference for some people than for others.

If civil rights are a favored instrument of social change in American society, yet they rarely become active through formal claims, what conclusions might we draw about the extent of change rights can actually produce? Since enactment of the ADA, those who have sought to make it effective (and those who have sought to limit its reach) have focused a great deal of attention on litigation strategies and on the courts' interpretations of the statute's meaning and purpose. Commentators have tended to follow this example and have measured the ADA's success or failure in terms of appellate court decisions. We do not dispute the importance of these doctrinal battles, but we think they provide an extremely limited and at times distorted picture of the difference the ADA has made. Our study points to the need to understand and evaluate a far broader range of effects. We need to assess the positive and the negative consequences of the ADA as it has become active in each of the ways we have identified, rather than to limit our inquiry to the latest decisions handed down by the appellate courts.

In order to measure the difference a civil rights statute makes in terms of its broad spectrum of effects, we must consider factors that go beyond the outcomes of formal rights claims. Using the ADA as an illustration, we suggest that considerations such as the following might be included in the analysis:

The employment provisions of the ADA make a difference primarily for individuals who realize that they have a disability and especially for those who are willing to reveal this fact to an employer. For example, individuals with learning disabilities often go undiagnosed for part or all of their lives and receive no benefit from the ADA's provisions concerning nondiscrimination and reasonable accommodation. Even among those who recognize that they have a disability, many fear the stigmatizing consequences of revealing their diagnosis to others. The benefits they receive from the ADA, if any, are confined to shifts in self-understanding, but without accommodations they may never have the opportunity to perform to their true ability in the workplace.

For individuals whose disability has been revealed or is apparent to others, the benefits of the ADA may vary according to their knowledge of rights and their propensity to embrace or reject them. If individuals do not have knowledge of their rights, then they will benefit only from the ADA's indirect, context-creating effects or from the interventions of others. But even individuals who know about their rights may not want to invoke them because they dislike conflict, because they think rights entitle them to more than they deserve, or because they fear that others will denounce the perceived "special treatment" that the ADA mandates. These individuals may benefit from the ADA's indirect or symbolic effects, but they are unlikely to use the ADA to seek individual accommodations or protest against discriminatory treatment.

Social class, race, and gender interact in very complex ways with ADA rights and with careers. In some cases, these social circumstances produce societal expectations that are consistent with high career aspirations and with the goal of attaining particular types of jobs, but in other cases they do not. The benefits of the ADA, even those that are primarily indirect or symbolic, may vary accordingly. In the absence of expectations that certain kinds of work are appropriate, denial of access to such work may not be perceived as a violation of rights, and the ADA may not be seen as relevant to an act of exclusion. But when social circumstances and other identity-related factors are consistent with expectations of a successful career, then the ADA is more likely to confer a broad spectrum of benefits.

Considerations such as these help us to understand not only whether civil rights laws can make a difference but when and how. By asking in this way what difference rights make, it becomes possible to envision different kinds of strategies for enhancing their effects and realizing the goals of a statute such as the ADA. For example, legal activists or policymakers may determine that it is more beneficial to concentrate efforts on institutional or community level change rather than focusing primarily on individual claims. The context-creating effects of rights described in our interviewees' life story interviews are often very powerful and are perhaps more prevalent than other effects. Also, our interviewees provide strong evidence of the importance of early life influences. Identities formed in childhood around the assumption of social inclusion have been key to the success of individuals like Sara Lane, Beth Devon, and others. Strategies aimed at introducing the norms and concepts of the ADA to young children, including children who do not (yet) have disabilities, could prove particularly important. Such strategies should be directed not only at schools, where our interviewees recounted mixed success in achieving inclusion and reasonable accommodations, but also at social service providers, medical providers, churches, business leaders, and community groups. We might also note that education directed at children sometimes has the unexpected benefit of leading parents to recognize they have the same hereditary disability and hold the same rights under the ADA.

Our study raises further questions about the difference that rights make. We are struck by the fact that two of our most successful interviewees, Sid Tegler and Beth Devon, constructed fulfilling lives and successful careers without ever invoking rights. Indeed, each offered thoughtful and well-reasoned arguments why rights would not have worked for them and have perhaps been overvalued by others. Unlike many interviewees, however, Sid and Beth were able to use the resources their families and their social circumstances provided in order to create an identity distinct from the effects of their disability and to maintain a successful career notwithstanding their use of a wheelchair. We learn from Sid and Beth that invoking rights may require difficult or complex choices, that rights can have costs as well as benefits, and that while many individuals may find ways to benefit from rights, others will, for equally good reasons, reject them entirely.

We are impressed by the thoughtful, and often profound, assessments of the possibilities for rights offered by our interviewees. Most of them believe that rights are "right," that is, rights are just and appropriate, yet many also believe that the outcome of invoking rights can be uncertain or problematic. Such cautionary conclusions help to explain why none of the sixty interviewees used rights explicitly and confrontationally in situations of perceived injustice. Yet some of the interviewees maintain that a formal assertion of rights could be justified as a matter of principle, and they describe circumstances under which they themselves might take such a step. They would do this, they say, to prove a point to an employer who is clearly in the wrong or because they believe that rights can, in some situations, confer a favorable outcome, which might include a more desirable identity for themselves and future employees. More often, however, our interviewees are highly selective about the situations in which they say rights should be invoked. Some of our most thoughtful interviewees spoke to us about the importance of education, which they took to be a more important strategy for bringing about inclusion than rights-based claims. Their statements remind us that identities can be transformed and rights can become active in many ways. A recursive theory of rights must consider identity as a precursor as well as a consequence of rights, and rights as a result as well as a cause of change.

We conclude with an account of an intergenerational conversation about rights. The participants are a father and daughter who have similar learning disabilities. Deeply devoted to one another, they nevertheless differ in their perspectives on rights, identity, and disability. We hear them speaking across a generational divide, reflecting the difference between growing up with rights and without them.

Epilogue

When Dick Seaton (see pages 219–20) appears for his interview, he is accompanied by a young woman whom he introduces as his daughter, Joanna. At first we are surprised that he has invited her to sit in, but he explains that he came to understand his own learning disability as a direct result of Joanna's diagnosis early in her childhood. Their life stories are intertwined. When Joanna was ready to enter college, Dick also applied, and now they are both working toward their bachelor's degrees.

Joanna listens as Dick describes a painful childhood growing up with a learning disability that no one recognized or understood. He went to school before the concept of "dyslexia" was defined, before special education existed, and before the ADA was even imagined. Dick Seaton was the child of impoverished tenant farmers, and his teachers viewed his academic difficulties as consistent with what they considered his inferior social class. Dick resisted his relegation to the "shop track" by sneaking into some college preparatory classes, but on the whole he accepted the view that he lacked intelligence.

Dick recalls a big schoolmate named Wilbur Lassiter, a "farm kid," who was "retarded." "I kind of thought, well maybe this was my situation." When Joanna was diagnosed, Dick took the same tests and discovered that he had an IQ of 140. But throughout his childhood and much of his adult life, he assumed that his identity and his prospects were much like Wilbur Lassiter's: "I just felt I was retarded or a slow learner or dumb. To me, there were two different segments of people. There were people who were intelligent that were going on to school, and there were people who were just going to be laborers for their life. . . . I haven't thought of myself that way since I was tested."

Pursuing a career consistent with his earlier-held identity as a laborer, Dick eventually became a successful painting contractor and an active member of the local Republican Party. His distaste for oppressive government regulations colors his perception of disability rights, even though he now realizes that he—and Joanna—are potential beneficiaries of the ADA: "If you're an employer that's running a business . . . and somebody can produce more profit for you than someone who . . . [has] some form of disability . . . it's unfair of society to say to you, as an employer, you have to accommodate this person." Dick contends that employers should not be forced to provide accommodations for employees with disabilities: "Maybe we have to educate rather than passing all kinds of laws."

At this point, Joanna speaks up. Although she and her father are extremely close and have shared many experiences, she does not agree with Dick's statement about the role of rights. She tells her father, "If you just want to educate them, they're not going to take it upon themselves to be educated unless they have a law that says they have to. . . . I don't think people are just going to take the initiative on their own. I just don't think so."

A year later, we are sitting in the living room of Dick Seaton's spacious house, interviewing Joanna. It is a hot summer day, and Joanna's mother appears with a tray of lemonade. Three cockatoos in the next room interrupt our conversation from time to time with loud squawks. It soon becomes clear that there is no Wilbur Lassiter in Joanna's memory of early childhood, but she does recall the day when she appeared in this very room to make an important announcement:

> I was just around five years old. I came to my parents and told them that I had a problem. . . . I knew that I looked at the world differently than other people did. . . . I still remember I was standing right there and I had my pajamas on . . . and I don't know for sure why it was that I realized that things were different to me than they are to other people. . . . There's a real line there between how other people think and how I think.

When Dick Seaton's difference had become apparent, his parents and teachers reacted harshly. Dick had told us that his father was "a very nasty person" who would yell at him "and you could never do anything that satisfied him." As we listen now to Joanna's memories of childhood, we are struck by the difference between her warm and comfortable family surroundings and the cold and impoverished household in which her father grew up. Her parents soon took her for testing and diagnosis. They supported, encouraged, and "inspired" her, never doubting that she was capable of academic success. For Joanna, unlike her father, learning specialists were available with sophisticated under-

standings of dyslexia, and a legal framework existed to protect her educational rights. Recently, as Joanna is well aware, the ADA was enacted.

Despite her early diagnosis and the special education services that
were available, Joanna has faced many obstacles. Her parents fought
with the local school district over her accommodations and eventually
decided to withdraw her from special education and hire a private tutor
instead. She struggled throughout high school and had only a few close
friends. When she entered college, she requested and received testing
accommodations, and she has maintained an A average. Even in college,
however, Joanna keeps her disability a closely guarded secret. She participates actively in student government and fears that "it would tarnish
my image" if anyone learned that she was dyslexic. She is preparing to
become a schoolteacher to work with children who confront the challenges she has faced throughout her life.

Joanna Seaton is by no means an ardent advocate of disability rights,
but her perceptions are based on life experiences unlike her father's. As
we talk on this hot summer afternoon in the comfortable house that
Dick Seaton built for his family, Joanna reflects a viewpoint shaped by a
different upbringing in a different historical era. She does not share her
father's negative perception of rights. She is not sure exactly whether
or how she would invoke her rights as long as she remains determined
to conceal her disability from professors, friends, classmates—and the
school administrators who might hire her. But Joanna, unlike Dick, believes that the ADA appropriately expresses the obligation of employers
toward employees, including teachers like herself who have disabilities:

> I can help these children, because I've been there. I know how they
> perceive the world. I can . . . help them in the same way that I was
> helped, so in that respect I would think that I would be an asset to
> them, and I would think they should do as much as they could to
> see to it that different children have the best education that they
> could. And if that meant providing me with some small measure
> that's going to help, then I think that should be their obligation.

Joanna, unlike Dick Seaton, has known since early childhood that
there is a name and an explanation for the difference she first articulated
while standing in her pajamas in the living room where we now sit and
talk. Her experiences, unlike his, always occurred in proximity to the
practices the law mandates for people with disabilities. She has never
fully embraced these practices and is wary of the negative consequences
the law might have. Joanna differs from her father, however, in that
she perceives herself as a *bearer of rights,* and she believes those rights
to be necessary and just. Although she is not sure she will ever invoke

the ADA, her thoughts about the future that she expresses to us today, on the threshhold of graduation from college and a career as a teacher, must be very different from those her father would have expressed when he was her age, twenty-five years ago, as he embarked without rights on an even harder journey.

References

Statutes and Cases
Americans with Disabilities Act (ADA), 42 U.S.C. §§12101 et seq. (1994)
Individuals with Disabilities Education Act (IDEA), 20 U.S.C. §§1400 et seq. (1994 & Supp. IV 1998)
New York Education Law §§1001 et seq. (McKinney 1988 & Supp. 2000)
Occupational Safety and Health Act of 1970 (OSHA), 29 U.S.C. §§651 et seq. (1994)
Rehabilitation Act of 1973, 29 U.S.C. §§701 et seq. (1994 & Supp. IV 1998)
Brown v. Board of Education, 347 U.S. 483 (1954)
City of Cleburne v. Cleburne Living Center, 473 U.S. 432 (1985)
Deas v. River West, 152 F.3d 471 (5th Cir. 1998)

General References
Abel, Richard L. 1973. "A Comparative Theory of Dispute Institutions in Society." *Law and Society Review* 8:217–347.
Amott, Theresa L., and Julie A. Matthaei. 1996. *Race, Gender, and Work: A Multicultural Economic History of Women in the United States.* Rev. ed. Boston: South End Press.
Asch, Adrienne, and Michelle Fine. 1988. "Introduction: Beyond Pedestals." In *Women with Disabilities: Essays in Psychology, Culture, and Politics,* ed. Michelle Fine and Adrienne Asch, 1–37. Philadelphia: Temple University Press.
Bartlett, Katharine T., and Rosanne Kennedy, eds. 1991. *Feminist Legal Theory: Readings in Law and Gender.* Boulder, CO: Westview Press.
Berg, Paula. 1999. "Ill/legal: Interrogating the Meaning and Function of the Category of Disability in Antidiscrimination Law." *Yale Law and Policy Review* 18:1–51.
Bickenbach, Jerome E. 1993. *Physical Disability and Social Policy.* Toronto: University of Toronto Press.
Biklen, Douglas. 1992. *Schooling without Labels: Parents, Educators, and Inclusive Education.* Philadelphia: Temple University Press.
Black, Donald J. 1973. "The Mobilization of Law." *Journal of Legal Studies* 2:125–49.
———. 1976. *The Behavior of Law.* New York: Academic Press.

Blanck, Peter David. 1994. "Employment Integration, Economic Opportunity, and the Americans with Disabilities Act: Empirical Study from 1990–1993." *Iowa Law Review* 79:853–923.

———. 1998. *The Americans with Disabilities Act and the Emerging Workforce: Employment of People with Mental Retardation.* Washington, DC: American Association on Mental Retardation.

Blanck, Peter David, and Millie Weighner Marti. 1997. "Attitudes, Behavior, and the Employment Provisions of the Americans with Disabilities Act." *Villanova Law Review* 42:345–406.

Blau, Peter M., and Otis Dudley Duncan. 1967. *The American Occupational Structure.* New York: Wiley.

Bowles, Samuel, and Herbert Gintis. 1976. *Schooling in Capitalist America: Educational Reform and the Contradictions of Economic Life.* New York: Basic Books.

Brown, Clair, and Joseph A. Pechman. 1987. *Gender in the Workplace.* Washington, DC: Brookings Institution.

Brown, Dale S. 1994. "Personal Perspective—Problems and Promises: Adults with Learning Disabilities in the Past and in the Present." In *Learning Disabilities in Adulthood: Persisting Problems and Evolving Issues,* ed. Paul J. Gerber and Henry B. Reiff, 46–51. Stoneham, MA: Andover Medical Publishers.

Brown, Dale S., and Paul J. Gerber. 1994. "Employing People with Learning Disabilities." In *Learning Disabilities in Adulthood: Persisting Problems and Evolving Issues,* ed. Paul J. Gerber and Henry B. Reiff, 194–203. Stoneham, MA: Andover Medical Publishers.

Brown, Mark S. 1995. "Letter to Editor: Column by Rosemond Does Disservice to ADD." *Buffalo News,* February 11. Editorial, p. 2.

Bruner, Jerome. 1990. *Acts of Meaning.* Cambridge, MA: Harvard University Press.

———. 1997. "A Narrative Model of Self-Construction." *Annals of the New York Academy of Sciences* 818:145–61.

Bumiller, Kristin. 1988. *The Civil Rights Society: The Social Construction of Victims.* Baltimore: Johns Hopkins University Press.

Burkhauser, William. 1997. "The Americans with Disabilities Act: Social Contract or Special Privilege?" *Annals of the American Academy of Social and Political Science* 549:71–83.

Burstein, Paul, and Kathleen Monaghan. 1986. "Equal Employment Opportunity and the Mobilization of Law." *Law and Society Review* 20:355–88.

Cohen, Elchanan, and Terry G. Geske. 1990. *The Economics of Education.* 3rd ed. New York: Pergamon Press.

Cole, Melissa. 2000. "The Mitigation Expectation and the *Sutton* Court's Closeting of Disabilities." *Howard Law Journal* 43:499–555.

Colker, Ruth, and Bonnie Poitras Tucker. 2000. *The Law of Disability Discrimination.* 3rd ed. Cincinnati, OH: Anderson Publishing.

Crenshaw, Kimberlé. 1988. "Race, Reform, and Retrenchment: Transformation and Legitimation in Antidiscrimination Law." *Harvard Law Review* 101:1331–87.

Crenshaw, Kimberlé, Neil Gotanda, Gary Peller, and Kendall Thomas, ed. 1995. *Critical Race Theory: The Key Writings That Formed the Movement.* New York: New Press.

Curran, Barbara A. 1977. *The Legal Needs of the Public: The Final Report of a National Survey.* Chicago: American Bar Foundation.

Deegan, Mary Jo. 1985. "Multiple Minority Groups: A Case Study of Physically Disabled Women." In *Women and Disability: The Double Handicap,* ed. Mary Jo Deegan and Nancy A. Brooks, 37–55. New Brunswick, NJ: Transaction Books.

Deegan, Mary Jo, and Nancy A. Brooks, eds. 1985. *Women and Disability: The Double Handicap.* New Brunswick, NJ: Transaction Books.

Delgado, Richard, and Jean Stefancic. 2000. *Critical Race Theory: The Cutting Edge.* 2nd ed. Philadelphia: Temple University Press.

Elshtain, Jean Bethke. 1995. *Democracy on Trial.* New York: Basic Books.

Emerson, Robert M. 2001. "Producing Ethnographies: Theory, Evidence and Representation." In *Contemporary Field Research: Perspectives and Formulations,* ed. Robert M. Emerson, 281–315. 2nd ed. Prospect Heights, IL: Waveland Press.

Engel, David M. 1984. "The Oven Bird's Song: Insiders, Outsiders, and Personal Injury in an American Community." *Law and Society Review* 18:551–82.

———. 1991. "Law, Culture, and Children with Disabilities: Educational Rights and the Construction of Difference." *Duke Law Journal,* 166–205.

———. 1993. "Origin Myths: Narratives of Authority, Resistance, Disability, and Law." *Law and Society Review* 27:785–826.

———. 1995. "Law in the Domains of Everyday Life: The Construction of Community and Difference." In *Law in Everyday Life,* ed. Austin Sarat and Thomas R. Kearns, 123–70. Ann Arbor: University of Michigan Press.

Engel, David M., and Frank W. Munger. 1996. "Rights, Remembrance, and the Reconciliation of Difference." *Law and Society Review* 30:7–53.

———. 2001. "Re-Interpreting the Effect of Rights: Career Narratives and the Americans with Disabilities Act." *Ohio State Law Journal* 62: 285–333.

Etzioni, Amitai. 1993. *The Spirit of Community: Rights, Responsibilities, and the Communitarian Agenda.* New York: Crown Publishers.

———. 1996. *The New Golden Rule: Community and Morality in a Democratic Society.* New York: Basic Books.

Etzioni, Amitai, ed. 1995. *New Communitarian Thinking: Persons, Virtues, Institutions, and Communities.* Charlottesville: University Press of Virginia.

———. 1998. *The Essential Communitarian Reader.* Lanham, MD: Rowman and Littlefield.

Ewick, Patricia, and Susan S. Silbey. 1998. *The Common Place of Law: Stories from Everyday Life.* Chicago: University of Chicago Press.

Feldblum, Chai. 2000. "Definition of Disability under Federal Anti-Discrimination Law: What Happened? Why? And What Can We Do about It?" *Berkeley Journal of Employment and Labor Law* 21:91–147.

Felstiner, William L. F. 1974. "Influences of Social Organization on Dispute Processing." *Law and Society Review* 9:63–94.

Fike, Hilary Greer. 1997. "Comment: Learning Disabilities in the Workplace: A Guide to ADA Compliance." *Seattle University Law Review* 20:489–541.

Fine, Michelle, and Adrienne Asch. 1988. "Disability beyond Stigma: Social Interaction, Discrimination, and Activism." *Journal of Social Issues* 44:3–21.

Fineman, Martha Albertson. 1999. "Cracking the Foundational Myths: Independence, Autonomy, and Self-Sufficiency." *American University Journal of Gender, Social Policy and the Law* 8:13–29.

Finkelstein, Victor. 1980. *Attitudes and Disabled People: Issues for Discussion.*

World Rehabilitation Fund, Monograph No. 5. New York: International Exchange of Information in Rehabilitation.

Finlan, Thomas G. 1994. *Learning Disability: The Imaginary Disease.* Westport, CT: Bergin and Garvey.

Foucault, Michel. 1972. *The Archaeology of Knowledge and the Discourse on Language.* Trans. A. M. Sheridan Smith. New York: Pantheon Books.

———. 1991. "Politics and the Study of Discourse." In *The Foucault Effect: Studies in Governmentality,* ed. Graham Burchell, Colin Gordon, and Peter Miller, 53–72. London: Harvester Wheatsheaf.

Franklin, Barry M. 1987. *Learning Disabilities: Dissenting Essays.* Philadelphia: Falmer Press.

Freeman, Alan D. 1998. "Antidiscrimination Law: A Critical Review." In *The Politics of Law: A Progressive Critique,* ed. David Kairys, 285–311. 3rd ed. New York: Basic Books.

French, Rebecca R. 1998. "Lamas, Oracles, Channels, and the Law: Reconsidering Religion and Social Theory." *Yale Journal of Law and the Humanities* 10:505.

Funk, Robert. 1987. "Disability Rights: From Caste to Class in the Context of Civil Rights." In *Images of the Disabled, Disabling Images,* ed. Alan Gartner and Tom Joe, 7–30. New York: Praeger.

Galanter, Marc. 1974. "Why the 'Haves' Come Out Ahead: Speculations on the Limits of Legal Change." *Law and Society Review* 9:95–160.

———. 1983a. "The Radiating Effects of Courts." In *Empirical Theories about Courts,* ed. Keith O. Boyum and Lynn Mather, 117–42. New York: Longman.

———. 1983b. "Reading the Landscape of Disputes: What We Know and Don't Know (and Think We Know) about Our Allegedly Contentious and Litigious Society." *UCLA Law Review* 31:4–71.

———. 1985. "Vision and Revision: A Comment on Yngvesson." *Wisconsin Law Review,* 647–54.

Gallet, Jeffry. 1988–89. "The Judge Who Could Not Tell His Right from His Left and Other Tales of Learning Disabilities." *Buffalo Law Review* 37:739–50.

Gerber, Paul J., and Henry B. Reiff. 1991. *Speaking for Themselves: Ethnographic Interviews with Adults with Learning Disabilities.* Ann Arbor: University of Michigan Press.

Gerber, Paul J., and Henry B. Reiff, eds. 1994. *Learning Disabilities in Adulthood: Persisting Problems and Evolving Issues.* Stoneham, MA: Andover Medical Publishers.

Gilliom, John. 2001. *Overseers of the Poor: Surveillance, Resistance, and the Limits of Privacy.* Chicago: University of Chicago Press.

Glendon, Mary Ann. 1991. *Rights Talk: The Impoverishment of Political Discourse.* New York: Free Press.

Glennon, Theresa. 1995. "Race, Education, and the Construction of a Disabled Class." *Wisconsin Law Review,* 1237–1338.

Gliedman, John, and William Roth. 1980. *The Unexpected Minority: Handicapped Children in America.* New York: Harcourt Brace Jovanovich.

Gluckman, Max. 1955. *The Judicial Process among the Barotse of Northern Rhodesia.* Glencoe, IL: Free Press.

Goffman, Erving. 1963. *Stigma: Notes on the Management of Spoiled Identity.* New York: Simon and Schuster.

Greenhouse, Carol J. 1986. *Praying for Justice: Faith, Order, and Community in an American Town*. Ithaca, NY: Cornell University Press.

Greenhouse, Carol J., Barbara Yngvesson, and David M. Engel. 1994. *Law and Community in Three American Towns*. Ithaca, NY: Cornell University Press.

Greenwood, Judith Goodwin. 1996. "History of Disability as a Legal Concept." In *Disability Evaluation,* ed. S. L. Demeter, G. B. J. Andersson, and G. M. Smith, 5–12. St. Louis, MO: Mosby Year-Book.

Groce, Nora Ellen. 1985. *Everyone Here Spoke Sign Language: Hereditary Deafness on Martha's Vineyard*. Cambridge, MA: Harvard University Press.

Habermas, Jürgen. 1979. *Communication and the Evolution of Society*. Trans. Thomas McCarthy. Boston: Beacon Press.

———. 1996. *Between Facts and Norms: Contributions to a Discourse Theory of Law and Democracy*. Trans. William Rehg. Cambridge, MA: MIT Press.

Hahn, Harlan. 1985. "Introduction: Disability Policy and the Problem of Discrimination." *American Behavioral Scientist* 28:293–318.

———. 1994. "Feminist Perspectives, Disability, Sexuality and Law: New Issues and Agendas." *Southern California Review of Law and Women's Studies* 4:97–144.

———. 2000. "Accommodations and the ADA: Unreasonable Bias or Biased Reasoning?" *Berkeley Journal of Employment and Labor Law* 21:166–92.

Hale, Thomas W., Howard V. Hayghe, and John M. McNeil. 1998. "Persons with Disabilities: Labor Market Activity, 1994." *Monthly Labor Review* (September): 3–12.

Handler, Joel F. 1987–88. "The Transformation of Aid to Families with Dependent Children: The Family Support Act in Historical Context." *New York University Review of Law and Social Change* 16:457–533.

Handler, Joel F., and Yeheskel Hasenfeld. 1991. *The Moral Construction of Poverty: Welfare Reform in America*. Newbury Park, CA: Sage Publications.

Hanna, William John, and Betsy Rogovsky. 1991. "Women with Disabilities: Two Handicaps Plus." *Disability, Handicap and Society* 6:49–63.

Harrington, Christine B. 1985. *Shadow Justice: The Ideology and Institutionalization of Alternatives to Court*. Westport, CT: Greenwood Press.

Harrington, Christine B., and Barbara Yngvesson. 1990. "Interpretive Sociolegal Research." *Law and Social Inquiry* 15:135–48.

Haskell, Thomas L. 1987. "The Curious Persistence of Rights Talk in 'The Age of Interpretation.'" *Journal of American History* 74:984–1012.

Hofrichter, Richard. 1987. *Neighborhood Justice in Capitalist Society: The Expansion of the Informal State*. New York: Greenwood Press.

Hooper, Stephen R., and W. Grant Willis. 1989. *Learning Disability Subtyping: Neuropsychological Foundations, Conceptual Models, and Issues in Clinical Differentiation*. New York: Springer-Verlag.

Jans, Lita, and Susan Stoddard, eds. 1999. *Chartbook on Women and Disability in the United States*. Washington, DC: U.S. Department of Education, National Institute on Disability and Rehabilitation Research.

Kahn, Robert L. 1981. *Work and Health*. New York: Wiley.

Kanter, Rosabeth Moss. 1993. *Men and Women of the Corporation*. 2nd ed. New York: Basic Books.

Karst, Kenneth. 1989. *Belonging to America: Equal Citizenship and the Constitution*. New Haven, CT: Yale University Press.

Kelman, Mark, and Gillian Lester. 1997. *Jumping the Queue: An Inquiry into the*

Legal Treatment of Students with Learning Disabilities. Cambridge, MA: Harvard University Press.

Kennedy, Duncan. 1997. *A Critique of Adjudication (fin de siècle).* Cambridge, MA: Harvard University Press.

Kessler-Harris, Alice. 1982. *Out to Work: A History of Wage-Earning Women in the United States.* New York: Oxford University Press.

Kritzer, Herbert M. 1980–81. "Studying Disputes: Learning from the CLRP Experience." *Law and Society Review* 15:503–24.

Laumann, Edward O., ed. 1970. *Social Stratification: Research and Theory for the 1970s.* Indianapolis: Bobbs-Merrill.

Livneh, Hannoch. 1983. "Death Anxiety and Attitudes towards Disabled Persons." *Psychological Reports* 53:359–63.

Macaulay, Stewart. 1963. "Non-Contractual Relations in Business: A Preliminary Study." *American Sociological Review* 28:55–67.

Mannheim, Bruce, and Dennis Tedlock. 1995. "Introduction." In *The Dialogic Emergence of Culture,* ed. Dennis Tedlock and Bruce Mannheim, 1–32. Urbana: University of Illinois Press.

Mayerson, Arlene. 1993. "The History of the ADA: A Movement Perspective." In *Implementing the Americans with Disabilities Act: Rights and Responsibilities of All Americans,* ed. Lawrence O. Gostin and Henry A. Beyer, 17–24. Baltimore: Paul H. Brookes Publishing.

Mayhew, Leon H. 1968. *Law and Equal Opportunity: A Study of the Massachusetts Commission against Discrimination.* Cambridge, MA: Harvard University Press.

Mayhew, Leon H., and Albert J. Reiss Jr. 1969. "The Social Organization of Legal Contacts." *American Sociological Review* 34:309–18.

McCann, Michael W. 1994. *Rights at Work: Pay Equity Reform and the Politics of Legal Mobilization.* Chicago: University of Chicago Press.

McCann, Michael W., and Tracey March. 1995. "Law and Everyday Forms of Resistance: A Socio-Political Assessment." *Law, Politics, and Society* 15:207–36.

McNeil, John M. 1993. *Americans with Disabilities: 1991–1992; Data from the Survey of Income and Program Participation.* Washington, DC: U.S. Department of Commerce, Economics and Statistics Administration, Bureau of the Census.

Miller, Richard E., and Austin Sarat. 1980–81. "Grievances, Claims, and Disputes: Assessing the Adversary Culture." *Law and Society Review* 15:525–65.

Milner, Neal. 1986. "The Dilemmas of Legal Mobilization: Ideologies and Strategies of Mental Patient Liberation Groups." *Law and Policy* 8:105–29.

———. 1989. "The Denigration of Rights and the Persistence of Rights Talk: A Cultural Portrait." *Law and Social Inquiry* 14:631–75.

Minow, Martha. 1990. *Making All the Difference: Inclusion, Exclusion, and American Law.* Ithaca, NY: Cornell University Press.

Moore, Sally Falk. 1978. "Law and Social Change: The Semi-Autonomous Social Field as an Appropriate Subject of Study." In *Law as Process: An Anthropological Approach,* 54–81. London: Routledge and Kegan Paul.

Morello-Frosch, Rachel, Manuel Pastor, and Carlos Porras. 2001. "Who's Minding the Air at Your Child's School?" *Los Angeles Times,* June 3, Opinion, Part M, 3.

Moss, Kathryn, Michael Ullman, Matthew C. Johnsen, Barbara E. Starrett, and Scott Burris. 1999. "Different Paths to Justice: The ADA, Employment, and Administrative Enforcement by the EEOC and FEPAs." *Behavioral Sciences and Law* 17:29–46.

Munger, Frank W. 2002. "Dependency by Law: Welfare and Identity in the Lives of Poor Women." In *Lives in the Law,* ed. Austin Sarat and Thomas R. Kearns, 83–121. Ann Arbor: University of Michigan Press.

Munger, Frank W., and David M. Engel. 1998. "Civil Rights and Self-Concept: Life Stories of Law, Disability, and Employment." *Droit et Cultures* 35:43–73.

Murphy, Robert F. 1987. *The Body Silent.* New York: Norton.

Newman, Katherine. 1988. *Falling from Grace: The Experience of Downward Mobility in the American Middle Class.* New York: Free Press.

N.O.D./ Louis Harris. 1998. *The 1998 N.O.D./Harris Survey of Americans with Disabilities.* Washington, DC: National Organization on Disability.

O'Brien, Ruth. 2001. *Crippled Justice: The History of Modern Disability Policy in the Workplace.* Chicago: University of Chicago Press.

Oliver, Michael. 1990. *The Politics of Disablement: A Sociological Approach.* New York: St. Martin's Press.

OuYang, Elizabeth R. 1990. "Women with Disabilities in the Work Force: Outlook for the 1990s." *Harvard Women's Law Journal* 13:13–33.

Pijl, Sip Jan. 1994. "United States." In *New Perspectives in Special Education: A Six-Country Study of Integration,* ed. Cor J. W. Meijer, Sip Jan Pijl, and Seamus Hegarty, 55–78. London: Routledge.

Pospisil, Leopold J. 1971. *Anthropology of Law: A Comparative Theory.* New York: Harper and Row.

"Progress in Special Education." 2001. *New York Times,* May 1. Editorial, §A, p. 22.

Reiff, Henry B. 1997. "On the Front Line: Thoughts from Persons with Learning Disabilities in the Workplace." In *Learning Disabilities and Employment,* ed. Paul J. Gerber and Dale S. Brown, 333–48. Austin, TX: Pro-Ed.

Reskin, Barbara F., and Heidi I. Hartmann, eds. 1986. *Women's Work, Men's Work: Sex Segregation on the Job.* Washington, DC: National Academy Press.

Reskin, Barbara F., and Irene Padavic. 1994. *Women and Men at Work.* Thousand Oaks, CA: Pine Forge Press.

Rosemond, John. 1994a. "Learning Disability Seen as a Challenge." *Buffalo News,* January 9. Lifestyles, p. 3.

———. 1994b. "Managing ADD without Drugs." *Buffalo News,* November 6. Lifestyles, p. 3.

Rosenberg, Gerald N. 1991. *The Hollow Hope: Can Courts Bring about Social Change?* Chicago: University of Chicago Press.

Rosenwald, George C. 1992. "Conclusion: Reflections on Narrative Self-Understanding." In *Storied Lives: The Cultural Politics of Self-Understanding,* ed. George C. Rosenwald and Richard L. Ochberg, 265–89. New Haven, CT: Yale University Press.

Saks, Michael J. 1992. "Do We Really Know Anything about the Behavior of the Tort Litigation System—and Why Not?" *University of Pennsylvania Law Review* 140:1147–1292.

Sarat, Austin, and Thomas R. Kearns. 1995. "Beyond the Great Divide: Forms of

Legal Scholarship and Everyday Life." In *Law in Everyday Life,* ed. Austin Sarat and Thomas R. Kearns, 21–61. Ann Arbor: University of Michigan Press.

Scheer, Jessica. 1984. " 'They Act Like It's Contagious': A Study of Mobility Impairment in a New York City Neighborhood." In *Social Aspects of Chronic Illness, Impairment and Disability,* ed. Stephen C. Hey, Gary Kiger, and John Seidel, 62–69. Salem, OR: Willamette University, Society for the Study of Chronic Illness, Impairment and Disability.

Scheingold, Stuart A. 1974. *The Politics of Rights: Lawyers, Public Policy, and Political Change.* New Haven, CT: Yale University Press.

Schneider, Elizabeth M. 1993. "The Dialectic of Rights and Politics: Perspectives from the Women's Movement." In *Feminist Legal Theory: Foundations,* ed. D. Kelly Weisberg, 507–26. Philadelphia: Temple University Press.

Scotch, Richard K. 1984. *From Good Will to Civil Rights: Transforming Federal Disability Policy.* Philadelphia: Temple University Press.

———. 2000. "Models of Disability and the Americans with Disabilities Act." *Berkeley Journal of Employment and Labor Law* 21:213–22.

Shalit, Ruth. 1997. "Defining Disability Down." *New Republic,* August 25. Pp. 16–22.

Shapiro, Joseph P. 1993. *No Pity: People with Disabilities Forging a New Civil Rights Movement.* New York: Times Books (Random House).

Shapiro, Joan, and Rebecca Rich. 1999. *Facing Learning Disabilities in the Adult Years.* New York: Oxford University Press.

Shklar, Judith N. 1991. *American Citizenship: The Quest for Inclusion.* Cambridge, MA: Harvard University Press.

Shostak, Marjorie. 1981. *Nisa: The Life and Words of a !Kung Woman.* New York: Random House.

Silberman, Matthew. 1985. *The Civil Justice Process: A Sequential Model of the Mobilization of Law.* Orlando, FL: Academic Press.

Silvers, Anita. 1998. "Reprising Women's Disability: Feminist Identity Strategy and Disability Rights." *Berkeley Women's Law Journal* 13:81–116.

Simpson, Eileen. 1979. *Reversals: A Personal Account of Victory over Dyslexia.* Boston: Houghton Mifflin.

Slonaker, William M., and Ann C. Wendt. 1995. "Patterns of Employment Discrimination toward Workers with Disabilities." *Business Forum* 20:21–25.

Speece, Deborah L., and Barbara K. Keogh, eds. 1996. *Research on Classroom Ecologies: Implications for Inclusion of Children with Learning Disabilities.* Mahwah, NJ: Lawrence Erlbaum.

Sternberg, Robert J. 1999. "Epilogue: Toward an Emerging Consensus about Learning Disabilities." In *Perspectives on Learning Disabilities: Biological, Cognitive, Contextual,* ed. Robert J. Sternberg and Louise Spear-Swerling, 277–82. Boulder, CO: Westview Press.

Stone, Deborah A. 1984. *The Disabled State.* Philadelphia: Temple University Press.

Tocqueville, Alexis de. 1945. *Democracy in America.* Vol. 1. New York: Vintage Books.

Tomasic, Roman, and Malcolm M. Feeley. 1982. *Neighborhood Justice: Assessment of an Emerging Idea.* New York: Longman.

Torgesen, Joseph K. 1998. "Learning Disabilities: An Historical and Conceptual

Overview." In *Learning about Learning Disabilities*, ed. Bernice Y. L. Wong, 3–34. 2nd ed. San Diego, CA: Academic Press.

Trubek, David M., et al. 1983. "The Costs of Ordinary Litigation." *UCLA Law Review* 31:72–127.

Tucker, Bonnie Poitras. 2001. "The ADA's Revolving Door: Inherent Flaws in the Civil Rights Paradigm." *Ohio State Law Journal* 62:335–89.

Tushnet, Mark. 1984. "An Essay on Rights." *Texas Law Review* 62:1363–1403.

Weis, Andrew. 1998. "Jumping to Conclusions in 'Jumping the Queue.'" *Stanford Law Review* 51:183–219.

Weisberg, D. Kelly, ed. 1993. *Feminist Legal Theory: Foundations*. Philadelphia: Temple University Press.

Wendell, Susan. 1996. *The Rejected Body: Feminist Philosophical Reflections on Disability*. New York: Routledge.

West, Jane. 1993. "The Evolution of Disability Rights." In *Implementing the Americans with Disabilities Act: Rights and Responsibilities of All Americans*, ed. Lawrence O. Gostin and Henry A. Beyer, 3–15. Baltimore: Paul H. Brookes.

West, Michael, et al. 1993. "Beyond Section 504: Satisfaction and Empowerment of Students with Disabilities in Higher Education." *Exceptional Children* 59:456–67.

White, Lucie. 1991. "Subordination, Rhetorical Survival Skills, and Sunday Shoes: Notes on the Hearing of Mrs. G." In *At the Boundaries of the Law: Feminism and Legal Theory*, ed. Martha Fineman, 40–58. New York: Routledge.

———. 2002. "Care at Work: Inside the Life World of a Government Program." In *Laboring below the Line: The New Ethnography of Poverty, Low-Wage Work, and Survival in the Global Economy*, ed. Frank Munger, 213–44. New York: Russell Sage Foundation.

Williams, Patricia J. 1987. "Alchemical Notes: Reconstructing Ideals from Deconstructed Rights." *Harvard Civil Rights—Civil Liberties Law Review* 22:401–33.

Wing, Adrien Katherine, ed. 1997. *Critical Race Feminism: A Reader*. New York: New York University Press.

Wingert, Pat, and Barbara Kantrowitz, with Tara Weingarten in Los Angeles. 1997. "Why Andy Couldn't Read." *Newsweek*, October 27. Pp. 56–64.

World Health Organization. 1980. *International Classification of Impairments, Disabilities, and Handicaps: A Manual of Classification Relating to the Consequences of Disease*. Geneva: World Health Organization.

Wright, Beatrice A. 1983. *Physical Disability—A Psychosocial Approach*. 2nd ed. New York: Harper and Row.

Yelin, Edward H., and Patricia P. Katz. 1994. "Making Work More Central to Work Disability Policy." *Milbank Quarterly* 72, no. 4: 593–619.

Yngvesson, Barbara. 1985. "Re-Examining Continuing Relations and the Law." *Wisconsin Law Review*, 623–46.

———. 1988. "Making Law at the Doorway: The Clerk, the Court, and the Construction of Community in a New England Town." *Law and Society Review* 22:409–48.

———. 1993. *Virtuous Citizens, Disruptive Subjects: Order and Complaint in a New England Court*. New York: Routledge.

———. 1997. "Negotiating Motherhood: Identity and Difference in 'Open' Adoptions." *Law and Society Review* 31:31–80.

Ysseldyke, James E., and Bob Algozzine. 1982. *Critical Issues in Special and Remedial Education.* Boston: Houghton Mifflin.

Zemans, Frances Kahn. 1983. "Legal Mobilization: The Neglected Role of the Law in the Political System." *The American Political Science Review* 77:690–703.

Zola, Irving Kenneth. 1993. "The Sleeping Giant in Our Midst: Redefining 'Persons with Disabilities.' " In *Implementing the Americans with Disabilities Act: Rights and Responsibilities of All Americans,* ed. Lawrence O. Gostin and Henry A. Beyer, xvii–xx. Baltimore: Paul H. Brookes.

Index

accommodations: ambivalence toward accommodations received, 99; citizenship
and negative view of, 125–26; employers and, 121, 155, 208–9; entitlement
viewed through self-concept, 128–29;
individual's expectations of, 75–76,
187, 201–2; individual's strategies used
to gain, 207–8, 224; limits to options,
174; in market forces discourse, 154–55,
157–58; "reasonable accommodations"
meaning misperceptions, 121, 155; by
schools, negative experiences, 71–72,
206–7, 221–22; by schools, positive
experiences, 22–23, 134–35, 184, 185,
191
ADA. *See* Americans with Disabilities Act
affirmative action: disability rights and
connotation of racial rights, 151; racial
justice discourse and, 144, 145
Algozzine, B., 60n. 7
Americans with Disabilities Act (ADA,
1990): constitutive effects, 121–22,
125; constitutive rights basis, 83;
contribution to activation of rights
for an individual, 102–3; criticisms
of disability-related social welfare
policies in US, 54–55n. 3; education
process impact, 38; employers' attitudes
impacted by, 26, 200; employers'
obligations, 13–14, 68; entitlements
misperceptions, 209–10; factors to
consider, 250–51; federal agencies
overseeing, 6n. 5; formal assertion of
rights as gauge of effectiveness, 240;
individual's avoidance of invoking
(*see* interviewees' view or knowledge
of ADA); individual's perception of
affirmative action-like approach, 146–
47; inexplicit application to gender,
226; intention of, 130, 131–32; judicial
decisions regarding, 6; legislation leading to, 5; measuring success of, 250–52;
moral force through racial justice
analogy, 145; narrative evidence of
true effects, 79–80; paradox of equality
gained through proof of difference, 88–
89, 120; paucity of formal complaints
of violations of, 91–92; perspective
of disability reflected in, 119; from
perspective of rights vs. relationships
model, 84, 85–86; promises of equal
treatment and inclusion, 81; provisions,
5–6, 89n. 10; qualified person definition, 120; questions about difference
rights make, 252; "reasonable accommodations" meaning misperceptions,
155; "reasonable accommodations"
requirement, potential limitations
from, 121; self-concepts as barrier
to, 131; study approach, 4; theories
of disabilities and, 119n. 8; timing's
relationship to resource availability
and use, 254–55; "undue hardship"
definition, 153; unemployment rates
among disabled, 92n. 16; ways rights
become active and, 243–45
Asch, A., 14, 216, 228nn. 9, 10
Avery, Dianne, 228n. 8

Berg, P., 119n. 8, 121n. 10
biomedical paradigm theory of disability,
119n. 8
Black, D., 84
Blanck, P. D., 92n. 18
Brown v. Board of Education, 82
Bruner, J., 12, 41, 115
Bumiller, K., 93, 94n. 21

SELMA AND DALLAS COUNTY LIBRARY

3 6054 00118 0921

PUBLIC LIBRARY OF
SELMA & DALLAS CTY
1103 SELMA AVENUE
SELMA, AL 36701